Practical Smart Device Design and Construction

Understanding Smart Technologies and How to Build Them Yourself

Christopher Harrold

Apress®

Practical Smart Device Design and Construction: Understanding Smart Technologies and How to Build Them Yourself

Christopher Harrold
Denver, CO, USA

ISBN-13 (pbk): 978-1-4842-5613-8   ISBN-13 (electronic): 978-1-4842-5614-5
https://doi.org/10.1007/978-1-4842-5614-5

Managing Director, Apress Media LLC: Welmoed Spahr
Acquisitions Editor: Natalie Pao
Development Editor: James Markham
Coordinating Editor: Jessica Vakili

Distributed to the book trade worldwide by Springer Science+Business Media New York, 233 Spring Street, 6th Floor, New York, NY 10013. Phone 1-800-SPRINGER, fax (201) 348-4505, e-mail orders-ny@springer-sbm.com, or visit www.springeronline.com. Apress Media, LLC is a California LLC and the sole member (owner) is Springer Science + Business Media Finance Inc (SSBM Finance Inc). SSBM Finance Inc is a **Delaware** corporation.

For information on translations, please e-mail booktranslations@springernature.com; for reprint, paperback, or audio rights, please e-mail bookpermissions@springernature.com.

Apress titles may be purchased in bulk for academic, corporate, or promotional use. eBook versions and licenses are also available for most titles. For more information, reference our Print and eBook Bulk Sales web page at http://www.apress.com/bulk-sales.

Any source code or other supplementary material referenced by the author in this book is available to readers on GitHub via the book's product page, located at www.apress.com/978-1-4842-5613-8. For more detailed information, please visit http://www.apress.com/source-code.

Printed on acid-free paper

This book is dedicated to everyone who wants to know more. I hope it helps.

Table of Contents

About the Author ix

About the Technical Reviewer xi

Acknowledgments xiii

Part I: Smart 1

Chapter 1: A Brief History of Smart Things 3

The Computer 3

    Small 5

Sensors and Industrial Controls 9

Summary..14

Chapter 2: The DIY Smart Era 15

Instant Gratification...15

    The Minimum DIY Lab...17

    Software Considerations 33

Summary..35

Chapter 3: Beyond the Hype – Smart Today and Tomorrow..............37

The IoT That Wasn't...38

Taking the I out of IoT..39

Connected 40

Why Not?...43

Where We Go Now..44

Summary..45

Part II: Smart Hardware..47

Chapter 4: EE for the Total N00b....................................49

Resistance 53

Circuits..57

Circuit Diagrams 67

Summary..72

Chapter 5: Advanced Circuit Components 73

The Transistor...73

    BJT Transistors (N-P-N or P-N-P) 74

FET Transistor...77

The Capacitor 79

Diodes 85

Other Common Elements 91

Summary..94

Chapter 6: Circuit Building Lab....................................97

A Series Circuit 98

A Parallel Circuit..103

    A Transistor Controlled Circuit 108

    A Diode-Based OR Gate 121

    A Capacitor Test Circuit 128

Summary..138

Part III: Smart Software...139

Chapter 7: Touch, See, Hear, Smell, Taste 141

Touch, See, Hear – The Big Three...................................142

Smell and Taste – The Other Senses...............................146

Sensor Considerations 147

Analog vs. Digital...148

Advanced Devices 150

To the Library!..155

Arduino Libraries 157

Python Libraries..158

Summary...159

Chapter 8: The Small Computer...................................**161**

Small-ish..161

The Magic of GPIO and the Humble Pin 165

A0 or D0 168

Digital IO 169

Analog 170

The Software of Smart 172

A Brief Word on Tools 173

Smart System Basics 176

Let's Get Ready to Rumble!...178

Raspberry Pi Prep 180

Arduino Prep 190

A Word on Code..195

Summary...201

Chapter 9: Smart Device Building Lab **203**

What Are You Going to Make in These Labs? 214

Let's Take a Quick Look at That Code...............................237

Hello World Recap 239

A VERY Brief Look at the Code 260

Again, a VERY Brief Code Recap.......................................281

Basic Sensor Recap 283

Chapter 10: Smart System Building Lab..**285**

   Smart System Recap 355

Part IV: Permanence **357**

Chapter 11: Your First Circuit Board....................................**359**

   Locking It Down 361

   Maintaining Good Iron..370

   Semi-permanent..375

      Your First Circuit Board Lab...383

   Summary...395

Chapter 12: Your First Good PCB **397**

   When Bits of Resistor Just Aren't Good Enough 399

   On Closer Inspection 400

   Your First Traces..405

      Add a Component to Your Board.......................................407

      Add Your First Traces 414

      A Note on PCB Fails 421

      Getting Fancy...423

Index...**427**

About the Author

Christopher Harrold is a 25-year veteran of IT, starting from help desk and tech support through to leading technology organizations and departments. Throughout his career, he has been privileged to witness one of the most exciting times in technology as the rapid pace of innovation and growth has driven technology from the realm of the corporation into the hands of the consumer. This has also spawned a rise in the creation of smart devices – devices that extend our own abilities and reach through the application of technology.

As a maker and creator, this ability to build things that can do tasks is innately exciting to Chris, and so he has stayed close to the smart device space and has learned and built numerous things in that time. It is that process of building his skills in hardware, engineering, and product design that prompted Chris to write this book. While there is no way to convey a career of learning and study in a single book, his aim in writing this is to help others like him get started in the smart device space, by giving them the basic background, context, tools, and guidance to build on as they take their own projects to the next level.

About the Technical Reviewer

Rebecca Stewart is a lecturer in the School of Electronic Engineering and Computer Science at Queen Mary University of London, where she completed her PhD in 2010. She works with e-textiles and signal processing to build interactive, body-centric wearable computing systems, often incorporating performance, fashion, music, and/or design. In 2011, she co-founded Codasign, an arts technology company that taught children and adults how to use code and electronics in creative projects. She regularly collaborates with artists and fashion designers and has had work featured by the BBC, *The New York Times*, and NPR.

Acknowledgments

As with anything, this book took a village to produce. I would like to thank my family who tolerated so many hours of writing and the mess of the lab and was patient to no end as I worked to finish. I would also like to thank the team at Apress who was so supportive as I went on this journey. Lastly, building knowledge is never something you do alone, and I am eternally grateful to everyone who shared knowledge and skills with me along the way. I especially want to thank Louis Frolio for his support and friendship in this project. I could not have done it without him.

PART I

Smart

The real purpose of this book is twofold for you as a reader. First is to give you a grounding in the basics that are required to build any smart device. These fundamentals are universal and will not change because of advances in computers or in new sensor developments. The fundamentals of smart devices are based in scientific laws and basic engineering, so they will be effective tools for you for a very long time. The second purpose is to bring together a background and context for *why* things are how they are and where smart devices are going. It is fair, and perhaps even an understatement, to say that this technology is changing rapidly. This book is not meant to cover everything ever that is possible, as it could never hope to do so. It will, however, give you the critical grounding in the basics of smart device theory and fundamentals so that even as the tools and capabilities change, you can keep pace with them.

This first section provides a historical context for you to understand why smart devices have developed the way they have and where they came from. This historical background is not explicitly needed of course, but as it is one of the stated purposes of this book, and one of my core beliefs in building materials for educating others, context matters. Understanding what has come before and influenced these developments can help you to understand how to use the results to their best effect.

CHAPTER 1

A Brief History of Smart Things

Welcome, reader, and I am glad you've chosen to pick up this book. I wrote this book for two reasons: I think that people struggle with approaching smart devices because the hardware side of the process can be intimidating if you are unfamiliar with the concepts and basics of working with hardware like circuits and components. The second is that I have seen in my speaking and teaching efforts that having a little bit of context around what you are learning and working on can help inform the process and make it more relevant. That is what I will take you through in the first chapter of the book, the context of the smart device: where did they come from, why are they here, and how they can be used to change and improve the environment around us.

The Computer

According to the *Oxford English Dictionary*, the first known use of the word "computer" was in 1613 in a book called *The Yong Mans Gleanings* by English writer Richard Braithwait: "I haue [sic] read the truest computer of Times, and the best Arithmetician that euer [sic] breathed, and he reduceth thy dayes into a short number." This usage of the term referred to a human computer, a person who carried out calculations or computations.

C. Harrold, *Practical Smart Device Design and Construction*,
https://doi.org/10.1007/978-1-4842-5614-5_1

This usage continued until well into the modern era with "computers" being literally "people who did calculations." As the book *Hidden Figures* pointed out, these computers were oftentimes women, who were doing some of the most important mathematical work of their time. In that same movie, we also see the arrival of the first mainstream modern computer, the IBM 3070 mainframe, at NASA. This new digital computer promised the ability to complete complex calculations in a fraction of the time of human computers. It was not without its flaws, and took an army of human computer experts to get it installed and working, but it represented a huge leap forward into the digital age that we now inhabit.

There is an axiom coined by Arthur C. Clarke that states that "any sufficiently advanced technology is indiscernible from magic." Certainly, to anyone not familiar with the operation of those computers they must have felt like a truly magic device. They were able to take a mundane task and allow the operator to focus on the inputs and outputs as opposed to all the dense mathematical operations in the middle part. This is also arguably the first instance of a digital assistant; something that a human controls, but that works digitally. Fundamentally all modern computers are really digital extensions of the controller, providing the ability to perform basic tasks faster and more easily without having to resort to math on paper, and by delivering capabilities that far exceed the user's own. The ability of these digital assistants to perform complex calculations is not lost on the business world, and the rise of the tabulating machine and the now common spreadsheet begins shortly after the appearance of the first computers in the 1970s.

From that point until the late 1980s, computing power was generally the domain of academia and large companies, owing to the extreme cost and complexity of the devices, and the difficulties encountered in building and maintaining them. During the late 1970s, we do see the beginnings of the homebuilt movement, where engineers and gifted amateurs begin assembling and developing their own computers literally in garages and basements all over the world. These smaller and simpler computers are the forerunner of the modern computing age, resulting in the development of the PC and the Mac that are now the standards of personal computing. They relied on two basic components to make them functional, the modern Central Processing Unit, or CPU, and the software that allows a computer to function, the Operating System, or OS.

Since their creation, CPUs have increased in processing power roughly every couple of years following Moore's law. This expansion of capability has fueled a massive growth of the computing market, and its expansion into new areas and uses that were never imagined during the earliest days. Digital medicine, computerized cars, and our smart phones are all the results of this increasing power in a decreasing physical footprint. In recent years, the explosion of cloud, virtualization, distributed computing, miniaturization, and the ubiquity of the connectivity has brought us to an age where computing power is relatively limitless compared to the large, monolithic computers of those early times.

We have such a proliferation of "computers" now that there are often things with computers embedded in them that you would not expect, or indeed not even want sometimes! This is where the history of the computer joins up with our smart devices, because it is the combination of increasing compute capability with the miniaturization of the computers that allows us to place sensors and controls close to the things we wish to act on. Without this development, the smart device would still be as much of a dream as Dick Tracy's watch phone (which I just replied to a text with).

Small

In April of 1981, a company that is now long since defunct and lost to computing history, Osborne Computer Corporation, announced what was the first production portable computer. "Portable" is probably a stretch as it weighed in at about 25lbs and had a screen that was just 5" wide (marginally smaller than your cell phone today). This was not, strictly speaking, the first portable; IBM, Apple, and others all had ideas or prototypes for portables, but it was the first one you could buy. The bigger "wow factor" was that it was relatively cheap at only about $1800. As Osborne himself said in an interview with *InfoWorld*, "It is not the fastest microcomputer, it doesn't have huge amounts of disk space, and it is not especially expandable." None of that mattered, because it was functional and was the first true portable that was semi-practical and worked. Why do we not have Osborne computers today? Through a series of bad bets and bad tech, as well as poor management of the company, by 1984 Osborne had filed for bankruptcy, and the race to miniaturize was fully in effect as Compaq, IBM, Apple, and others got their early portables into the market.

We continue to see this effect today of course, with small laptops retailing for under $200 in some cases, with significantly more functionality than the $1800 luggable of the early 1980s! What's more, as this pace of miniaturization has increased, the ability to put a computer in just about everything has as well. The term "computer" doesn't always mean that it is a full-fledged computer system with an OS and display and peripherals and all that. More that it has computational capability and can run some level of embedded code to serve a function. Examples abound, but a simple one is the code in my electric toothbrush. It only operates the 30 second timer for the brushing cycles and the motor, and that's all it needs to do. It doesn't need to perform complex software tasks like rendering a display screen or running a web browser. That's what makes these programmable controllers the backbone of the Smart Device world. It has "just enough" capability to perform the function needed to control the smart device without too much or too little capability.

This idea of true Micro Controller Units, or MCUs, was first realized in the early 1970s with the creation of the TMS1000 by Texas Instruments engineers Gary Boone and Michael Cochran. They used an 8-bit microprocessor and included read-only memory (ROM), random access memory (RAM), a processor, and clock all on the single chip that was designed to be embedded in other things as a control mechanism. Not to be outdone, Intel released its own 8048 with a processor chip designed specifically for the embedded market. Shipping beginning in 1977, and this little chip would find its way into numerous devices including a billion PC keyboards alone. Embedding microcontroller units into peripherals was an easy way to offload some computing from the PC itself and allows peripherals to gain more functionality without needing extra parts in the base computer. This is a system that is still used today for peripherals, and results in the ability to have connected devices with many defined functions that do not take up resources on the computer itself.

These early microcontrollers had a major limitation in how they operated, and that was in the concept of programming them using ROM. ROM stands for "Read-Only Memory," and unlike regular storage we are all used to today, it is a form of storage that requires the memory chip holding the program to literally be "burned in" with the code which is then read to perform the contained instructions. Early ROM came in two flavors: OTP-ROM or "One Time Programmable" ROM that came with the code burned in already and ran what it ran. This was common for the aforementioned keyboards as they needed a lot of the same set of instructions. The second was PROM or "Programmable ROM" that could be programmed exactly once by the user. This meant your code was perfect or your ROM was trash! Obviously not ideal for prototyping and for experimentation. There was early reprogrammable ROM called EPROM, or "Erasable Programmable Read-Only Memory," but even this solution was not particularly easy to use, requiring the chip to be exposed to UV light to be erased before reprogramming. I can still remember having a UV light station in the workshop of several companies for this purpose.

In 1993, however, the introduction of EEPROM, or "Electrically Erasable Programmable ROM," meant that the ROM can be reprogrammed by sending the correct electronic signal to the chip and then reprogrammed as many times as required. As hardware developers breathe a sigh of relief at being able to debug and test, the microcontroller chip market explodes and the embedding of a microcontroller into pretty much everything booms. By 2002, about 55% of all compute power sold was made up of 8-bit microcontrollers and microprocessors. By 2017, the market had shifted to include 16- and 32-bit MCUs as well, but there is still a staggering number of microcontrollers sold each year, and they are incredibly inexpensive. 1000 32-bit MCU's will set you back about $50 – a very small number when you consider the cost of more powerful computing chips.

Obviously, with this type of cost-per-unit and abundance of manufacturing, there are now MCUs everywhere. By one account, the typical home in a developed country has roughly 4 full-blown computers and at least 40 MCUs. A typical midrange car has around 30 MCUs for example. I personally do not have a typical home, as I have a ton of tech, but I put this to the test as I was writing this chapter, and tried to observe from my couch the number of MCUs I could see:

- TV – My Smart TV has multiple MCUs – I counted 8 on the picture from the service guide

- Soundbar and subwoofer – Soundbar has 4 and the sub has 2

- Cable box – I counted 6 on the picture I found of the guts

- Gas fireplace – 3

- Wireless speakers (Sonos Play 1) – I counted 4

- 3D printer – 12 or more

- Wireless router – 20+ and a real Broadcom processor too!

- Game consoles – Easily 20 each plus real processors

- My laptop I am typing on – Another 20 easily and a real CPU of course

- Thermostat (NEST) – 6 I could see

- Smart lock (also NEST) – 8 I could find on the picture

So, you can see I am well above the "typical home" (although I suspect with the rate of computerization you are too!). I have found in a quick look around without getting up from where I am sitting, almost 100 MCU and control units. I am sure with a full search I could push that to over 200 easily and that's before I count all the NodeMCUs and Raspberry Pis I have for workshops (which feels like cheating a little).

Why does this matter? Because this immense amount of supply and relentless drive to increased miniaturization have driven down the cost of small MCUs to the point where they can literally be used for fun. This tipping point probably really takes hold sometime around the early 2000s with the advent of the Arduino and associated community of hobbyists, but there are many families of MCU now that afford the hobbyist the ability to embed a logic and program into just about anything they could want. The current smallest MCU was unveiled in June of 2018 and the entire package clocks in at about 0.3 mm. Yes, 1/3rd of a millimeter from edge to edge. It is dwarfed by a grain of rice and includes the ability to send and receive signals and measure temperature. That is some serious Sci-Fi stuff right there, but in the realm of "things you might actually use" there are hundreds of practical modules for your own projects, depending on what you need.

Sensors and Industrial Controls

Departing the computer for a moment, the other part of any smart device is the humble sensor. Sensors were not always called sensors, in fact the history of the "sensor," as we know it, begins with the concept of the "Industrial Control." All smart devices today are simply a digital descendant of these industrial control concepts. If I want to measure and control an action of a thing, without having to constantly manage it directly myself, I need a means to measure and report on that thing's state, and then react to that state with the appropriate action. That statement, more than any other, is what leads to some of our greatest breakthroughs, and it is the genesis of the modern smart device. If you thought that the "computer" has a long history, the history of the theory and uses of the industrial control is mind bogglingly long.

For many centuries, people have sought to measure and manage things accurately; from time, to capacity, to distances, there is always a need to keep accurate measures, generally as it applies to commerce. Knowing the change of seasons, when to harvest and when to plant, the migrations of animals, these are all critical things early people needed to measure accurately in order to not just survive but expand as a civilization. The economic drivers behind invention cannot be ignored, not just in terms of monetary gain, but in terms of "intangible" assets like time. If I can reliably know when things are supposed to happen without constantly checking the soil or the skies or going out and seeing if the herds are where I think they should be, I free up time to do other things. Time is just as critical an asset of expansion as money, and the idea of reliably measuring time is a basic premise of early science.

The biggest hurdle to accurately measuring time on our particular ball of rock is that it moves. That means that different things are in different places at different times. This can be staggeringly difficult to overcome, and early people relied on something that was fixed. They used the sun and its regular rise and set cycle to measure time passing. This works pretty well and allows for the sort of "gross" time measurement that would have been critical to early civilizations: time to plant, time to harvest, time to hunt. When civilization starts to become more predicated on trade and the supply of goods to far-flung places, this type of gross timekeeping starts to fail. Fruits and vegetables go bad in a number of days, not many months. A more accurate means of keeping time is needed for enabling the next expansion.

It is because of this need that the concepts of industrial controls and the modern smart device are created. It starts with the simplest concept in automation: the feedback loop. A feedback loop is a system of control in which the device being controlled responds to a state condition via some means of feedback. One of the first feedback control devices on record is believed to be the ancient water clock of Ktesibios, which was kept in Alexandria, Egypt, around 250 B.C. Ktesibios's water clock was an amazing design using water to fuel and regulate an accurate timekeeping mechanism. The clock kept more accurate time than any clock invented until the pendulum clock of the 17th century. This is an example of the answer to "how do I manage this thing without having to check that it has water a million times a day?" By designing a system that regulated the flow of water, and the use of a regulating mechanism, the clock could essentially be self-maintaining as long as it was supplied with water. Move that concept into the modern age, and apply electricity to replace the water, and a modern industrial control is born!

Throughout the Renaissance and Age of Enlightenment and into the Industrial Revolution, the concepts and means of providing these industrial controls were perfected and refined. In 1620, Cornelis Drebbel designed a control system based on the volume of mercury in a tube to operate a furnace, effectively designing the first thermostat. Another early control mechanism was patented by Edmund Lee in 1745 and was used to tent the sails of windmills in order to control the gap between the grinding stones driven by the sails. The concept he introduced in his discovery led to one of the most fundamental controls for the Industrial Revolution, the Steam Governor, produced in November 1788 by James Watt and later improved on by both William Siemens and James Clerk Maxwell.

The Industrial Revolution primarily focused on controlling the temperatures and pressures of steam to ensure continuous operation of steam-driven machinery. In the early 1900s, however, the need for control over increasingly larger and larger machines of war necessitated the rapid development of new types of controls and actuators. It is during this period that the servomotor (servo) is developed, along with huge advances in pneumatic, hydraulic, and most importantly electrical controls and means of detecting different states and alerting based on those states. A major revolution in command and control of industrial systems comes in the 1920s when power plants get central control rooms, and the concept of color-coded lights is put into common practice to alert operators to issues.

Fast forward a bit, past the World Wars, and into the late 1960s and early 1970s, the computer is already on the scene (NASA now has several, and has sent men on the way to the moon with them), and the need for a more robust and most importantly adaptable system to monitor and control industrial systems is becoming more and more pressing. It is at this point that the Programmable Logic Controller, or PLC, is developed in 1968. This device allowed a control scheme to be configured, and most importantly, changed without the need to completely refit the whole environment with new devices. The PLC was manual, with wires needing to be connected to different logic points to build the control flow, but this was far and away better than the idea of ripping out entire manufacturing lines, for example, just to change the process of one or two steps. This simple change revolutionized the ability of manufacturers to retool production lines without having to build an entirely new set of tooling and processes as well as the monitoring of those steps from scratch every time.

The development of the PLC, along with the advancements in computing power, memory, and speeds, meant that it was possible now to incorporate hundreds, and eventually many thousands, of sensors and actuator controls into a single logic matrix, enabling the control of massive environments. It is the utility companies that push this forward as the primary consumers of these networks building out and developing them in what are known as Supervisory Control and Data Acquisition networks, or SCADA networks. SCADA networks are the most complete progenitor to the concept of the smart environment we started out describing and are still in common use today. They allow a utility company to monitor remote transformer stations, power stations, power lines, and with the emergence of smart metering they can even monitor the individual consumer. SCADA networks allow utilities to pinpoint demand spikes, generation issues, and device faults from a central location without the need to drive out to the middle of nowhere and physically look at the devices.

The convergence of all the technologies: the idea of a network of devices, working together to alert on changing conditions and actively mitigate them has met up with the growth of computing power, and the rapid advances in communications and storage capacity, means that we can now collect and store all the data from anywhere at any time. Now again enters the eternal question "what if I could do that without having to manually manage it?" It seems in this telling, a natural offshoot of the SCADA concept that the smart device would follow-on, but it took many further decades of development before the underlying technology was ready for truly smart devices. Primarily the issues were in miniaturization, communications mechanisms, and the ability to power devices for long enough to make them functional as portable and remote units.

In wearables, for example, after the introduction of the watch in 1500, it isn't until the 1980s that we get the calculator watch and 2009 that we get the first Fitbit. The first personal use sensors don't really hit the market until around 2010, and until we get the Raspberry Pi and Arduino boards in and around 2012, there isn't much to do with them on your own, if you are not building industrial sensing gear. The release of smaller, lighter, and cheaper computing devices and sensors (both in real dollars and in terms of their power consumption needs) that allow the assemblage of devices that we carry around with us in smartphones, watches, our cars, and increasingly in our homes is the final piece of the Smart Device puzzle. Once those devices became more mainstream and were readily available to the general public, the Smart Device era really began to take off.

Summary

And so, you have arrived at the end of the history lesson. The rise of computing and its relentless drive to miniaturize and pack more power into smaller spaces. The desire for industrial control over processes and systems so we can manage more without being physically present. And finally, the advent of our modern, digital age, replete with a variety of small sensors, computers, and the ability to get them in hand to make your own smart systems. This history is important in understanding the general why of smart devices, and from here we will embark into the how. The next chapter focuses on building up your own lab of hardware to both complete the later exercises in the book and also to experiment on your own. From there we will take a brief look at smart systems themselves, and then work our way through basic EE theory and designs to complex smart systems, and eventually to building your own circuit boards and PCBs. Let's start though by looking at the things you need most to get a well-stocked workbench of things to build your own smart devices.

CHAPTER 2

The DIY Smart Era

What do you need to have to get your own Smart Device journey under way? While that is obviously a highly subjective question, I have tried to get the basic sort of starter kit and options together in this chapter to get you ready and going with a basic home workbench. The options I have cited will also be required to complete the labs "as built," but as I will point out throughout the process, half the fun of the smart device world is experimentation with new devices and options! So, in this chapter then, a quick look at the rise of the availability of smart device components, and then a "shopping list" if you will to get your lab in order.

Instant Gratification

There have always been the home-brew crowd that was pushing the boundaries of what computing could do. The emergence of homebuilt and self-programmable computers in the 1970s and 1980s is evidence of this and progresses through the 1990s to the early 2000s when the first Ultra-Portable computing devices emerge. It is easiest to describe them as the now familiar "Arduino" devices and others like them – small, single-board computers with limited capabilities that were designed to support a single objective of allowing the device to interface with sensors and actuators. These immediately became the controller of choice for many industrial systems and were copied and cloned in thousands of different configurations. The inclusion of wireless, Bluetooth, Bluetooth/Mesh,

© Christopher Harrold 2020
C. Harrold, *Practical Smart Device Design and Construction*,
https://doi.org/10.1007/978-1-4842-5614-5_2

and an increase in the reliability and availability of these units has created an opportunity for anyone who wants to make and control devices and elements with these powerful and small computers. The possibilities for wearable, personal, home control and automation, manufacturing, agriculture, medicine, city management, indeed just about anything you interact with could be instrumented and managed with these types of devices.

The DIY era of the smart device has benefited from this rapid proliferation of hardware and software, to be sure, but without a distribution mechanism to get that hardware into your hands, there is no DIY smart revolution. No history of the smart device can, therefore, be complete without mentioning Amazon, Alibaba, MicroCenter, Fry's, and every other mega retailer that handles technology components. It is not far off to make an argument that the ability to buy literally anything under the sun and have it sent directly to your door in a minimum amount of time has done more for DIY smart devices than any single other technology. Certainly, this is a grossly over-simplified way of saying that the global supply and manufacturing system, the advances in shipping and logistics, combined with the development of large-scale warehousing and fulfilment logistics are all the foundation on which the DIY movement depends, but the most visible and ubiquitous face of that series of developments is the retail engine that supports this marketplace, and the endless supply of parts and tools for building smart devices.

Recognizing this market trend, there are also many vendors that have responded by creating "ready to go" kits with an MCU/Computer and sensors allowing the DIYer to get up and running in a matter of a few minutes from the time they crack open the box to the time their first LED blinks. The need to potentially go to multiple stores to get breadboards, wires, sensors, MCU or computer, soldering gear, and other tools and parts requires time and effort, and that creates a logical barrier to entry for smart devices; if I have to spend a long time gathering the parts, I lose time building. Rapid fulfilment is something that makes the DIY movement more mainstream, and the response is a market that is well stocked with the tools needed for the assembly of nearly any smart device you can conceive.

While by no means conclusive, the following is a basic shopping list for you as you prepare to build your own devices. This is not an endorsement of any specific manufacturer, or even a recommendation except that I have used these devices myself and know that they will work in the projects in the book. The items on the list will give you the basics needed for all of the projects in this book, as well as many others. Once you get started building smart devices, I am sure you will find as I do that there is always that "one more/better/newer sensor/chip/MCU" you need to build the next thing you dream up. This book will lay the foundation for you to incorporate any type of sensor or Computer/MCU into your devices, but this list will give you the bare minimum to get a lab running without a lot of effort or expense!

The Minimum DIY Lab

A minimal lab for your own prototype projects should not be a barrier to entry for you to get started with smart devices. There are a variety of all-in-one kits that will let you build with a specific MCU and a variety of sensors that are already included in the kit. There are also many, many sensor kits with a variety of sensors. I have avoided putting a price on these as I was mildly surprised when I compared them from 2016/2017 to 2019 when I looked again at how much they had gone up in price. Because prices can and do change rapidly, I did not want to put a price here that might be inaccurate, but I have tried to focus on keeping a total kit an under $100 investment. (Also if you type the first few words of the **BOLD** description into the search, you should find the referenced item at the top of the results list in an Amazon search.)

MCU Kits

- **Elegoo EL-KIT-001 UNO R3 Project Complete Starter Kit with Tutorial for Arduino**

  A very good kit for Arduino, with a massive sensor selection for a starter kit, including some uncommon ones like a display screen and radio-frequency identification (RFID) sensor.

- **CanaKit Raspberry Pi 3 B+ (B Plus) Ultimate Starter Kit (32 GB Edition, Clear Case)**

  Cana Kits are the "gold standard" for Raspberry-Pi all-in-one kits as they give you all the parts to make the Pi immediately useful, such as a case, SD card, and power supply. The Pi starter kits are at a premium however, and as such there are no sensors in this kit, only LEDs and buttons. Adding a small sensor starter kit is an inexpensive way to make this kit more useful.

- **OSOYOO NodeMCU IOT Starter Kit 2018 Open Source Programming Learning with NodeMCU ESP8266 Wi-Fi Development Board and Free Tutorial for MQTT Broker**

  A nice little kit for the NodeMCU (ESP8266–based MCU) with an emphasis on servos and motors, but with a couple of regular environmental sensors as well.

Sensor Kits

- **KOOKYE 16 in 1 Smart Home Sensor Modules Kit for Arduino Raspberry Pi DIY Professional (Smart Home Kit)**

- **ELEGOO Upgraded 37 in 1 Sensor Modules Kit with Tutorial for Arduino UNO R3 MEGA 2560 Nano**

- **HiLetgo 37 Sensors Assortment Kit 37 Sensors Kit Sensor Starter Kit Arduino Raspberry pi Sensor kit 37 in 1 Robot Projects Starter Kits for Arduino Raspberry Pi**

All of these kits have a good variety of sensors and a couple of unique ones here and there that might make you want one or the other. I have tried to focus on kits that are affordable, but still offer enough sensors to make the kit worthwhile. The reality is that, if you get started on building smart devices and really start to invest, you will spend the bulk of the money on sensors and devices to connect to your MCU in the long run. These kits are all designed to give you something to get going with quickly as you get the basics down and begin to embark on building out your project(s).

Build Your Own

Of course, one of the best things about the DIY Smart Era is that you get to build your own things from scratch, and your selection of project materials is no different. To complete the build-along exercises in the labs in this book, as well as for your own explorations, this is the absolute minimum requirements for your own home lab kit, and even if you purchase the starter kits discussed, there may be things in this list they do not include, so it is worth checking!

- Double A or "AA" battery boxes (see Figure 2-1) – No kit is ever complete without one!

Figure 2-1. *Various "AA" battery holders (1, 2, 3, and 4 battery versions)*

- Breadboard(s) – Covered in detail in Chapter 4; they are indispensable! (See Figure 2-2.)

Figure 2-2. *Various breadboards (full-length, half, and solderable perfboard style)*

- Resistors – Also covered in Chapter 4, you can never have enough! (See Figure 2-3.)

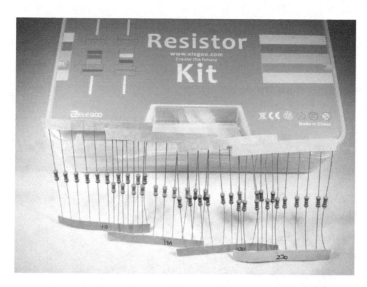

Figure 2-3. *Various resistors and a resistor kit*

- LEDs – Again, you can never have enough or enough variety. (See Figure 2-4.)

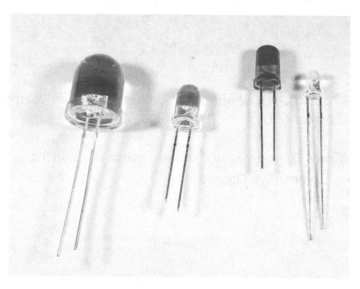

Figure 2-4. *A variety of LED sizes and colors – don't let the clear dome fool you, they can be different colors as well!*

21

- The MCU of your choice – The kits I recommended earlier have one of each of the "big 3" for DIY use, but there are many others. See Figure 2-5 for images and Chapter 5 for more detail.

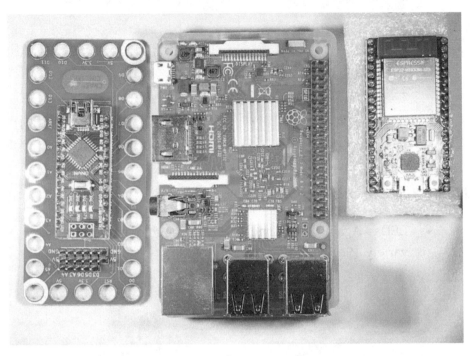

Figure 2-5. *Various MCU options (L-R Arduino Nano, Raspberry PI 3B+, ESP32 NodeMCU)*

- Wires – There are many, and you will need them for prototypes. (See Figure 2-6.)

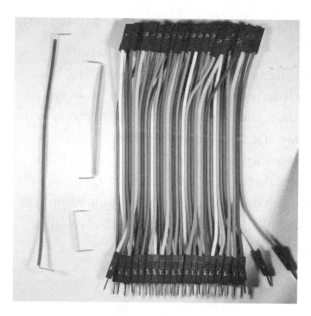

Figure 2-6. *Various wires (L-R pre-cut "breadboard wires," M-F wires in a bundle)*

As for sensors, minus the fact that like LEDs, you can probably never really have enough, you are going to need the following basic devices to complete the lab builds. I have focused on using relatively inexpensive sensors and devices here, not top of the line sensors, but for experimenting and lab prototypes, these devices are functional if not exactly "commercial grade." **Note:** You can of course use your own sensor(s), but the associated code may not work without modifications. I will try and call out any places where this could be an issue.

To Complete the "Build It" Exercises As Written

Just to note, I will explain the details of all of these parts in the book, so if you don't understand a term or acronym, they are explained, but since you need the gear to get going on the build labs, I want you to have the list first instead of at the end of the book.

- **4 Pcs Radial Electrolytic Capacitor 25V 10000UF
  105C**

  OK, so these are optional strictly speaking, because
  other than providing a ridiculous amount of
  capacitance for the lab build, they are probably not
  super useful. You will find smaller (physically and
  capacitance wise) versions in many of the other
  kits, and do not need this one, but your build will
  not match the pictures in the lab guide without it,
  so I included it for completeness. They look like
  Figure 2-7 for reference.

Figure 2-7. *10,000 Microfarad Capacitor – OVERKILL is thy name!*

- **LAMPVPATH (Pack of 8) AA Battery Holder Bundle
  2Pcs Single AA Battery Holder, 2Pcs 2X 1.5V AA
  Battery Holder with Leads, 2Pcs 3X 1.5V 3 AA Battery
  Holder with Wire, 2Pcs 4X 1.5V 6 Volt Battery Holder**

I used this exact kit in the labs, but really any type of basic battery holders will work. This kit is nice, and inexpensive, with a couple of each type of holder to provide some flexibility for your projects as you see in Figure 2-8.

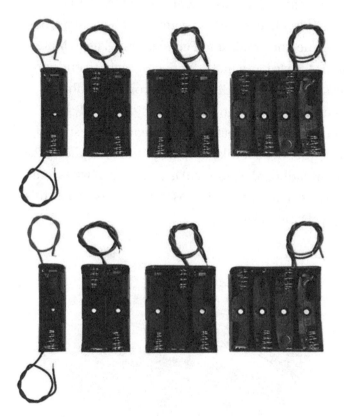

Figure 2-8. *Battery holders for a variety of voltage levels*

- **LANDZO 120pcs Multicolored 40pin Male to Female, 40pin Male to Male, 40pin Female to Female Breadboard Jumper Wires Ribbon Cables Kit for Raspberry Pi and Arduino**

You will probably get some wires of this type with a kit, but again, for completeness I included this set here. Wires like these for prototyping have two types of connectors: Male and Female. The Male to Male. or MM, style has a male connector on both ends and is useful for connecting the holes on a breadboard together. The Male to Female version, or MF, is often used to connect from the header on a small computer header (like the ones on the Raspberry Pi) to a breadboard. Figure 2-9 is a nice kit of wires, and there are packages for just MM and FF as well as this type of combo kit.

Figure 2-9. *Wire kit*

- **AUSTOR 560 Pieces Jumper Wire Kit 14 Lengths Assorted Preformed Breadboard Jumper Wire with Free Box**

  Again, probably a bit of a "nice to have" item, but these Breadboard wires are nice to use in complex prototypes as they can help keep the wiring mess a little more controllable. Plus, Free Box! The kit looks like Figure 2-10 for reference.

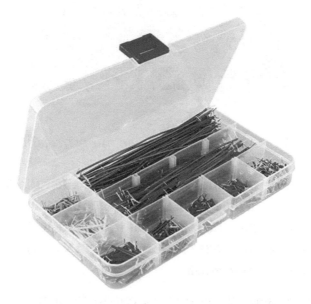

Figure 2-10. *Breadboard wires are a nice wiring convenience*

- **Hilitchi 675-Piece 15 Values 2N2222-S9018 NPN PNP Power General Purpose Transistors Assortment Kit**

  This one is for sure overkill only because you need one for the lab, but again, this is the kit I used the transistor from for it. There are transistors in the other kits I mentioned as well, so check before you buy the one you see here in Figure 2-11 as you may not need it. (It won't hurt, just trying to save you a few $$.)

Figure 2-11. *Transistor kit with way too many transistors*

- **Chanzon Fast Switching/Schottky/Rectifier Diode Assorted Kit (200pcs 14 Values 1N4001 1N4004 1N4007 RL207 1N5404 1N5406 1N5408 UF4007 FR107 FR207 1N5817 1N5819 1N5822 1N4148) Electronic Assortment**

  I am sensing a theme of giving you overkill items, but this is the kit I got the diodes from for the lab build, and just wanted to be complete. Again, check your other kits as there are usually one or two mixed into a few of the starter kits, but if not, then Figure 2-12 is the kit I got with a big selection of them for future projects as well.

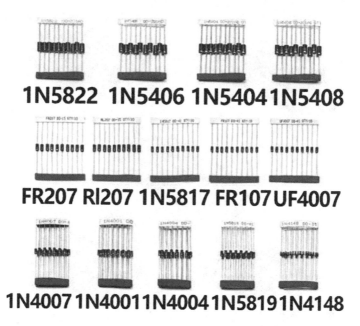

1N5822 1N5406 1N5404 1N5408

FR207 RI207 1N5817 FR107 UF4007

1N4007 1N4001 1N4004 1N5819 1N4148

Figure 2-12. *Diode kit, with way too many diodes*

- **DAOKI 5PCS High Sensitivity Sound Microphone Sensor Detection Module for Arduino AVR PIC**

  You only need one, but I got them in this 5 pack for a reasonable price. The sound sensor that comes with the Elegoo kit is similar and works with the same code. See Figure 2-13.

Figure 2-13. *DAOKI sound sensors (there are lots that are identical sold under different names)*

- **Gikfun Capacitive Soil Moisture Sensor Corrosion Resistant for Arduino Moisture Detection Garden Watering DIY (Pack of 2PCS) EK1940**

  Again, you will only need one of these for the lab, but it is a great sensor that is really sensitive and provides a nice analogue output (I will cover outputs later). Soil moisture sensors that come with the other kits are similar but may require tweaking your code. See Figure 2-14.

Figure 2-14. *Gikfun capacitive moisture sensor – there are also similar variants for less money, but quality varies widely!*

- **eBoot 30 Pieces Photoresistor Photo Light Sensitive Resistor Light Dependent Resistor 5 mm GM5539 5539**

  Last bit of overkill I promise, but this was the smallest/least expensive kit I could find the Light Dependent Resistors for the smart system build later. It never hurts to have a few of these on hand, so it's not wasted to get the bigger kit that you see in Figure 2-15, but like the others, check the starter kit as it may have one already to save a few bucks.

Figure 2-15. *Light Dependent Resistors in the kit*

Pretty much everything else used in the labs came from one of the starter kits I mentioned earlier, or was from other stuff I had lying around. There are a lot of buttons in one starter kit, as well as LEDs, but both can also be ordered in a larger "bulk" package for a few dollars each via a quick search.

I did a quick add up and all in, with all the overkill kits included, I spent just over roughly $120 for everything that shows up in the labs (including the MCU and RPi). You can easily spend a lot on the kit over time, and as your needs/wants grow, you probably will, since you will likely want to purchase increasingly sensitive, powerful, and complex sensors and gear, as well as just needing additional bits and pieces like transistors, diodes, and capacitors for your circuits. You do not have to do so of course, and you will find that even the inexpensive sensors and components are useful for smaller and less demanding projects.

Software Considerations

The other major thing you are going to need to decide on is the language(s) you want to code in. As mentioned before, there are a myriad of software tools and languages for you to choose from, but I would advise anyone just starting in smart devices to get a solid foundation in at least C/C++ and Python. Those two languages are the most common to find examples for and are also the most functional depending on the platform you choose. Most Arduino compatible MCU platforms will use some variant of C/C++ and the Raspberry Pi is very easy to program using Python and its massive collection of libraries that will allow you to get running quickly.

In Chapter 8, I will go into some specifics of both languages for smart devices, but it is by no means a comprehensive education in either. There are countless tutorials and guides for both languages in books and online that will get you through the basics and help you get going with confidence.

It is also obvious, but should be mentioned now, that you will need some sort of computer for programming your MCU. I am a Mac user, but there are specific limitations with using the latest gen Mac and Mac OS to program ESP8266-based MCUs in particular, which I found out after a great deal of pain while preparing for a workshop. My recommendation is to have at least a basic Windows machine for the programming of the Arduino and compatible MCUs, if not the development element of the code. You will need to be able to work with, save, and load code to your MCU to complete all but the most basic "build it" exercises in this book. You do not need something powerful to program the devices themselves, just something capable of an Internet connection, and running the IDE for passing the code, generally over USB.

One other incredibly important note – you will be using A LOT of standard 5v USB cables, like the kind you use for charging various devices around your house. However, it is critically important that you know that there are actually two types of those cables, one that is just for power and another that actually is for data transmission. The ones that come in the kits mentioned earlier are the latter, but if you buy the MCU outside a kit, or you just grab a random USB cable that you have around the house, you will very likely NOT have the right cable. I recommend these only because I have validated personally that they work:

Rankie Micro USB Cable High Speed Data and Charging, Nylon Braided, 3-Pack 3FT

They are very inexpensive and will save you a massive headache later when you cannot understand why your computer cannot connect to the device!

Software Used in the Book

If you really just want to be able to use exactly the same software I did for the examples and screenshots (and I can understand why – much easier to complete the exercises when everything looks the same), here is the list:

- **Visual Studio Code** – Microsoft's free IDE – A very good tool for developing code

- **Arduino IDE** – Required for deploying to both Arduino and NodeMCU devices

- **GitHub** – An account is free, and it is a very useful too beyond just what I show you in the book

- **Node-Red** – Node-Red is a graphical programming tool that is included on the Raspberry Pi

- **Mosquitto** – Mosquitto is a very lightweight message broker server that you can run on an RPi or your own computer for using MQTT messaging

Keep in mind that versions change, and so the screenshots and processes I show in the book may have changed from the time I documented them until now. Fundamentally though, the tools and programs used *should* be pretty much the same from version to version. One place this is also a factor is in the code itself. The code I have provided as a companion to the book, via a repository on GitHub, is written using the common version of the languages (Python and C++) that were in use at the time of writing. However, a great example of the change that could occur is that the Python code had some version 2.x elements, and that version is set to be discontinued for version 3 this year (2020), and so my exceptional reviewer noted it during one of the editing rounds, and I updated it accordingly. This is not to say that it won't change again, so if you are looking at this book in the future, it is possible that the code may have changed again, the UI of a tool might be different, and even whole lines of computers, MCUs, and sensors may not exist anymore. The good news is there is lots of backward compatible consideration given to this phenomenon and so *mostly* things just work when moving from version to version, but it is worth considering as you begin building your own projects.

Summary

You've now got the basic ingredients to get through this book and also to expand beyond what you learn here and branch out to your own projects. The introductory kits found here will help you build out a great many projects and give you lots of room to experiment as you learn more and develop your skills. Even if you don't have something you need, it is always close at hand with the ability to get parts and kit quickly via the global supply chain that has evolved alongside the expansion of smart device capabilities. One last stop before you dig into the theories and foundations of basic electronic engineering concepts, and then on to working with sensors and building smart device. Smart Devices are inextricably linked to the concept of the IoT, or Internet of Things, but I want to spend a little time talking through the IoT, and why smart devices and the IoT are not the same and do not have to be, before you get into the building.

CHAPTER 3

Beyond the Hype – Smart Today and Tomorrow

Before we start building, there is one last foundation I want to lay for you to begin your projects. Smart devices are a class of small device that performs various functions in extension of the user. These could be as simple as a device to check the temperature or a complete set of devices that are used to form the basis of a complete agriculture solution that measures temperature, moisture, and sunlight for optimizing crops. The purpose of this book is to distil the *concept* of an entire smart farm into the building blocks, the smart devices that make up that smart farm solution. It is at this point that anyone who is technically savvy or aware of trends in tech will likely start to equate it to IoT, or Internet of Things, which is the omnipresent buzzword for all things that are connected and form smart systems. As I mentioned before, I am purposely avoiding using IoT in this book, but I feel that it is worth bringing up conceptually, and then laying to rest before we move on.

© Christopher Harrold 2020
C. Harrold, *Practical Smart Device Design and Construction*,
https://doi.org/10.1007/978-1-4842-5614-5_3

The IoT That Wasn't

I do not favor the term IoT, as it is both a misnomer and a term that engenders specific responses, both good and bad. IoT stands for "Internet of Things", which is just a buzzy, marketing speak way of saying "connected devices." The misnomer that I spoke of is that by saying it is the "Internet of Things," it has to include the Internet. Much like the hype around "Big Data," which was just a buzzy way to say analytics, implied that you had to have a ton of data to do meaningful analytics on it, using the word "Internet" in the name almost forces you to conclude that your device must be on the Internet to be a smart device. Nothing could be further from the truth!

In point of fact, you can successfully build entire smart systems that have no connection to the Internet at all. The Internet provides a convenience for certain things in terms of user interfaces, and access to advanced capabilities that cloud-based tools can give you, such as machine learning or AI, but it isn't *REQUIRED*. In fact, more and more of those technologies are being adapted to run at the point of data collection on smaller systems such as Raspberry Pi, Intel NUC, and other small computers. Indeed, there are already several "edge" adaptations for image recognition, and other ML/AI type functions that can be deployed on a Raspberry Pi, eliminating the need to access cloud resources. The Internet can also be a huge advantage for the user experience of certain devices, for example, the Nest line of home products. Having access to my home thermostat, locks, doorbell, and others can be hugely useful and provide an additional layer of interaction that gives me extra value. However, I don't explicitly *have* to have this in order for the devices themselves to function; my thermostat continues to work just fine even without Internet access, as do the other devices. I can use them while in my home on the same network, with the same functionality I enjoy from out of the house.

Taking the I out of IoT

I have done a series of talks about "taking the I out of IoT" that encourages people to find ways to make their smart devices work without needing Internet access – something that is totally possible with planning and good design. The reality is that industrial controls and automation have been around for a very, very long time, and the hyperbole and hype around IoT makes it sound as though this is a new invention, only made possible with the advent of the Internet. The hype machine would have everyone believe that you need a full and aggressive IoT strategy in order to stay relevant. Frankly, this is a lot of marketing and very little fact.

There are so many things for which smart device capabilities make a lot of sense, such as asset tracking through RFID, or smart cars, or manufacturing and assembly-line management. Even in the home, the proliferation of smart thermostats, lights, heat, and so on all help us combat the growing threats from climate change. Wearables help us with our fitness and keep us connected. Many, if not all, of these do not require any sort of Internet connection to be useful and powerful in the hands of their users. They need to be accessible, of course, but that doesn't mean they *have* to be on the Internet to be useful. That is a tool of convenience, not necessity, and one that, while very useful in terms of me turning on my thermostat from the airport, isn't strictly required for my smart thermostat to work.

In this book, we are talking about the basics of a smart device, but there is so much more involved in a full connected solution that combines hardware and sensors, data collection, processing, visualization, responses, and automation means. I said earlier that any smart system is really just sensors connected to a central processing device, and that is 100% true. The smart devices then make up a *part* of the IoT ecosystem, but not the whole. In this way they form a critical component, but they themselves are actually just a small part of the overall solution. However, they are also where the most intensive use of hardware comes into play, and as such, that is the hurdle I want to help you as the reader get over. The reality is you do not need the Internet to tell if the sun is shining or the temperature is hot or cold, and a simple smart device will do all of that with even minimal capabilities. (In fact, you will build one later in the book.)

There is another facet to consider which is having the ability to access the *output* of the smart system you are building kind of implies the use of the Internet. Yes, it is really nice to be able to raise and lower my temperature at home from anywhere, see my yard and door, check my watering schedule, and so on, but that means that a sufficiently motivated attacker can do all of that too, and that risk is a chance we take with IoT. That said, you can do a whole lot locally, and in point of fact with things like webhooks and other tech you can probably do a lot remotely that you may not have thought of. We will talk about some of this in the later chapters of this book, because it is my firm belief that the highest barrier to people getting into the connected world is the hardware and how to handle it, but having that result be something you can see and interact with is what makes smart devices powerful.

Connected

A modern, connected system is made up of five key parts:

- Sensors, actuators, and their controllers (the focus of this book)

- A transport method (Bluetooth, Wi-Fi, really long wires – all qualify)

- A central control gateway (provides the interface to the collection devices)

- A place to store the collected data (databases, files, etc.)

- A way to visualize it (some sort of UI that makes the data and information consumable and actionable)

Really any smart system follows this basic pattern with these basic parts. Sensors collect the data about the conditions around what is being monitored. Moisture, light, humidity, and temperature for a garden or farm. The speeds, position of items, and number of items for an assembly line. The speed, position, surrounding distances, nearby objects, and distances for a car. The only thing that really changes in the smart system is the sensing devices and the things being measured. From there you send that data to a central "brain" that does the heavy lifting. Why? Because the local computing power of the collectors will never be able to match the computing power of a central system. This is also the rationale behind the I in IoT in large part. The UI access is nice but not required. Processing billions of data points however is almost certainly going to require a massive amount of computing power. Also, it is worth noting that having things centralized is *easy*. You don't have to change the code on potentially thousands or even tens of thousands of devices to change your views, results, and so on. You can change one central command setting and that takes care of all the devices.

The downside to smart devices is that if your sensing devices are this distributed and thus "hardwired" to do a single function, then changing that function can become prohibitive, or really just impossible outright. You aren't likely to be able to take the sensors out of your car and change what they do with any level of convenience anytime soon. Same with thousands of soil sensor on a farm. It's not that you couldn't collect and modify them, but that's just a lot of work! You want your sensors doing the same thing, pretty much forever, because changing them out is a giant hassle and means that while you are doing that, you are either taking an outage of the system or not monitoring at least some part(s) of it. Thus moving the heavy lifting and "thinking" part of the system to a central, consolidated location means that you take the need to update potentially hundreds or thousands of collecting devices away, and instead have the big work done at the central spot, leaving the collectors to just function the same way all the time.

This is the main issue to overcome that made the Internet the cornerstone of "IoT"; by using the Internet as a "cheap" means of collecting data from myriad devices and consolidating it onto "cheap" cloud-based storage and compute, you can overcome the computing hurdle for huge numbers of devices. This completely ignores the advances in networking speeds and capacities, computing and storage costs and capacities, and the ability to do much more with smaller and smaller computers. Just like the huge push for "big data" was geared to make huge amounts of storage relevant, the "Internet of Things" is meant to push you logically to the cloud for your IoT platform. There isn't anything outright *wrong* with this approach, and it does meet that goal, but it also suffers massively from the unintended consequences that exposing any device to the Internet creates.

Thus, if you are going to really, truly, build a connected system to perform a function, there is one thing that needs to be done right, from the beginning, and has to just work, all the time. That is why I chose purposely to focus on the smart devices, the building blocks themselves, and the foundational skills needed to build them. The reality is that there is no IoT without smart devices, and they don't explicitly require the Internet for functionality. They can be programmed and built to perform locally with minimal direct access, providing greater security and the same functionality. Certainly, as you build your first prototypes, they will very likely not connect to the Internet as there is no need. In fact, you will likely just do the work on the device itself, since you don't have hundreds of collectors and the amount of data in terms of size is very small. The basic functions of sensing and processing inputs do not warrant sending data outside the device itself very much, but as you progress in terms of skills and complexity, the need will likely present itself, and you might want to move your computing power to a centralized location. Thus, my guidance to you is to minimize your dependence on the Internet for your smart device and find ways to keep it local when possible.

Why Not?

Why not use the Internet for your smart devices and all the tools that it offers? As the bard said, "therein lies the rub." The fact is for everything you do there is a trade-off. Having access to the Internet for transporting data, using cloud-based services, and storing and analyzing data is not undesirable in itself. Quite the contrary, there are many use cases where having your smart device access the Internet could provide increased functionality and capability. Using computer vision modules on a cloud service, for example, could make your camera-based sensor more intelligent by giving it classification ability without having to train models remotely and then load them to your smart device locally, which is time consuming and technically/administratively difficult. The trade-off is that every connection you make to the Internet is a vector for traffic going the other way, not all of which will be benign. One only needs to look at the spread of the Mirai botnet to see the risk of having smart devices with poor security in place, and exposed access to the Internet.

Internet connectivity means your attack surface is bigger and you have created a target on your virtual back. This means that security has to be a primary consideration if you intend to use anything enabled for Internet connectivity, and those considerations can be very tricky. Good device security will often be contrary to simple operation and development, and in many (far too many) cases, it gets ignored completely in favor of convenience. Identifying and remediating security risks in your designs is also not limited to software if you are going to look at anything commercial. There is an entire legion of hardware hacking practitioners out there who are just waiting to get hold of your device and rip it apart for analysis, and if you have left insecure access in place such as poor passwords or hardware access, then this is an easy task. The devices I am walking you through here are basic, and designed to be something that has no Internet connectivity, and so I have willfully avoided the discussion of security as it is a topic for a book all its own, but it is something you should keep in your mind as you go through the design process because it is important, and represents the major weak spot in IoT.

Where We Go Now

Well, the hype around IoT is starting to die down a bit, which is good, but it isn't dead yet, and there is still a pretty constant barrage of buzz and fluff about connected solutions, IoT, smart everything, and the overall push to connect our entire world. I suppose I am adding to that in a way by even writing this book, but I hope that it provides a much more practical and meaningful introduction to the connected world. There is no IoT without smart devices, and understanding how they work and more importantly how to build them is crucial to allow all the great things that our connected world can offer.

There is a silver lining to the hype around IoT which is that it has led to a lot of investment into the development of smart devices. This means that the future vision I teased in the introduction is coming closer and closer to reality. We already see self-driving tech coming to a variety of cars from different manufacturers, and the pace of smart home technology development shows no signs of slowing. There are devices for monitoring and interacting with just about every physical thing in your home from the outlets and lights to the sprinklers in the yard to the furnace in the basement. The future of smart devices is one where the power to use local services currently reserved for powerful cloud-based solutions is a reality, and the ability of the devices to support and extend us as human beings is greatly increased. Long after the IoT hype has died off, smart devices will still be supporting us and our ability to improve our lives, through their ability to augment our own.

Summary

The IoT while a buzzword does have practical implications and uses for smart devices, in fact relying on them to even exist. The underlying premise it creates, specifically that the Internet is required for Smart Devices to work, simply is not the truth. There can be many reasons you might want to use Internet-based services, access, and connectivity, however, the cautionary warning is just to be very aware of the exposure this can create. The development of the connected devices of the world is going to be an area where there will need to be people who understand the basic concepts of hardware, sensors, MCUs, and how those things connect together and work to make something happen in a smarter way. That journey starts in the coming chapters, with an introduction to the concepts and theories you need to understand to build the sensing hardware, connected systems, and ultimately how to make those things permanent, reliable, and smart.

PART II

Smart Hardware

As I worked on developing the concept for this book, one thing became immediately clear: the real struggle with Smart Devices is not the software, it is hardware. Hardware is scarier I think, because it is more tangible. Computer code failures generally just result in annoyances and lots of headdesk moments. Hardware failures, on the other hand, can cause pain and death. Electricity is no joke, and it should be treated with care and respect. Although the electricity we will be using in our smart devices is far less lethal than the stuff running in your household wires, it is this fear that I think keeps people from trying to get into smart devices. The prototypes you will build in your own home lab are not anywhere near powerful enough to kill you, and the types of projects that you find on the Internet and even in this very book are all meant to show you that the hardware is not scary. You can absolutely short out a circuit board or Raspberry Pi without proper wiring, but the whole point of this book is to make sure you don't!

I have spent a lot of time developing workshops to introduce people to the concepts and principles you will read about here which I hope will help to make the hardware for smart devices more approachable to you. As you progress through the projects and build out increasingly complex devices, you will encounter new bridges to cross with hardware. Certainly, when you move into printed circuit boards, there is a new challenge of permanence, but I am skipping too far ahead. We must begin with the most important things you need to know to build smart devices.

PART II

Smart Hardware

CHAPTER 4

EE for the Total N00b

Electrical Engineering, or EE, as a discipline is a very deep and fascinating area of study. It deals with the laws and principles of controlling electricity and how that electricity interacts with our environment. A single chapter in a book cannot hope to give you a full grounding in the deep concepts and theory of EE. Instead, I am going to focus on the applicable theories and, more importantly, the practical applications of those theories that you will need to account for and understand in designing smart devices specifically. This focuses primarily on the law governing electrical currents, voltages and resistance, and the various types of circuits.

In electronics there are three key things we need to always be aware of as we design our hardware for our Smart Device. They are Voltage, Current, and Resistance. These three forces are present in all electronic devices and the control of them is what makes those devices function. The reason they are so critical to the design of electronics is that they govern the ability of smart things to actually function. Too much voltage delivered to a pin on a sensor or MCU, and you just fried it because it cannot handle that much load. Not enough current flowing to an LED? The light it outputs could be dim or even not lit at all. Knowing the requirements of and the function of each of these fundamental forces is key to designing your device.

When thinking of these forces, I like to refer to a simple analogy that most people are familiar with, which is that electrical flow is a lot like water flowing through pipes. If we use that analogy, voltage is the water pressure, current is the flow rate, and resistance is analogous to the size of the pipe the water is flowing through. In our plumbing analogy, if we increase

© Christopher Harrold 2020
C. Harrold, *Practical Smart Device Design and Construction*,
https://doi.org/10.1007/978-1-4842-5614-5_4

the water pressure (Voltage), the flow of the water (Current) increases, provided the pipes are able to handle the capacity (Resistance) without either bursting or impeding the water's flow. Larger pipes can handle more flow, but if there is not enough pressure then they will mostly be empty. Figure 4-1 illustrates this analogy.

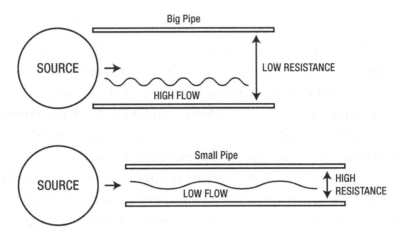

Figure 4-1. *Pipes showing different flow and resistance*

Luckily for us, there is a simple rule that governs the relationship between these forces. It is perhaps the most important rule in EE as it applies to Smart Devices: Ohm's law. Before I get to the law itself, a fascinating bit of history to impress your friends with: Ohm's law is one of those laws of science that, when you think it through, seems like a pretty self-evident conclusion.

It is written simply as

$$V = IR \text{ or } I = V/R \text{ or } R = V/I$$

When he first published it in 1827, however, it was derided as fantasy, even prompting the German Education Minister of that time to say that "a professor who was willing to publish something so obviously false was unfit to teach in Germany"! Ohm was roundly ridiculed and persecuted for his publication of the law and subsequently had a pretty rough go of it in the academic and scientific circles he worked in. Of course, we know now that Ohm's law has been proven out and it is not over-stating fact to say that, without it, the modern era would largely not exist. It is the simplest fundamental rule of electrical systems, and our understanding of it, and its 100% guaranteed proof, is what allows us to have everything we have that is powered by electricity today.

Thanks to the rules of mathematics, all of these say the same thing: The Current (Symbol: I; Unit of measure: Amperes or Amps) through a conductor (like a piece of wire) between two points is directly proportional to the Voltage (Symbol: V; Unit of measure: Volts) across those two points. This proportionality of Voltage and Current introduces the concept of Resistance (Symbol: R; Unit of Measure: Ohms), and the three work together to define how electricity flows and the means with which it can be controlled.

The simplest example is that if you have a 1V battery, delivering 1A of current, you also have 1 Ohm of resistance:

$$R = V/I$$

$$R = 1/1$$

$$R = 1$$

Translating this to electrical wiring, we can start to plan out what force of electricity needs to arrive at what device, and in what volume. Devices in electrical circuits are rated for voltage and current levels, and exceeding them will cause bad things to happen, which we want to avoid. It is very important to check the outputs and inputs of your devices to make sure you do not exceed these values. Generally, electronics come with a spec sheet (generally you can find them online – in the olden days they were printed and included with the element in question) that you can use to find the operating voltage, current limits, temperature range (important for outdoor applications! I have fried a few computers in the Colorado heat), and other pertinent operational parameters.

Having these operating parameters allows you to use Ohm's law in one of the most common ways you will find yourself using it as you build out your projects, "how much current do I need to make this thing work?" mode. Using Ohm's law allows us to calculate the missing part of a circuit in order to deliver the correct flow of energy to our devices. Generally, we will be working with the R =V/I form, because most often we know what the power source is putting out in terms of Voltage and Current (e.g., it is easy to find that a 1.5v AA battery outputs 1.5v (duh) and 50mA (50 milliamps) of current). So, you often need to reduce that amount by introducing resistance to get what you want.

It is also important to know that all conductors that you will work with have some level of resistance. That means that if you have a very precise meter, your measured voltage at the two points along a wire would be higher at the source and lower at the end. That is because the wire itself does not perfectly transfer the electric flow from one end to the other, causing some loss of voltage during the transfer. This gets markedly worse the longer the transmission distance becomes, which in the case of small devices is usually not an issue. It is worth being aware of if, for example, you want to have a sensor that is many feet away from the physical power source. This is why big power lines carry such high voltages – the loss from crossing great distances has to be offset by sending a lot of juice through the lines. This is also why we have transformers closer to people's houses, so that the current can be lowered to the 110/220v we are familiar with instead of the much higher voltages of the big transmission lines.

In addition to understanding the forward flow of current through your electronic circuits, part of any full circuit design should include some sort of circuit breaker or fuse mechanism to prevent over-current conditions. For very, very small circuits, this is often unnecessary, (certainly for all of the labs in the book you do not need it) but for anything of a commercial nature, or something that may be in a place that is remote or not easily accessed, this is a critical consideration.

Resistance

Resistance is the key concept in respect to controlling electric flows, and something that is worth investing some extra time in. It is the other mode you will use Ohm's law for in your own design and planning. "How big a resistor do I need?" mode is the other most common mode of solving Ohm's law equations, as resistance is the single most reliable and simple method for controlling the current and voltage of your own smart devices. It is critically important when you are constrained by a device's voltage requirements not matching your power supply for example, or where you need to reduce the current flow of a circuit to protect a device.

It is possible to control both the current and the voltage of a circuit with your resistors, and in this way, you can manage to pull off integrating components that otherwise would not match the available power supply. A simple example, an LED can be powered by a 9v battery, but without a resistor it will destroy the LED very quickly as it is not rated for that much voltage and current, but a proper resistor in the circuit ensures that the LED lights and functions. In fact, it would simply just stay happily lit until the battery ran out, which is how we want our circuits to function all the time.

Resistors themselves are usually very small components as you can see in Figure 4-2. They don't look like much, but their one job is to be stubborn; they are the Gandalf of current (you shall not pass!), and they resist the amount of flow per their rating. A resistor will be rated in Ohms (named for the Ohm whose law they are governed by of course) – and the resistance value is represented by the Ω symbol. Resistors are commonly available in values of 0 Ω, 10 Ω, 12 Ω, 15 Ω, 18 Ω, 22 Ω, 27 Ω, 33 Ω, 39 Ω, 47 Ω, 51 Ω, 56 Ω, 68 Ω, 75 Ω, 82 Ω, and 100 Ω and then multiples of each such as 510 Ω, 5.1K Ω, 51K Ω, and so forth. Generally, any kit you buy of resistors, including the one in this book, will have a good assortment of resistors that you can use to create the amount of resistance you need.

Resistors are not "perfect," meaning they will be pretty close to this value, but generally the resistors used in DIY projects (e.g., the kind you get for very little money on Amazon) have a tolerance of about ±5%. You can, of course, pay much more for exact precision resistors with much less variability, but for these types of devices it is generally not needed in prototype situations or even in a commercial application with proper planning.

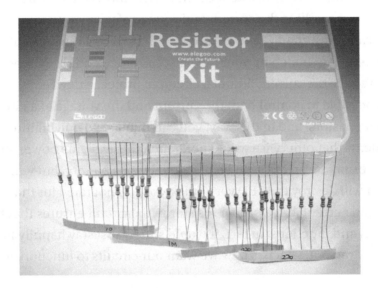

Figure 4-2. *Examples of resistors wiring diagram symbols*

You will also notice in Figure 4-2 that the standard barrel resistors have colored stripes on them. These stripes are how you "read" the resistance of that resistor. There is an excellent online tool provided by DigiKey (https://www.digikey.com) that gives you a guide and a simple "pick the colors" calculator to see what resistance you are working with. This calculator doesn't tell you how much resistance you **need** though, just what you have for a given resistor. Figuring out what you need to provide for resistance is where our buddy Ohm comes in.

Let's use a practical example:

CALCULATING RESISTANCE FOR A SIMPLE LED

Resistance reduces the current flow to devices along the path of the current, which is useful in this case, because LEDs will burn out if supplied with too much current for too long (if you want to try this, connect an LED directly to a 9v battery, it will light for a moment, and then you will hear a small *pop* as it burns out). This can also completely ruin your MCU! By having too much "live" voltage or too much current coming back to the MCU, you can burn out the board itself, which is obviously not ideal. We control the voltage by putting a resistor between the power source and the component (in this case, the LED), thus limiting the flow and keeping the LED or other devices from burning out.

Let's make a calculation using the law for our LED. To plug in the values to the formula, you need to know what voltage the LED operates at, and the current it needs to operate effectively. LEDs (or indeed any device/sensor/etc.) will usually have the required voltage in their datasheet or information – this is the voltage they operate at, and thus consume and remove from the total voltage available.

For an LED, this is generally called the forward voltage, and it is the amount of voltage that the LED takes out of the electrical energy flowing through it to do work. For a basic 5mm Red LED, they generally operate at around 1.8 volts at around 20 milliamps for maximum brightness. You can operate an LED at MUCH less than this, but you trade power efficiency for brightness – more current flow drains your battery faster, and your LED will go out sooner, but less current means your devices get less power and, in some cases, can mean they will not work at all.

So, we know two values for our three-part formula: the total voltage we have available (3V - this is the standard voltage output from most MCUs, as well as 2 1.5V batteries) and the voltage our LED uses up (1.8V), as well as the current it wants to receive to operate the best (20mA). Calculating the resistance needed to achieve that in our simple circuit is now just plugging in the values to the formula. Our conversion to Ohm's law looks like this:

(Total voltage − Consumed voltage) = Current in Amps X Resistance

$$R = 1.2V / 20mA$$

First, we subtract the voltage the LED consumes from the total voltage (3 − 1.8 = 1.2V leftover). Then we solve for "R". Because our current is in milliamps, we need to convert it to amps, by dividing by 1000 (Milli) which gives us 0.020A. After the conversion and computing the voltage, we end up with

$$R = 1.2V / .020mA$$

$$R = 60$$

We will need a 60 Ohm resistor to protect our LED. If you look back at the list of resistor sizes, you will see that 60 Ohm isn't in the list. That's OK, because of the variance, we can get away with picking the closest one. When using resistors in your projects, unlike on "The Price is Right", you want to definitely go over, so generally, you should pick the next highest value, which in this case is 68 Ohm.

You can also place resistors one after the other in a series (you'll learn about circuit types in the next section) – this will create resistance equal to the total of the resistors. So, if you needed a 20,550 Ohm resistance (which is a lot, but sometimes you need it!), you could put two 10k Ohm, a 512 Ohm, and four 10 Ohm resistors together which would put you just over that number. 20k, plus 512, plus 40 would put you at 20,554 Ohm which is well within the +/- of the resistor rating.

So now you know to light a Red LED with a 3V supply you need to add a 68 Ohm resistor to the path of flow! Can you use a higher resistance? Yes, and often I will just lazily throw a 100Ω resistor in my circuits because those are VERY common in the resistor kits you buy, BUT, using a higher resistance means less current reaching the component. If you want full brightness, you need full current flow. A 100 Ohm resistor works just fine, but the LED will be dimmer. Will it be a lot dimmer? Probably not enough that you could tell, but if you put a sufficiently high enough resistor in the flow, you could in effect cancel out the current altogether to such a level that the LED is not visible at all. You would certainly use much less of your battery, but a dark LED is not nearly as useful as one that lights up!

Calculating the flow of electricity is the basic function of electrical device design, and understanding how these forces relate and how to manipulate them is the most basic hardware design principle. You will spend a lot of time on this math during the planning phase of your projects and it is part of the fun of building out these smart devices; figuring out how to squeeze every last drop of amperage out of your batteries or MCU to power that one more LED or sensor. When you get it right and complete all the calculations to define the current and voltage flows, the result is the creation of a circuit.

Circuits

Circuits are the basic element of all smart devices. (Figure 4-3 illustrates a very basic circuit.) In fact, every electronic device from your garage door opener to the most powerful computers is made up of circuits. A circuit is just a path for electricity to flow through, that consists of a voltage source, a conductive pathway, power consumers, and ultimately a ground that closes the loop and acts like drain in our plumbing analogy. It is where the "used" electricity goes to complete the circuit. Circuits can be incredibly simple, or incredibly complex, but they follow a few basic sets of rules of membership:

1. You need a power source to supply fresh electrons into the circuit.

2. You need a path for those electrons to flow through the circuit – these are called conductors, and the simplest example is a wire.

3. You need a place for that current to flow to; this is the ground that completes the circuit.

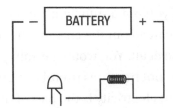

Figure 4-3. *Basic circuit*

An incredibly simple scenario that illustrates this: taking a wire and holding the ends to the ends of a battery. If you have not done this before as a kid, PLEASE DON'T DO IT NOW. It just causes the battery to get hot and it can definitely explode. That's because the battery is expecting what comes back to it to be less energetic than what left, and if you do not have anything else in your circuit, then you are just sending the raw voltage back, unchanged. This is bad, and seriously, with bigger batteries, can cause explosions and lots of pain.

That's why we need things in our circuit to consume the electrons that are flowing and to use that energy to do some sort of work. There are a few members of the circuit that are the parts that do the work:

1. Load devices – This could be an LED, a sensor, a motor, or truly anything that needs a supply of current to do something meaningful.

2. Protection devices – Fuses/breakers and the like that prevent a circuit from becoming damaged or uncontrolled if there is a power surge or failure of something in the circuit.

3. Control devices – Switches/buttons that turn the flow on and off and thus control the operability of the circuit.

Once we understand this, it becomes possible to create the fundamental architecture of the circuit, and thus the smart device itself. There are really only two types of circuits:

- **A series circuit** is a circuit where the power source, the consumers, and the ground are along a single path of conductivity (Figure 4-4).

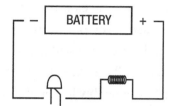

Figure 4-4. *Series circuit*

- **A parallel circuit** is one where there are multiple paths for electricity to flow to consumers before ending in a ground (Figure 4-5).

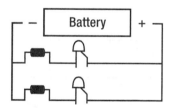

Figure 4-5. *Parellel circuit*

What is most important to understand about these circuits is the way each supplies its consumers with power. For example, you might think that a parallel circuit would supply less Voltage to each branch of the circuit, but (minus the resistance of the conductor), all paths start out with the **same** voltage. Their **current** however, that is the force of the current trying to flow into each path, is reduced by the number of paths that are present in the circuit. Electrically, the battery that supplies our electrical circuit supplies it with X number of Volts and amps per circuit path. The flow is not evenly distributed between these paths either. The flow of the current is divided between each path, *based on its resistance*. This last part is really important, because it means that high-resistance paths get less flow than those that are less resistant.

If you think back to our plumbing example, this makes sense when you draw it out. This is because in the plumbing example, as in the circuit, the water pressure supplied by the city (Voltage) isn't changed by having multiple faucets, but if you run all the faucets in your house at the same time there will be some with noticeably lower amounts of water coming out of them (less current). The pressure is a fixed value based on the supply, but if you give that pressure lots of routes to exit the system, then the flow will get smaller and smaller with each additional path, until only a trickle remains in each. Conversely, if you start turning off faucets (adding resistance) to some of the paths, the water will reroute to the open paths and the flow will increase for those paths. Figure 4-6 illustrates this.

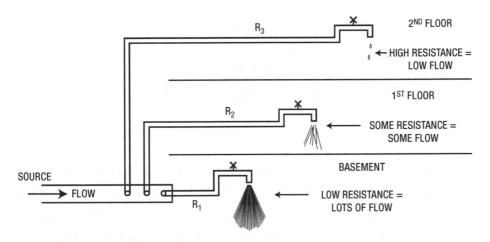

***Figure 4-6.** Parallel paths based on resistance*

This concept is important when planning out complex devices with multiple parallel circuits, as the difference in current could cause issues with your devices, and if you inadvertently have a fully open route back to the ground, you can cause a short that leads to bad things. As a general functional rule, parallel circuits are very often multiple series circuits connected in parallel paths to reduce or increase resistance and modify the flow of current. This is how you can ensure that the circuit is whole and does not cause power issues while still supplying the right amount of current to the devices on each circuit.

In a series circuit, the flow rate of the current is the same all through the circuit, because it is all travelling through the same "pipe." However, each consumer is in the same path of the flow of electrons, and each one reduces the voltage (water pressure) by the amount it requires. That means that the original 5v that leaves the battery drops some volts off at each load device, and it is possible to drop the voltage to zero with enough devices in the stream. Once this happens, the pressure of the flow is now at zero, and nothing will happen past that point in the circuit. Thus, the combination of series and parallel wiring is important to designing circuits that can drive multiple load devices without having to supply huge amounts of power which makes small devices impractical by requiring massive power sources. This understanding is critical for supplying multiple load devices that need a specific voltage, such as lights, without interference from other devices.

A parallel circuit can provide a certain level of redundancy, where, if a consumer is missing, and thus the path is broken, the remaining paths all still work. You can see this in a car, where a single turn signal light might burn out, thus not passing electricity anymore, but all the other turn signals and lights still function. While you need to ensure the other paths can handle a sudden influx of extra current, in smart devices the additional load of this is measured in milliamps, or thousandths of an amp, and doesn't generally result in overpowering of these small current circuits. (See Figure 4-7.)

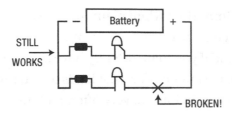

Figure 4-7. *Parallel circuit still partially works*

Series circuits on the other hand fail when one of the parts of the circuit fails. (See Figure 4-8.) You can see this in Christmas lights where a single bulb failure means the whole string fails. You can commonly find series circuits as part of the power supply of batteries, where several cells connected in series are used to obtain the target voltage. Two AA batteries, each with 1.5 volts in series, would provide a total of 3 volts. By connecting batteries in series, you can create a lot of voltage flow from the same 1.5V AA depending on how many you connect. This is also important in creating restrictive flows of electricity, since anything that is "in front of" another on a circuit's path of flow will take away voltage on that path. This is the reason the resistors we talked about earlier work to control the voltage to a device and allow you to have a power source that could be many times larger than required, but still allow the right amount of current to arrive at the target device, that meets the requirements of the device.

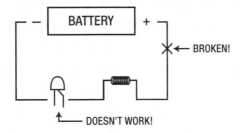

Figure 4-8. *Series circuit is broken*

So how do I connect these things together to actually form a circuit? Well, for the purposes of prototypes, you could just hold all the connections together, but once you have more than two of them, that will get a bit cumbersome, and is definitely not safe for high-voltage scenarios! Thankfully, there are a lot of ways to wire circuits ranging from prototypes to permanent versions, which we will cover the latter later on in the book. What you really need for prototyping circuits and connecting things temporarily is a means to connect all the load and power sources quickly and remove them just as quickly. It is here then that we will introduce the one tool that you will need for almost every prototype project: the humble, but indispensable, breadboard. (See Figure 4-9.)

Figure 4-9. *Various breadboard types (clockwise from left – full length, half-height, and solderable perfboard)*

The breadboard is a clever electrical connection platform for building circuits without making permanent connections. This means you can play around by putting objects in different orders and configurations without having to re-solder connections which can be very tedious in large configurations, and risks damage to the devices, the circuit board, and the connection pins. The breadboard gets its name from a literal breadboard, like the actual thing you cut bread on. In the earliest days of electronics, experimenters wanted a way to set parts of circuits down instead of manually holding all the connections together. This meant also that they needed to use a material that does not conduct electricity. It turns out that wood is very good for this, and there were already many flat pieces of it lying around in the form of breadboards. Today's breadboards are plastic and offer far more functionality than a simple flat board, but the name stuck, and we use them still, for much the same purpose.

The modern breadboard is an ingenious little object that makes wiring up circuits a snap. There are many variations in size and even shape, but the fundamental arrangement of the board is roughly the same. The breadboard is divided into areas for components and rails for power. Each hole in the breadboard is actually a connection point to metal rails embedded in the plastic. These rails run the full length of the board for the "+" and "–" rails, and up and down each column on either side of the central split. You can see this illustrated in Figure 4-10.

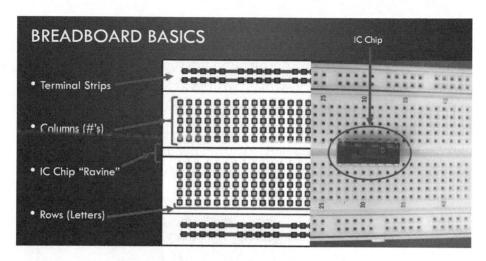

Figure 4-10. *Breadboard details with callouts*

By wiring up a common power and ground rail, we make it very easy to add new components with a jumper wire without having many wires coming from the voltage source. As you begin your prototyping, you will probably use wires that are pre-built with the proper male or female end depending on the connection you need. As you progress and want to build more complex prototypes, you will find that shorter wires on the breadboard will make it much easier to troubleshoot. I recommend some simple #2 doorbell wire that can be had at any hardware store for a few dollars for many feet worth. This should give you ample wires for your prototypes, even if you cut a lot of them into different lengths. For our first circuit project, you can use pre-made wires as we will only need two of them to make our connections.

Premade wires are convenient for prototyping because they are ready-made with connections for the pins on a breadboard or the header pins of a device such as a Raspberry Pi. There are two types of wire connections, male and female. This refers to whether they allow a pin to be plugged into them or they plug into a connector. They come from exactly the place you think they do and are named for what they are for exactly that reason. The connection points on the standard breadboard are Female, and in order to make connections on the breadboard, you will need either Male to Male or Male to Female wires (often written as M2M/MM or M2F/MF). MM will allow you to connect, for example, the power rail to a column on the breadboard where you have a sensor, and the MF wire will allow a connection from the breadboard to the header on a Raspberry Pi for example. Figure 4-11 shows a number of different wires.

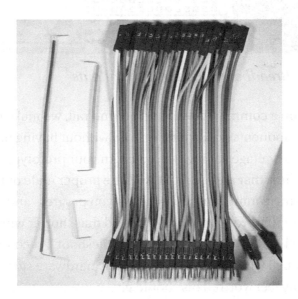

Figure 4-11. *Different wire types (left – M/M breadboard jumper wires; right – M/F bridge wires in a strip package)*

Circuit Diagrams

It would be the height of irresponsibility to conclude a chapter on basic EE concepts without going through a discussion of circuit diagrams. There are literally hundreds and hundreds of electronic components, types of circuits, and ways to diagram them, and so I will focus on two things:

1. Standards and practices that will help you read diagrams anywhere

2. Things that will show up further on in the book

So, we understand the basics of a circuit, and the two types of circuits (the third type is just a combination of the first two – a hybrid circuit that has parallel and serial components). Once you know what you want in your circuit, having a circuit diagram is a good way to remember how things hook up. No doubt that as you are learning to build devices and figuring out how circuits work, you will spend time looking at things like in Figure 4-12 with more than a little reservation! Once you understand the basics and how a circuit diagram is constructed, it is much easier to take a deep breath and just build from beginning to end.

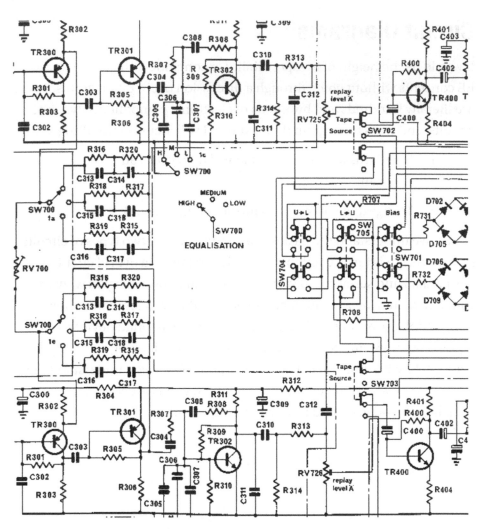

Figure 4-12. *Complex diagram – a stereo in this case*

Circuit diagrams are made up of symbols and lines. Lines represent connectors (wires, breadboard columns and rows, or copper connections on a circuit board) and form the route for electricity to flow in your circuit. The other symbols are all the controls and load elements. Here are some very basic symbols that you will encounter a lot on diagrams. We will add some more in the next chapter for some of the more advanced circuit components. Figure 4-13 shows these common circuit elements.

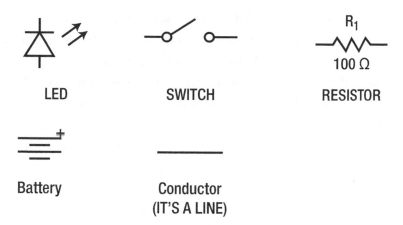

LED   SWITCH   RESISTOR

Battery   Conductor
                    (IT'S A LINE)

Figure 4-13. *Circuit symbols*

Let's take a less complex example and diagram out a circuit you are going to see and build later; a series circuit with a resistor and LED. I have drawn it out for you in parts, just like you would build it. So, for the first part, let's look at the power source. You can find this on any diagram by looking for the "battery" symbol. Figure 4-14 is our starting point. As you can see, it is just a battery delivering 3v. Now you know that is just two 1.5v batteries wired together – a two-battery pack will do just that.

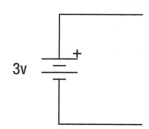

3v

Figure 4-14. *Part one – just the battery*

Next, we follow the current flow. As we see in Figure 4-15, the next object we hit is the resistor, labelled R1, and calling for 68 Ohm. Obviously, you will need to connect the battery to the resistor and so the line between them implies also that there is some sort of wiring present. It could be a breadboard, a physical wire, or a combination of both, but the point is that you need to connect those two things. Now you know that you can simply put those wires from the resistor and battery pack into the appropriate columns on a breadboard and they are connected!

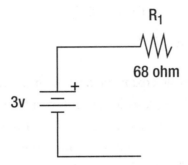

Figure 4-15. *Adding a resistor*

Now we come to the LED symbol in Figure 4-16. It is the symbol for a diode (you will learn about them in the next chapter) with the arrows pointing out showing it emits light. So, you will need to add an LED to your circuit, and it connects on one side to the conductor from the resistor. Easy enough plug it into your breadboard in the right columns.

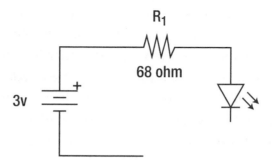

Figure 4-16. The LED

Last bit of the diagram, and the easiest of all – time to close the loop! Figure 4-17 shows the last connection in place, a complete circuit now created. This would be adding a wire to connect the last column on the breadboard to the ground rail, for example, and connecting the battery ground as well. The second you did that, your LED will light, and you will do just that in the circuit build lab later in the section!

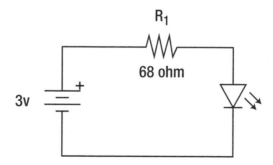

Figure 4-17. Closing the loop and completing the circuit

Obviously, this is an incredibly basic circuit with only a few parts, but once you have a basic understanding of the "follow the flow" logic, and can find the basic symbols to know what component is what, even the most complex diagram becomes legible. Always break it down to smaller chunks, and when building complex circuits out in the physical space make sure to take an additive approach – get one part working and then add in the next and the next and you will find before long you have built out the whole circuit!

Summary

You now have the basics for building your first smart device. A grasp of the fundamental properties of resistance, electrical flow, and the overall means for creating your basic circuits is the foundation all other smart devices come from. We will make one more deeper dive through the advanced electrical component world, and when we get to the labs at the end of this section, we will take all of the knowledge here, along with the advanced bits, and get to building some circuits and basic devices.

CHAPTER 5

Advanced Circuit Components

In our last chapter we explored some of the basics of electrical engineering and the fundamental concepts that form the basis of circuits and electronic components. As you grow your skills in smart device construction, you will inevitably come to a point where the limits of basic resistors and circuit design no longer allow you to progress. This happens fairly quickly after your first builds, and in this chapter, we will explore more advanced circuit topics, and some of the most commonly used components for advanced circuit designs – transistors, diodes, and capacitors – as well as discuss some basics around other control mechanisms you are likely to encounter. All of this groundwork leads up to the next section where we introduce the idea of a computer "brain" to control these devices.

The Transistor

The transistor is everywhere in modern electronics, and it is safe to say that without it we would not have the modern computing era. Transistors make up a huge part of the central processing unit (or CPU) of computers, as well as providing the processing power in MCUs. This is what allows them to process and calculate instructions from code; by controlling the flow of electricity they create the 1s and 0s which make up the language

© Christopher Harrold 2020
C. Harrold, *Practical Smart Device Design and Construction*,
https://doi.org/10.1007/978-1-4842-5614-5_5

of computing. This simple device is effectively an electrically controlled switch, but unlike a relay, which we will cover later, they offer a couple of significant advantages in terms of both size and power needs.

There are MANY types of transistors, and you will undoubtedly come across them in your own research, but the types we will focus on here fall into two categories: BJT (N-P-N or P-N-P) and MOSFET. The reason for focusing on these two is that, aside from needing a whole book to cover all the types in detail, these two types are the most common in smart devices. The BJT is used commonly as an electric switch, and the MOSFET is often employed in things like motor controllers for robotics.

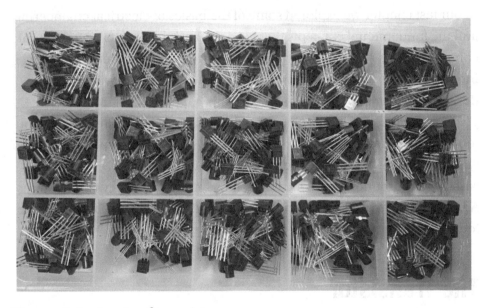

Figure 5-1. *A mix of transistors*

BJT Transistors (N-P-N or P-N-P)

This type of transistor is an excellent means of switching on a current using a minimal amount of power. Effectively, this type of transistor has two inputs for the circuit you are controlling, and one output. Unfortunately for first-timers, using a transistor can be a little confusing at first. That is because transistors operate on the flow of electrons, but circuits operate on what is called the "conventional flow," which, as we saw in the last chapter, is from + to – on our battery. When you first come to BJT transistors you will find this diagram (Figure 5-2) everywhere.

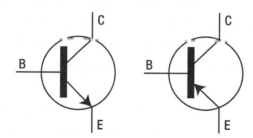

Figure 5-2. *Two types of BJT transistors – NPN on the left and PNP on the right*

The easiest way to think about the usage of a transistor of this type in your design is to follow the arrow. The arrow in the diagram points in the direction of conventional current flow, meaning that most likely you want your transistor to be an NPN type. Thus, the collector side of the transistor is where the current you want to turn on and off comes into the transistor, the emitter side is where it will exit, and the third connection is the control signal.

The reason for this is the switching mechanism of the transistor is controlled by a relative charge method that compares the emitter voltage to the base voltage. In an NPN, the way you "turn on" the switch is to apply a current to the base, thus raising that value above the value of the emitter voltage and allowing the current to begin to flow. In a PNP transistor, you would "turn it on" by actually turning off the current to the base and allowing the current to flow. To be clear, BOTH WORK FINE to control the current, but generally we think of turning on and off in terms of "having current" and "not having current" and so this distinction is as much for your own circuit designing sanity as anything. Certainly, in a simple circuit, where you are using the transistor in place of a switch, this makes the most sense.

There are instances where having a transistor in a "current-on" state might make sense in a circuit though. For example, you might want current to flow through the transistor if something is NOT happening. In the case of software-controlled devices, you could be holding up a signal for some length of time via your code or waiting for a condition to stop occurring via the output from a sensor. In both cases, having a "switch" that stops electrical current while current is applied to the base might be advantageous as a means of controlling other functions of the circuit. Having the flexibility of both types of transistor will give you better control in designing complex circuits. As you can see in Figure 5-3, the transistor has three areas inside it, the collector side, the control (also called the base), and the emitter.

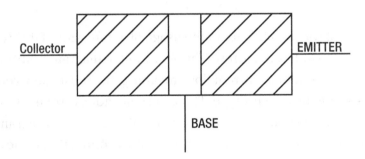

Figure 5-3. *Internal of a BJT transistor*

In an NPN transistor, applying power to the base means the current can "jump" over to the emitter side. In a PNP, you must turn off the flow to the base to allow the current to cross through the base material.

Some huge advantages of this model is that you can switch a very high voltage current with a very low voltage signal – for example, in the smart device world, if you wanted to control a 5v current with the 3v pins that are common on most MCU devices, a transistor will allow that, whereas a relay may not, due to its higher power needs. This could be used to perform a variety of actions like powering on and off an array of sensors all at once instead of with individual pins. This would give you the net effect of having control over their power consumption but only require the use of a single general-purpose input/output (GPIO) pin on the MCU, a critical concern when you are dealing with a finite amount of usable IO pins on your MCU. (GPIO is covered in detail later in the book.)

Another powerful function of the transistor is its ability to amplify the voltage passing through it. While this is not common in smart devices per se, it is hugely powerful for things like sound and video, and you will find transistors in every major piece of audio and visual gear you have around.

Transistors come in a variety of ratings and sizes for use in your devices, as you can see from Figure 5-1. The most important considerations are the voltage it is rated to handle and the type it is meant to be used for (switching types for the purposes of most smart devices). The only other consideration is the form factor, and if it can be mounted into your breadboard or soldered to a printed circuit board (PCB) later. Fundamentally, for working with basic switching concepts, an NPN transistor rated to handle 5v would be best to use for most smart device applications where you want to use it as a switch.

FET Transistor

The FET style of transistor (of which the MOSFET is arguably the most common) refers to the way the current is passed through the transistor through what is called the Field Effect Transmission method. This method relies on the creation of an electromagnetic field to control the flow of power. (Incidentally, the MOS refers to the material the MOSFET is made from in this case, Metal Oxide Semiconductor.) The big advantage of FET over BJT is that they are generally smoother in operation (the current flow is better) and they require very low voltage to let A LOT of current flow through. This is what makes them ideal as motor controllers since most robotics motors are anywhere from 9 to 24 volts; a voltage which would immediately fry any common MCU device. With a MOSFET motor controller, you can turn the flow of current to the motor on and off using the available 3v pins on the MCU without danger to the device. Figure 5-4 shows the wiring for a MOSFET transistor. If it looks familiar, that's because it is the same as the BJT; the difference is all in the functionality and composition of the transistor itself.

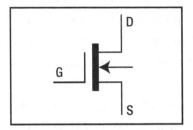

Figure 5-4. *FET cirucuit diagram*

Like the BJT transistor, there are three connections to the MOSFET style transistor: the source, gate, and drain (Figure 5-5). Just like in the BJT, these control the current flow. The source is exactly what it sounds like, the source of current you want to control. The drain is the destination (like the emitter in the BJT) for the current flow. The gate is the on/off switch and is what produces the magnetic field to allow the current to flow through the FET.

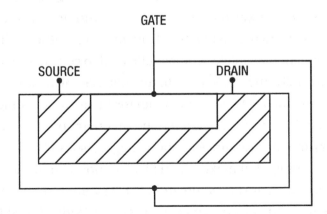

Figure 5-5. *FET diagram*

As you can see here, the internal mechanism of the FET is different from the BJT, and it is this difference that allows it to function much more smoothly, and to be miniaturized much more tightly than a traditional BJT transistor – a fact which obviously makes them valuable in smart devices! Transistors rely on impedance to control the flow of electricity, which is like hyper-resistance because it is a combination of the resistance we discussed before and the reaction of different conductive materials that allows or prevents electrical flow. The gate layer in the FET is what controls the flow of the current, and because this electromagnetic bridge has a very high impedance when the gate is closed, it allows the FET to control very large loads with very small voltage applied to the gate. For example, there are surface mount MOSFET transistors capable of controlling voltages in excess of 120v that are about the size of the head of a match. That is a lot of control in a very small package!

I would be remiss at this point not to note that there are a wide variety of other transistor types that you are likely to come across, but I have chosen to focus on these two types for the simple reason that one or more of them is often included with the various "starter kits" that are widely available on the Internet for people getting started with sensors and circuits. There is a myriad of information on the Internet for using other styles and applications of transistor tech for your own projects, but the FET and BJT styles presented here will be a very common piece in your workbench.

The Capacitor

Perhaps second only to the transistor in common use for smart devices, the capacitor has nonetheless a hugely important part to play in circuit design when you move into advanced circuits. The capacitor uses a similar principle to the battery, in that it can store electricity. Unlike the battery, it can accept and expend that electrical energy very quickly (nearly instantly

in some types of capacitors). This is incredibly useful in situations where
you have electrical noise or perhaps you are looking at using battery power
for a project. A capacitor can provide a "smoothing" effect to the power
supply that is causing electrical "noise" or spikes and dips in currents, and
in the case of batteries, having a correctly wired capacitor would allow
your device to continue to function while the battery is being changed.
Highly useful for things like wearables and other battery-specific devices.
As shown in Figure 5-6, there are many types of capacitors as well, due to
the need to have the right size for the load of current and discharge, as well
as the function they are performing.

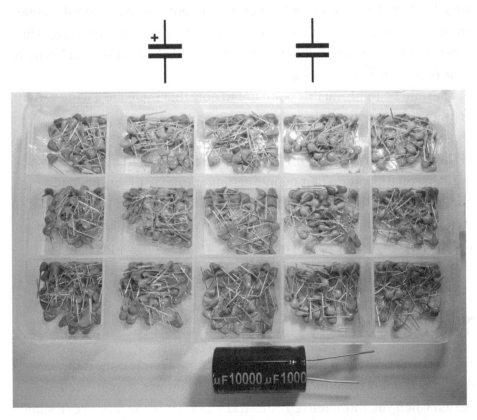

Figure 5-6. *Capacitors and their symbols (top left – polarized
capacitor; top right – basic symbol; under – various capacitor types)*

The measurement of the capacitor is not as simple as a battery, where an AA battery provides 1.5v, for example. The capacitor is measured in farads, and they are generally in fractions of a farad at that. A full farad (incidentally named for electrical pioneer and enemy of good cell phone signals, Michael Faraday) is an enormous amount of capacitance, and so most of the capacitors you would use are actually rated in fractions of a farad.

If we want to liken the capacitor to our plumbing example in our basic circuits, the capacitor would be akin to a water tower. It collects water from the system and stores it in the tower. Water continues to flow through, but "extra" water piles up in the tower. If we were to turn off the water flow, the water in the tower would still supply everything "downhill" – that is following the tower in the system – until it was empty, or the flow of water from the source started up again. The amount of water that the water tower can release and in what amount of time it can release it would be its capacitance.

This is a critical understanding point and leads to another important bit of math for EE that you should know. The rate at which a capacitor discharges, in other words, how long it can deliver power to the rest of the circuit, is determined by a really simple formula that you will recognize some elements from:

$$\tau = RC$$

Time Tau (τ) equals the product of the resistance and the capacitance.

Here's the funky thing about this formula, remember how I said a farad, or a unit of capacitance, is HUGE? Well if you assumed that the discharge time is essentially one times the resistance as the RC implies, it isn't. Generally, most capacitors you will use are rated in the milli, micro, or even nano and pico farads of capacitance. What this means is that, in order to get a meaningful rate of discharge (meaning you can actually see the LED dim and go out), you can do a few things to the circuit:

- Have an ASTRONOMICAL amount of resistance – for example, I used a 1M Ohm resistor and a 9v battery with a 100 nanofarad capacitor and I could just barely see the LED dim out in a pitch-black room. Of course, I could also only barely make out the LED since that much resistance meant VERY little current made it to the LED! So how long did my fade-out last?

    $\tau = RC$

    $\tau = 1,000,000$ ohms $\times$ 0.0000001 farads

    $\tau = 0.1$ seconds

  So, for all of that crazy high resistance, I bought 1/10th of a second?! Not really all that amazing to watch.

- Have a lot of capacitance in parallel – why parallel and not serial like a battery? Because capacitors in SERIES have a fractional relationship to capacitance, whereas those in parallel are equal to the SUM of the capacitance. So, if you take a bunch of reasonable capacitors, say something in the 100 μF range (100 micro farad), and maybe 10 of them?

    $\tau = RC$

    $\tau = 460$ ohms $\times$ (0.0001 $\times$ 10) farads

    $\tau = 460$ ohms $\times$ (0.001) farads

    $\tau = 0.46$ seconds

Well, that's actually starting to approach reasonable – if you switched it up with some bigger capacitors, say 1000 µF, and had a few of those, now you could get to a reasonable delivery of power in an observable time.

Have a large amount of capacitance and reasonable resistance. 100 nanofarads is infinitesimally small in the grand scheme of things, and even 100 µF is pretty tiny. What happens if I go for a big gun and bust out a 0.01 farad (10,000 µF) capacitor and put my resistance at something much more reasonable (a 9v battery lighting a basic LED needs 460 Ohms)?

$$\tau = RC$$

$$\tau = 460 \text{ ohms} \times 0.01 \text{ farads}$$

$$\tau = 4.6 \text{ seconds!!}$$

Well that's much more reasonable! I can actually see it dim and go out in that amount of time.

Now, if you repeat this experiment in the build lab later, you will see that in fact there is light coming out of the diode for MUCH longer than 4.6 seconds; that is because the discharge of the capacitor is not a linear or instantaneous discharge. Over time, the amount of voltage the capacitor is outputting starts out at full power, but gradually decays, producing less current as the amount of time gets longer. That means that your Tau value is *roughly* the amount of time you have BEFORE this decay kicks in – for comparison's sake, in the 0.01 farad example, I was actually trying to time it and I got as high as around 6 seconds (using the highly scientific "counting of 1-Mississippi" method) before I saw a noticeable decay in the amount of light from the LED.

In advanced circuit designs, you will see capacitors predominantly used where you want the flow of power to be smooth and even, or where you need a battery-like storage of energy in a shorter window of time (such as the battery powered device where you need it to stay alive long enough to change the battery). The Tau value then is the value you should consider in your design as the "safe time" before your power drops off. Also, WHAT gets powered is important here. In a smart device, very rarely would you want to power literally every part of the device in the event of a power loss. Much more likely you would want to design a circuit that provides power to the key part (like an MCU or memory for storing things) than to all the lights and sensors.

One additional common place capacitors are used that you will recognize is in camera flashes. The capacitor charges up from the camera battery, and when the flash is triggered, it dumps all that into the flash bulb to create a powerful light. You will also see them used anywhere there needs to be a strong signal like this to "kick off" an action, as they can power up to a much higher level than the input current over time. (Think about the noise an old-school flash makes charging up? That's the current rushing in to fill the capacitor.) They are often found in smart device applications in conjunction with motor wiring to provide a smooth start-up current as otherwise you would have a kind of "jolting" (no pun intended) inrush of current that could be unstable and cause odd performance of the motor (or damage even). You can see a couple of capacitors in Figure 5-7 on the wiring for this common MOSFET motor control circuit, and you will see them again in the circuit lab in the next chapter.

Figure 5-7. *MOSFET motor controller L298N with two big round capacitors on it (labelled with a 220 EZA)*

Diodes

Diodes are a very simple and common electrical component that gives two basic functions to the circuit designer – control of the direction of flow and protection from current going where it should not. Like all types of electrical components, there are many different types and sizes of diode (as you can see in Figure 5-8), but they all have the same basic function; they are the one-way valve of electrical circuits.

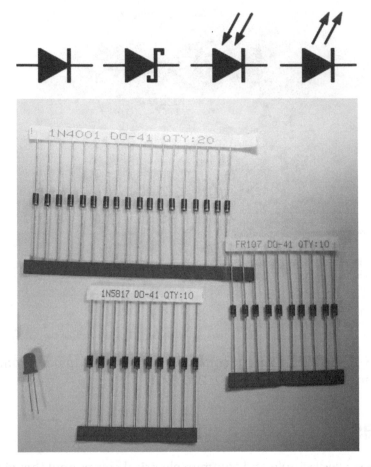

Figure 5-8. *Diodes and their wiring diagram symbols (top left – standard diode; second from left – Schottky diode; second from right – photodiode; far right – light emitting diode (LED); bottom – various diodes)*

As with so many electronic components, there are A LOT of options here. To keep the focus of the book on things you are likely to use and need in your own designs, I am focusing on just the more common diodes and their functions in this section. The basic diode you will get in most kits or diode collections is a silicon-based PN diode. These are great for basic circuits and can handle quite high voltages without bleeding current back through the diode and self-destructing. Yes, this is a thing. If the current trying to come back through the diode is too high, it can cause the diode to fail, and unfortunately part of that failure is allowing the current through the wrong direction. However, good circuit design and knowing your voltages and currents will mitigate this.

The Schottky style diode is made up slightly differently than the PN diode, much the way that the BJT and MOSFET are different but perform a similar function. The Schottky diode is more efficient when it comes to switching on and off when current is applied, resulting in much faster "on/off" state switching, which can be very useful in situations where high speed and precision are required. However, they have a much lower failure point than their PN brethren and will fail sooner, so care must be taken in ensuring that they are used in situations where they are not likely to be exposed to a lot of reverse current.

You might come across the need for diodes when you are building your circuits and connecting different wiring routes together into a single path. Having a diode in the path would ensure that no current goes the "wrong way" and comes back to a device that isn't expecting it. Practically speaking, there are not a lot of circumstances where you will **have to have** a diode to protect the flow of a circuit, generally electricity only wants to go one way. However, the diode has some really interesting other properties that you might want to exploit in a circuit. One of these is the ability to create light as the flow of electricity passes through the conducting material, and thus the Light Emitting Diode (you know it as an LED) is born! That's right, one of the most important components in any making project is a diode, which also means that by using one, you are ensuring that electricity flows only one way in that circuit!

Diodes, as a one-way entity, need to be installed in the correct direction! Larger diodes are usually labelled pretty clearly as to which end is the positive and which is the negative end of the diode. Figure 5-9 shows both an LED and a regular silicon diode.

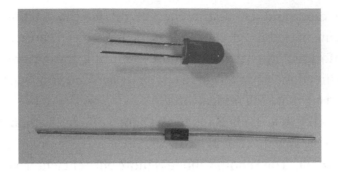

Figure 5-9. *Diode directionality*

The circuit diagram for a diode also shows the direction it is expected to be installed, with the positive arrow pointing to the negative bar as you can see in Figure 5-8. With smaller silicon-based diodes, the "bar" that is printed on the diode casing is the negative end and should be placed "facing away" from the source of your circuit's power. For LEDs – a diode that emits light – the long "leg" of the LED is the anode, and the shorter leg is the cathode. If for some reasons the "legs" are the same length, you can also feel the LED for a flat spot on one side of the plastic lamp. That flat spot faces toward the cathode, or negative, side and so should "face away" from your voltage source.

One other very important consideration in your designs for using diodes of any type is the concept of voltage drops. Any electrical component in a circuit has the potential to consume some of the flow of that circuit. This is totally normal and expected, but as you are going through your first circuits and building things out, it can lead to some unexpected results if you do not understand the reason why. In the case of the diode, there is a concept that you need to be aware of called Forward Voltage Drop. This is the amount of voltage the diode will "consume" as the current passes through it. Fortunately, this isn't an arcane art or something you need to divine! Diodes are generally clearly labelled with their operating voltages and forward voltage drop as relates to the current in the circuit. Luckily most modern diodes also "consume" very little current (something in the ranges of 200 or 300 mV even in circuits with loads as high as 1 amp). To put this in perspective, the max load from an ESP8266 based chip via one of its GPIO pins (not a dedicated 5v pin, but the regular GPIO defined pins) is 3v, so even with a diode in sequence, you lose VERY little of your overall voltage from the circuit. LEDs are an exception to this in that they consume more of the voltage for creating light than a regular silicon diode, but the loss of voltage through the LED is usually made up for by supplying more voltage, or isolating LEDs in your design.

One last thing to note about the diode in general, and LEDs in particular. Later in the lab section you will see one of the troubleshooting tips is to "turn the LED around." I have been making things with LEDs for many years now, and I still plug them in backwards. Remember that an LED is first and foremost a diode, and what does a diode do? Allows flow in one direction only! If you "plug it in backwards" with the anode and cathode legs reversed, no electricity will flow. It also means that you can simply switch that around, and voila, flow is established.

Lastly there are a couple of very interesting things you can do with diodes to create advanced circuits. These revolve around creating "gates" for electrical connections. In the case of an electrical circuit, a "gate" is a place where some set of conditions has to be satisfied to allow the flow of electricity to proceed. You will generally see them notated as the type of gate they are, and a diode or diodes can be used to create two very simple gates, the AND and the OR gate. Just like the type of gate they are, these gates match two criteria together to make a logical path of electricity flow. AND gates require the conditions to ALL be satisfied. OR gates require ANY of them to be satisfied. Here in Figure 5-10 is an illustration that will help.

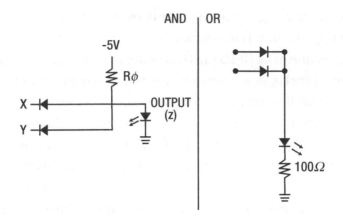

Figure 5-10. *AND and OR gates*

In your own project, you may want to have multiple circuits feeding into a single receiver. By using diodes to create an OR gate, you could allow the condition at the receiver to be TRUE, meaning that electricity is flowing, if ANY of the diodes are outputting current. This could be useful in detecting if one or the other of a sensor has triggered a finding on the same pin on your MCU, for example. It would also allow you to trigger an LED from two different places – like contact sensors, for example, on a door and window on opposite sides of a room. This would light up the LED if either of the two sensors was activated separately from one another.

Conversely, you could also set up a circuit that is wired so that you need ALL of the sensors to be sending current. That would be an AND gate. In the diagram, the voltage source passes through a resistor that controls the flow of current to an output – maybe an LED in this case. If only one of the diodes is activated (let's say that the door is open in our example, but not the window), the current that would flow to the output would be a fractional current and not enough to do anything with the output. If **both** diodes are activated though (the door and the window are both open) then the current would flow through the output at the full output of whatever is passing through the resistor.

The function of the diodes in these examples is not the logic itself since the wiring of the circuit determines that. It is to allow these circuits to be tied together without allowing electricity to "leak" into a place it is not expected.

Other Common Elements

There are a few other common elements that didn't really warrant the full section treatment but warrant some introduction as you will come across them commonly in many smart device projects. The first of these is the relay. This is like a transistor in that it allows turning the flow of current on and off. Unlike the transistor though, it is an electromechanical process (meaning it has moving physical pieces inside). This also means that it has different characteristics than a transistor in terms of operation. Primarily you will see relays employed in things like home automation where you want to control very large voltages (110/220) with your MCU devices. The main thing to know about the relay is that the switch requires a minimum voltage to activate. This means that you need to account for the activation voltage in your design since your MCU may not put out enough voltage to actually trigger the switch!

There are many types of relays, but generally you will find them pre-assembled in something like the picture in Figure 5-11: one or many relays pre-mounted to a circuit board, and ready for wiring with the screw terminals provided.

Figure 5-11. *Examples of relays on a pre-made circuit board*

Generally, the relay operates by introducing a voltage differential, much like the transistor, but with a MUCH higher required load. Relays are commonly used to control things like lights or lamps in a smart home application (at 110v) or motors and other larger electronic systems (usually 12 or 24v). This allows an MCU operating at 3 or 5v to activate the relay, although you may need to combine some current outputs using AND circuits to get enough voltage to the relay to activate it. Fundamentally though, relays provide a quick and easy way to get switched control to one or more devices from your MCU.

Headers are sets of pins that are pre-formed into neat packages and ready to mount on a circuit board. You will find there are as many headers as there are everything else, and you can trim and customize headers to your exact need as well. They are important in a circuit because it is not always possible to have everything on the same board, or sometimes you need to marry two circuit boards together. Headers give you the flexibility to do just that, without the permanence of soldered connections. Headers are also a great way to build in some expandability to a circuit since you can have a header connected to power, ground, and data sources/inputs and attach a device to it later. You can also find pin headers used as gates, where if pins are connected then current flows to a new location and a new function is activated. You can see a few examples of headers in Figure 5-12.

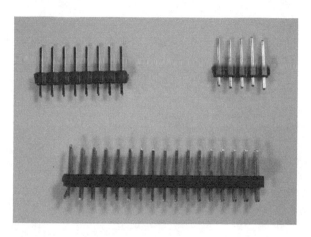

Figure 5-12. *Various sized headers*

Other connectors also deserve a mention here as you will often find the need to use things like network cables and USB in your circuits to extend your reach beyond the breadboard or circuit board. RJ-45 connections are an easy way to run wired sensor devices over long distances, for example, as they give you an easy way to connect structured network cable (category 6 is the current standard) to your circuit and pass the connections over great distances (50 feet or more) without huge voltage drop. USB ports are obvious power sources but can also provide output capability in more complex designs. Camera connections, display connections, audio ports, HDMI, you name it, all of them can be used in a smart device if you need that functionality.

The humble screw terminal deserves a mention here as they are an incredibly useful and basic connection used in all kinds of devices. Essentially just a clamp to hold wires with, they are a more flexible means of connecting wiring leads without soldering. You will find screw terminals on lots and lots of different pre-made circuit boards you will use, and you will probably use them yourself in some designs where you need to connect premade wired devices like motors and electrical cables. Figure 5-13 has some examples of the vast variety of connectors you will encounter.

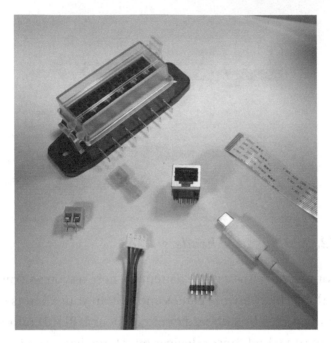

Figure 5-13. *Types of connectors you might encounter (clockwise from top left – a fuse-block with a bladed connector, a Flat Flex Cable [in this case a Raspberry Pi camera cable], a USB C connector, a 5-pin header an RJ45 cable connector, a four-wire cable connector, a "crimp" connector (the little blue thing - the wires are crushed inside it by the connector) and a screw terminal)*

Summary

I could continue on through so many exotic and amazing connectors, electrical components, and carry on down the rathole forever really. There are just so many possible ways to control and use electricity it is kind of overwhelming, but the topics and devices in these last two chapters are the ones you will *FOR SURE* use, even early on in your building of smart devices. The next step is to actually BUILD some of them! The build lab that follows is all about creating some functional and useful circuits that will do things, even without the use of the microcontroller. You can actually go quite a long way with just battery powered circuits and you will build some functional circuits in the lab that will show you the basics, help you get familiar with the concepts we've discussed, and give you a handy reference when you need it later.

CHAPTER 6

Circuit Building Lab

Let's look at a couple of really, really simple circuits that will not blow up your battery but will illustrate the principles we have covered to this point. This is the first project you will build, and it is the first prototype that many people build when they are getting started with smart devices (Figure 6-1).

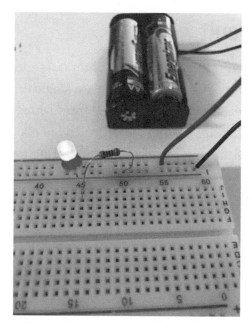

Figure 6-1. *Finished series circuit*

© Christopher Harrold 2020
C. Harrold, *Practical Smart Device Design and Construction*,
https://doi.org/10.1007/978-1-4842-5614-5_6

You can see in the picture that we have a power source (in this case, the "+" end of a battery), a power consumer (in this case, an LED), and the ground (in this case, the "−" end of the battery). The electrons will flow from the "+" to the "−" through the conductors that connect them to the breadboard. There are no control or protection devices, but we have added a resistor because, as mentioned before, LEDs can burnout if run at full current for too long. We don't really need to worry about a switch at this point, as we are just illustrating the barest basics of a circuit, and likewise a protection device such as a fuse would be overkill too.

Depending on how you connect the wires from the power, you can either build a series, parallel, or a combination circuit. We will do all three for good measure.

A Series Circuit

Technically, any circuit with a single consumer is a series circuit, and so this circuit is simply a series circuit with only a single thing wired to it. You could easily add a second LED to make it a "true" series circuit, and as an extra practice, what size resistor would you need to add to the circuit to make sure the resistance is correct? (I'll put the answer later in the exercise.)

In order to make this circuit, you need five parts as you can see in Figure 6-2.

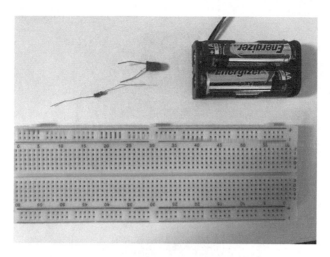

Figure 6-2. *Basic circuit parts*

To assemble the circuit follow these steps:

1) Place the batteries in the battery holder (easier when it is not connected to the breadboard!).

2) Connect the black or "–" side wire to the breadboard by inserting the bare end into one of the connection in the "–" rail. Do not connect the red wire yet! See Figure 6-3.

Figure 6-3. *Black wire connected to the breadboard*

3) Connect one side of the resistor to the "–" rail, and put the other end into any of the pins in the grid. The exact number isn't important, just that you know where it is. See Figure 6-4.

Figure 6-4. *Resistor on the breadboard*

4) Connect the short "leg" of the LED into the same
   column in the field as you place the resistor, and
   place the other leg into the "+" rail. See Figure 6-5.

Figure 6-5. *LED connected to breadboard*

5) Your circuit is now wired and you can "turn it on" by completing the circuit and plugging in the end of the red wire to the "+" rail, and lighting your LED. See Figure 6-6.

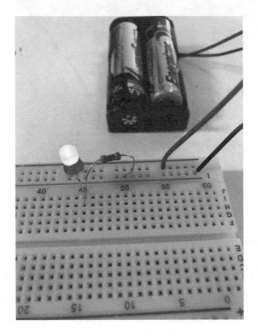

Figure 6-6. *Connecting the red wire will turn on the LED*

Note   If your LED did not light, there are three likely culprits:

1. Did you connect the batteries the right way in the holder? It should be labelled.

2. Pull the LED off and spin it around – I (far too often I admit) plug them in backward all the time.

3. Check that the leg of the resistor and the cathode leg of your LED are in the same column on the breadboard.

Note   Did your LED briefly light and then you heard a "pop" sound? Check your resistors. We are at the point where incorrect resistance and voltages can mean loss of electronic components. If you run a lone LED with the full 3v and no resistance, it will light for around 1 second before it goes out and you hear a "pop." That LED is now trash.

If you want to add another LED to this circuit, you will need to swap out the resistor, and simply plug the next LED in with one leg in the same column as the existing LED and the second in a different column. From there you will need to add the correct resistor. Did you figure that out yet from above? The answer is you need a 0 Ohm resistor from the other LED leg to the "−" rail and both should light. If you add a third, will they all light?

A Parallel Circuit

A parallel circuit is a little more complex in theory, but this simple version will build off of our existing series circuit, with a couple of minor changes. You can see the complete parallel circuit in Figure 6-7.

Figure 6-7. *Completed parallel circuit*

In order to make this circuit, you need six parts as you can see in Figure 6-8.

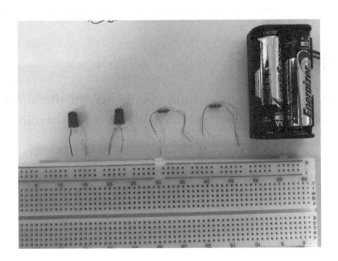

Figure 6-8. *Parallel circuit parts*

To assemble the parallel circuit, follow these steps:

1) Unplug the Red wire from the breadboard before starting!

2) Remove the resistor from the previous build and replace it in the same position with a 1 Ohm resistor instead of the one you used. See Figure 6-9.

Figure 6-9. *Resistor and LED in the breadboard*

3) Connect another 1 Ohm resistor in the same manner as before, with one pin in a new column on the breadboard and one in the "–" rail of the breadboard. See Figure 6-10.

Figure 6-10. *Second resistor on the breadboard*

4) Place a new LED in the same manner as you did
    before, with the long leg in the "+" rail and the
    other in the field of the breadboard, and NOT in the
    same column as the previous LED and resistor. See
    Figure 6-11.

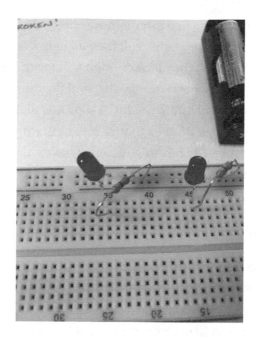

Figure 6-11. *Second LED on the breadboard*

5)   Now plug back in the Red wire and both LEDs
should light! See Figure 6-12.

Figure 6-12. *Completed parallel circuit*

Similar to the end of the first circuit, now comes the question, if you add a third LED to one of the paths, will they all light? The answer to both is no, they will not, because they lack enough voltage to light. How can I fix this? Ohm's law tells us we need more volts, and thus more battery supply. As we will see in the next chapter, the MCU pins are all fixed supply, and so all supply the same voltage from each pin, meaning your parallel circuits, instead of sharing a single 3v power source, all have a dedicated 3v source. Much more flexible for building complex designs!

ADVANCED CIRCUITS

Now that we have the basics of Ohm's law out of the way, we can move on to some more interesting hardware-only circuits. This may seem odd in a book about smart devices, but keep in mind that the vast majority of cool things you see the others have built all require some or all of this skill in order to function. I am constantly humbled at realizing that I actually know how to build a lot of what I see, simply because I understand these basic circuits and how they work. Once you get these down, building the rest becomes much easier (and WAY more fun!).

So, let's take a look at building some more advanced circuits using some of the other objects we discussed. If learning Ohm's law is like learning to count, and the basic circuits are 1+1, we are now going to work through multiplication and division with some more complex and advanced circuit designs. First up, let's build a switched circuit using a transistor to control a light.

A Transistor Controlled Circuit

Now we are going to start bringing in some of the other circuit concepts from previous chapters and use them in test circuits. This first circuit illustrates how to build a circuit that is controlled via a transistor. While simplistic, I am sure you will easily see where things like a switch could give way to a sensor later on, and where they can be controlled via an MCU. Building them in hardware first is always a good first step as it ensures you won't fry those MCUs when you build the real thing later! Here's the circuit diagram (Figure 6-13).

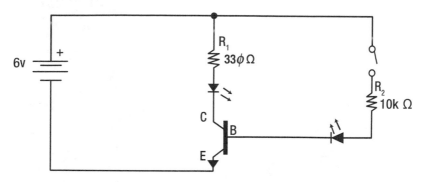

Figure 6-13. *Transistor circuit diagram*

In order to make this circuit, you need 10 parts. as you can see in Figure 6-14. You need

- A four-battery pack

- A 10k Ohm resistor

- A 330 Ohm resistor

- Two LEDs

- A button or other switch

- An NPN type transistor

- Two M/M wires

- A breadboard to put it all on

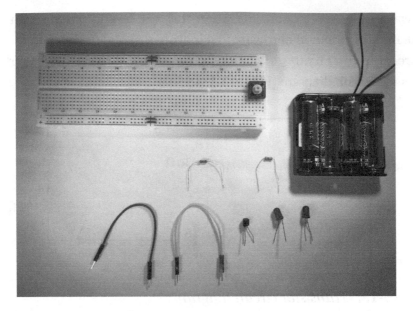

Figure 6-14. *Picture of transistor circuit parts*

To assemble the circuit, follow these steps:

1) Place the batteries in the battery holder (if they weren't there from an earlier build, this is, as always, easier when it is not connected to the breadboard!) and then set it aside – you will hook it up last.

2) Place the button on the breadboard, spanning the IC ravine. Be careful not to bend the pins on the button, which happens A LOT. Just straighten them up and make sure they all make a solid connection. See Figure 6-15.

Figure 6-15. *Button on breadboard*

3) Just like in the circuit diagram lab, you are going to build your physical circuit in parts. First, you are going to build the control side. (There is not a real reason for this, it was just what I chose to start with.) To begin, you will connect the + rail to the input side of the button as seen in Figure 6-16.

Figure 6-16. *MM wire plugged into the breadboard*

4) Next connect the 10k Ω resistor to the output side of the button as shown in Figure 6-17. The other end can go into any free column in reach.

Figure 6-17. *10K resistor on the breadboard*

5) Now plug in the first of the two LEDs. This LED is not required to make this circuit work per se, but it provides a visual signal that current is flowing through the control side of the circuit. Connect the anode to the same column as the 10k resistor and the cathode to the other side of the IC ravine in a free column as you see in Figure 6-18.

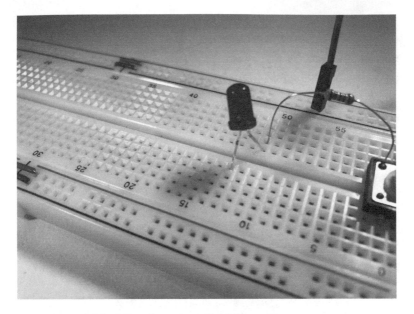

Figure 6-18. *LED bridged across the IC ravine*

6)   Next plug in your NPN transistor as follows: Connect the base to the same column as the LED you just plugged in. Connect the collector side to any empty column on the breadboard. Lastly, connect the emitter side to the "–" rail on the breadboard.

Transistors like the BJT one we are using have a flat side on the casing. If you look at the flat side of the casing, the pins are numbered in order, from, left to right. 1 is always the collector, 2 the base, and 3 the emitter. You can see the correct orientation in Figure 6-19.

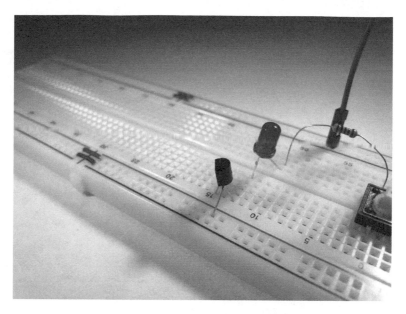

Figure 6-19. *Transistor on the breadboard – note the placement of the three legs*

7) Now you will build the other side of the circuit. First step is to take the 330 Ω resistor and plug one end into the + rail where you plugged the wire in earlier. The other end should go into any free column on the breadboard. See Figure 6-20 for the visual.

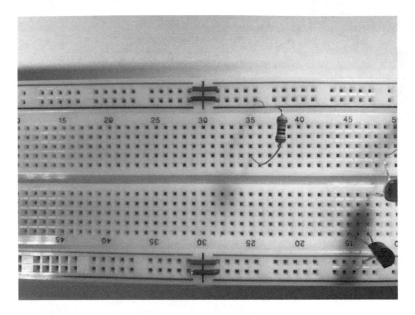

Figure 6-20. *330 Ohm resistor on the breadboard*

8) Now you will connect the other LED that will be
    lit by the circuit. Connect the anode to the same
    column as the end of the 330 Ω resistor, and then
    bridge the IC ravine with the cathode end, again into
    any free column. Figure 6-21 shows it connected.

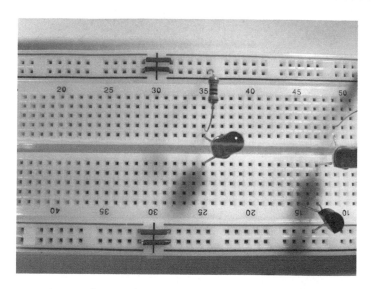

Figure 6-21. *Second LED bridging the IC ravine with the 330 Ohm resistor*

9) Now, using the other M/M wire, connect the column with the cathode from the LED to the collector of the transistor you plugged in earlier. Figure 6-22 shows them connected with the wire in place.

117

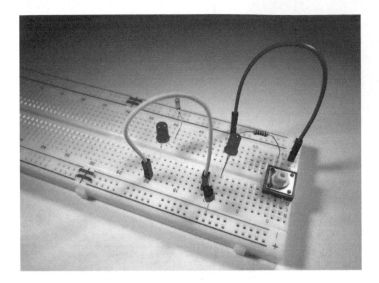

Figure 6-22. *Wire from second LED to the transistor*

10)   Last connection! The battery pack should now be
       connected with the red wire into the "+" rail at the
       top and the black into the "–" rail at the bottom.
       Figure 6-23 shows it connected and your circuit
       complete!

Figure 6-23. *Battery pack connected on the power and ground rails on the breadboard*

But wait... nothing happened?!

That's because we've introduced a switch into this circuit aside from just the transistor. Again, we didn't *have to*, but the circuit would be less visually illustrative without it. In order to make our circuit work, you have to push the button! Figure 6-24 shows both LEDs lit because we've started the flow of current through both paths of the circuit by opening the "gate" on the transistor.

119

Figure 6-24. *Activating the transistor by pressing the button*

Notice that one LED is much fainter than the other?
Do you know why? Remember our good friend Ohm
and his law and think about the resistors you used.
A 10kΩ resistor cuts off a LOT of current making that
second LED much dimmer – Ohm's law in effect!

Excellent work, and if you did not get lit up LEDs,
there are a couple of culprits:

- I kept missing the button pins. They are not at the
  EDGE of the button but inset by one column. I just
  plugged into the wrong column like a million
  times...

- LED rotation? It happens!

- Transistor hooked up the right direction? Make sure
  the C/B/E pins are right. Remember, looking at the
  flat side, they are left to right Collector-Base-Emitter.

A Diode-Based OR Gate

Time for the OR gate! This is a nifty little circuit to build, and quite easy, but the illustrative principle is very important. This circuit will only make one OR decision, but you could conceivably build out many, many OR decisions and make a much bigger circuit. In the spirit of fundamentals, I have kept it simple, but you will see very quickly where you could expand and add to it. Figure 6-25 is the wiring diagram version of the circuit.

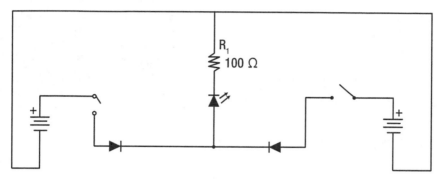

Figure 6-25. *Diode OR gate diagram*

Again, a fairly simple circuit that illustrates a very important concept, using hardware logic to control circuits.

In order to make this circuit, you need 12 parts as you can see in Figure 6-26. You need

- Two 2-battery packs

- A 100 Ohm resistor

- One LED (I used blue in the images)

- Two buttons or other type of switch

- Two diodes able to handle 3v

- Three M/M wires

- A breadboard to put it all on

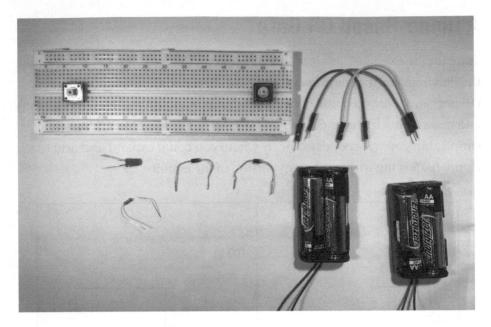

Figure 6-26. *Parts for the diode OR gate*

To assemble the circuit, follow these steps:

1) Place the batteries in the battery holders (if they weren't there from an earlier build, this is as always, easier when it is not connected to the breadboard!) and then set them aside – you will hook those up last.

2) Place the buttons on the breadboard, spanning the IC ravine. Be careful not to bend the pins on the buttons as before – make sure you have good contact from all four pins. See Figure 6-27 for the button arrangement on the breadboard.

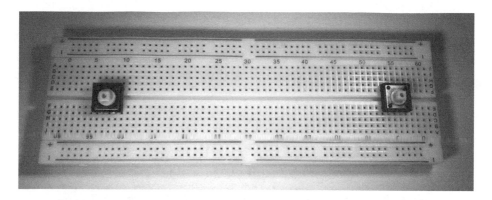

Figure 6-27. *Both buttons on the breadboard*

3) Next, place the two diodes on the breadboard with the positive end in the same column as one of the button outputs. See Figure 6-28. Make sure the negative end is not connected to the button; see the close-up in Figure 6-29 to find the marker on your diode.

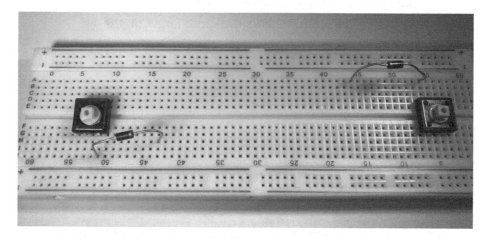

Figure 6-28. *Both diodes on the breadboard*

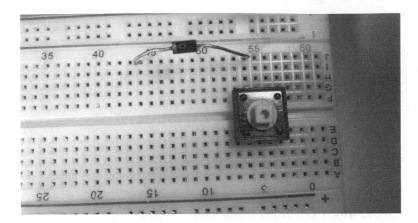

Figure 6-29. *Close-up of the diode showing the marker on the diode to the left in the picture (the gray stripe)*

4) Now take two of your M/M wires and connect one into the column with the negative end of each diode and then the other end into **the same** column on the breadboard. This is what makes this an OR gate since the source shares the same target on the circuit. Figure 6-30 to see them plugged up.

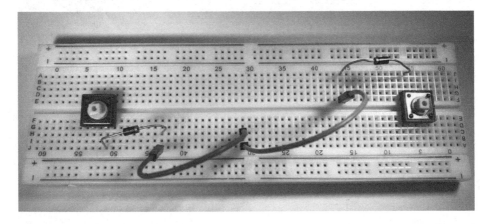

Figure 6-30. *Wires connected to the diodes and to the same column on the breadbaord*

5) Now place the LED in the breadboard, with the anode in the same column as the wires, and bridging the IC ravine to any free column on the other side, as seen in Figure 6-31.

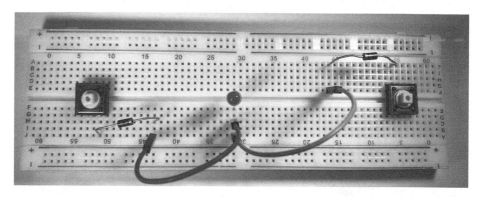

Figure 6-31. *LED connected across the IC ravine*

6) Next, we need the 100 Ohm resistor connected to the cathode of the LED, and into the "–" rail on the breadboard as seen in Figure 6-32.

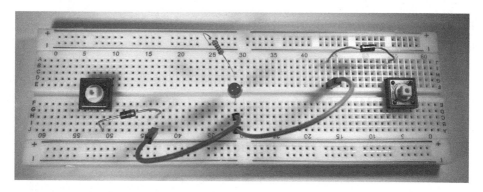

Figure 6-32. *Resistor connected to the LED and "–" rail*

7) This last connection might be optional for you –
the breadboard I used in this example does not
have contiguous power and ground rails – they are
separated in the middle of the board, so using the last
M/M wire, I simply jump the gap in the middle for
the ground rail. This just makes hooking the battery
packs up easier in the last step. See Figure 6-33 for
what this looks like on the board.

Figure 6-33. *Connecting the rails on the breadboard (you may not
need to do this)*

8) Last, it's time to hook up the battery packs.
The red wire from each pack will go in the same
column as one of the source sides on each
button, and the black wire into the "–" rail on the
breadboard. See Figure 6-34 to see them hooked up.

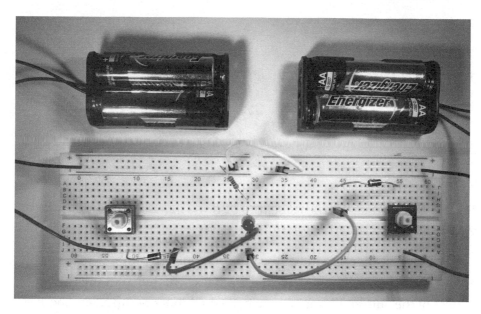

Figure 6-34. *Battery packs connected to the breadboard*

Again, like the transistor circuit, NOTHING HAPPENS! Except that it will when we push the button(s) as you can see in Figure 6-35, you can push either the button on the right or on the left to make the LED light up. You have created a hardware-only logic gate that allows the hardware to figure out the path for the electricity (with a little help by you pushing a button of course).

127

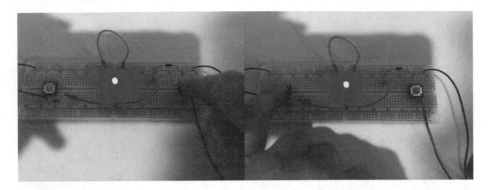

Figure 6-35. *Pushing the alternate buttons lights the LED, but the diode blocks the circuit from the other side*

One troubleshooting note - the button input and output sides are NOT across the IC ravine that you see in the pictures. Rather, they are the two "sides" of the button. Either "side" can be the input or output, and both pins on that side will be the same. Pressing the button connects these two sets of pins to make the connection. If you do not get a lit up LED, check that your inputs and outputs are connected as in the pictures. If your circuit has worked as planned, exciting times!! That's 2 of the 3 advanced circuits out of the way, now it's time for the third and final circuit, the capacitor test circuit.

A Capacitor Test Circuit

This simple circuit shows you how a capacitor functions in a circuit that is designed to charge and discharge a capacitor (Figure 6-36). We are going to use a button switch again to control whether the capacitor is charging or not, and will be using a 9v battery in this example as well, as we need a decent chunk of voltage.

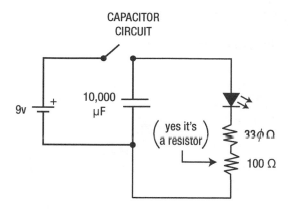

Figure 6-36. *Capacitor test circuit*

Out of our advanced circuits, this one is actually probably the simplest in terms of parts and wiring, but it illustrates such a critical thing that it finds a home in advanced circuits. Being able to operate without a power source, even for a few seconds, is a huge property for your smart device to possess and could really extend its capability – a great example is where solar power is involved. Using capacitors, along with solar and battery, could allow you to greatly extend the runtime of solar devices when there is a low power condition.

But enough of the hypotheticals, let's build it! In order to make this circuit, you need 12 parts as you can see in Figure 6-37. You need

- One 9v battery connector and a 9v battery.

- A 100 Ohm resistor.

- A 330 Ohm resistor.

- One LED (I used green in the images).

- One button or other type of switch.

- One capacitor – in the images I am using a BIG FAT CAPACITOR; if you don't have one that big, it's OK, use the biggest one you have. This one is a 10,000 µF (10,000 microfarad), which is frankly overkill in the extreme.

129

- Four M/M wires.

- A breadboard to put it all on.

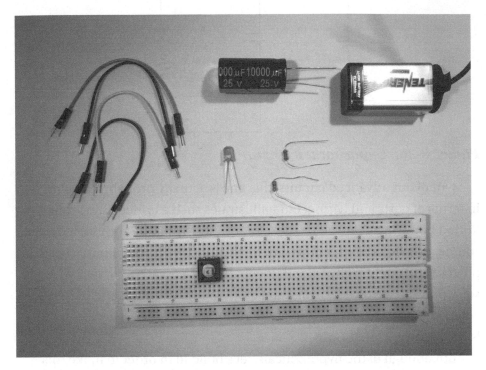

Figure 6-37. *Parts for the capacitor circuit*

To assemble the circuit, follow these steps:

1) Clip the 9v into the battery connector and then set
   it aside – you will hook that up last like the other
   circuits.

2) Place the button onto the breadboard like the previous
   builds (or leave it if you are reusing) again, minding
   the very likely to bend pins! Figure 6-38 for the visual.

Figure 6-38. *Button on the breadboard across the IC ravine*

3) Next place your capacitor. They have an anode and
    cathode like the diodes do and, in the case of the
    larger ones, are clearly labelled – you cannot miss the
    giant "–" signs on the side of the one in Figure 6-39.
    Make sure the anode is in the same column as the
    button output and the cathode is in a free column.

Figure 6-39. *10,000 microfarad capacitor showing the "–" label on
the cathode side*

4) Using one of your MM wires, connect the "+" rail to
    the input side of your button. See Figure 6-40 (which
    I had to rotate because of the crazy big capacitor in
    the middle!).

Figure 6-40. *Connecting the button to the "+" rail*

5) Using another MM wire, connect the cathode of
    your capacitor to the "–" rail on the breadboard as in
    Figure 6-41.

Figure 6-41. *Connecting the "-" rail to the same column as the capacitor*

6) Using a third MM wire, connect from the "-" rail to any open column on the breadboard; you will connect the LED part of the circuit here as in Figure 6-42.

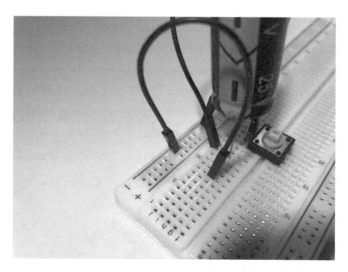

Figure 6-42. *Ground rail to an open breadboard column*

7) Taking the LED, plug it in with the short leg in the same column as your last wire and the long leg into any free column on the other side of the IC ravine as in Figure 6-43.

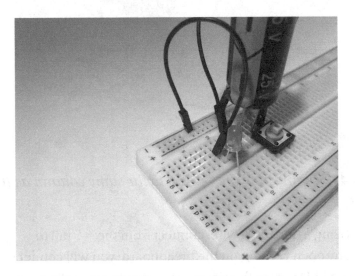

Figure 6-43. *Adding the LED across the IC ravine*

8) Next, connect the two resistors in series to create a total of 430 Ohms of resistance by connecting the leg of one to the same column as the LED anode and the other end into a free column. Then take the other resistor and connect one end into the same column as the last resistor's open end and the other end into a free column. Figure 6-44 shows how to hook them up in series on the breadboard.

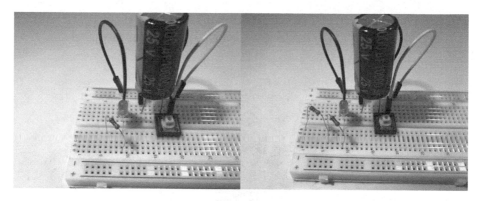

Figures 6-44. *Connecting the two resistors, in series, to create the total needed resistance*

9) Take your last MM wire and connect it to the output side of the button and the same column as the end of the resistor series as seen in Figure 6-45.

Figure 6-45. *Connecting the end of the resistor series to the button*

10)   And that's it, last step is to hook up the battery – red
        to "+" and black to "–" on the breadboard rails as in
        Figure 6-46.

Figure 6-46. *Battery wires connected to the power and ground rails*

Again, nothing happens right away because of the
introduction of the controlling switch. That's expected,
and we know we need to press the button to make the
magic happen. Now, what will happen when you press
the button is that the current from the 9v will rush
into the circuit, splitting itself between the LED and
the capacitor. (Even the thicc boi capacitor I am using
will fill up VERY quickly, a matter of under a second,
and will stop accepting current.) At the point that the
capacitor is full, all the current will start rushing to
the LED. When you let go of the button, the battery
will no longer be supplying power, and the capacitor
takes over. At that point you should see the decay of
the capacitor as it spends its charge trying to keep the

LED lit. The big capacitor in Figure 6-47 lasts a long
time, and the other ones show the LED gradually going
out over the span of several seconds (clockwise from
top left). A smaller capacitor, as we saw in the previous
chapter, will go out much faster and may not be visible,
but rest assured, whatever size capacitor you used,
it tried like heck to keep that LED lit for as long as it
could, even if it was a fraction of a second.

Figure 6-47. *LED fade-out from capacitor decay – From the
top: Full power from the battery, a few seconds after the battery
is "turned off" by letting go of the button, Dimmer still after a
few more seconds, and finally completely out*

Summary

You have now built your first circuits! Congratulations! These simple circuits are the basic foundation from which all smart devices are created. Obviously, the circuits themselves are simple, but you will find you will have many of these exact circuits in your future projects in fact, the same simple circuit you built to turn on your LED is also used to power your sensors, just replace the LED with the sensor you are going to use, and it has power and ground. As you will see in the following chapters, there are other connections for sensors, but at this moment, you have built the true, basic foundation of any smart project.

PART III

Smart Software

We depart now from our exploration of the basics of smart hardware and move into the software we need to truly make our smart devices smart. Before you begin this section, please note that this is not meant to be a complete guide to writing software, a complete reference for the languages mentioned, nor is it going to cover development cycles or the best practices for running a developer team as these are well beyond the scope of this book. There are many other excellent books to get you grounded in those concepts and abilities. I will also absolutely stay away from any speculation on which tools and frameworks are "the best," because the answer is that the best one is the one that works for you! I will make some recommendations where I feel comfortable, but they are simply that, a recommendation of something I am familiar with and that may help you. To this end we will focus on the practicalities of the software and how to handle common situations in smart devices with programming practices, and how to keep your smart software smart.

In the first chapter we will examine the different types of sensors that can provide you with access to the world around your smart device. From there, we will move into the MCU/SOC/Core of your smart devices and talk about preparing your systems to control your smart devices. The Arduino/Arduino Compatible and Raspberry Pi systems are covered here and will get you up and running with either or both. From there you will move into the smart device build lab and construct some devices that will put all your skills to work on circuits and devices.

When you have finished this section, you should have a fully functioning smart device prototype that will allow us to move into the next section on taking that prototype beyond the breadboard and into the truly "final product" realm.

CHAPTER 7

Touch, See, Hear, Smell, Taste

Alongside the rise of the programmable MCU and the proliferation of miniature computing devices has come the other required piece of smart devices. Since even the earliest days of scientific pursuits, there has been a goal to build human senses into automated systems. Even as early as the Greeks, and later the Romans, we were attempting to build humanoid forms of automata that had the ability to mimic human movements. These types of humanoid automata are a far cry from the AI-driven robotics creations we see performing backflips and opening doors on videos in the modern age, but they share the same end goal of building human capacity into inhuman devices.

One of the single most challenging elements in modern robotics is the seemingly insurmountable task of making human traits into digital skills. The "uncanny valley" is the sense of "not quite human" we get when interacting with humanoid robots, and it is a key hurdle to overcome in order to make robots more integrated with daily life. The other glaring facet of their lack of humanity is their inability to experience the world in human terms. They cannot apply the same basic senses we do to interact with their environment, and it is this limitation that sensing technology seeks to overcome.

The development of sensing and sensors that supply our digital systems with the ability to discern the world around them is critical to making smart devices that seamlessly integrate with our lives. One of the

© Christopher Harrold 2020
C. Harrold, *Practical Smart Device Design and Construction*,
https://doi.org/10.1007/978-1-4842-5614-5_7

secrets of smart devices is that they are not meant to "replace" humans, they are meant to "extend" them; to make us all *more* capable by removing the mundane, limiting, or simply dangerous tasks we need to perform. It is in this way that smart devices provide value to us as human beings; not as a replacement for our own senses, which have had millions of years of evolution to develop and be perfected. Rather they are an extension of our humanity. Sensing the world as we do is the most critical thing that smart devices do to extend our reach.

Touch, See, Hear – The Big Three

I purposely put the words of this chapter in this order, as they refer to the order in which these capabilities are likely to be important to a smart device. This is obviously subjective, but if you think about what a smart device, any smart device, could do for you, it is likely to come back to one of these three basic senses. This section is all about the context and rationale behind the *how and why* these senses are what they are and how they work, and their importance as the three core senses of smart devices is evident.

Touch – The ability to sense one's surroundings is a fundamental sense that is so basic that I am sure many of us take it for granted. It is so foundational to all other senses that even a blind person can still "see" by using their sense of touch to feel their surroundings and draw a mental picture of it. That is incredibly powerful, and the ability to touch and be touched is a critical element when considering smart devices for the simple reason that most, if not all, user interactions will likely come in the form of touch of some sort: buttons, switches, pressure sensor, contact sensor, something that registers the presence of a touch via an electronic signal.

The reality of the humble touch sensor is that it is primarily an outgrowth of a basic switch. Fundamentally a touch sensor really is taking the action of physical contact, be it with a button or pressure sensor or even something like the resistive screen technology in your phone screen, and closing or opening a circuit with it. This is the basic fundamental function of a switch, and in the case of a touch-based sensor it works the same way – on contact, the switch is placed in a new state (open or closed depending on the circuit) and then current either begins or stops flowing through the circuit. This, in turn, informs the circuit of the state change related to the circuit being either completed or interrupted and the device can take action. A practical example of this could be a bump sensor such as that on the front of a robot vacuum, telling it that it has hit the wall or some other obstacle. The response is written into the code of the vacuum's MCU and will generally be something along the lines of "if bumper is hit, then turn 90 degrees and move forward again." This ability to respond to the physical world is a critical element to smart devices.

Touch is also sometimes referred to as "feeling," and the other class of sensors that can fall into this are those that measure conditions like temperature, the level of water in the air or soil, or the weight of something. All of these require your device to detect something that we feel with our senses; hot and cold, wet and dry, heavy and light. These "feeling" sensors provide some of the most commonly used and basic functions in a huge number of smart devices, and understanding their use and functions is important. Figure 7-1 shows this most basic of sensors, the button.

Figure 7-1. *Example of a "touch" sensor – a simple button*

See – Perhaps no other sense is as important or difficult to mimic as sight. The power of sight is an incredibly complex and nuanced sense that science is even now not fully aware of the workings of. This makes bringing sight to our smart device an interesting challenge, but one that we have a variety of tools to perform. From infrared sensors to ultrasonic sensors, full ranging and mapping with LIDAR to the good old camera, there are a myriad of options for "seeing" the surrounding terrain.

Obviously, the concept of sight as it relates to smart devices is not limited to the idea of truly imaging the surrounding of the device in a visual sense. There is often not a need for literal photographic imaging in a smart device; however, that does not mean that awareness of the surroundings of the device is not important. There are multiple methods of sight for smart devices (you can see some examples in Figure 7-2), but they fall into two basic types:

a)   Imaging that creates a full and literal image of the surroundings – This could take the form of a regular photographic camera method or even something as advanced as LIDAR capability that produces a truly digital map of the surroundings.

b)   Imaging that gives a relative image of the surroundings – This could be done with ultrasonic sensors that provide a distance measurement to the nearest solid object from the sensor or something like an infrared sensor that measures reflected infrared light or the absence of it that would indicate the device is close to or far from an object, like the ground, for example.

Other types of simple sight would be things like motion sensors and light sensors, both of which are very common in a variety of smart devices, and which we will use later in the book.

Figure 7-2. *"See" sensors (clockwise from top left – ultrasonic distance, Raspberry Pi camera, and IR proximity sensor)*

Hear – Hearing is becoming more and more important to the smart device world as more devices are being developed with voice recognition as a key capability. Certainly, we wouldn't get very far using an Alexa or Google Home if the device couldn't hear us speaking! The basis for all of the sound sensors is the basic microphone, a simple device that uses a vibrating membrane to turn sound waves into an electric signal. That electric signal can then be used to decipher the sounds and use them in the device for things like voice commands or even just sensing that sound is occurring.

There are a great variety of sound-based sensors available for smart devices, depending on the use case that is required. A full microphone capable of capturing sounds and being used for recordings and voice activation is more complex to work with but has significantly more capability for the builder. There are also a variety of sounds sensors, literally sensors that detect the occurrence of sounds. These can be used to alert to the presence of loud noises in an otherwise quiet place, or to sense sounds in a specific range of frequency (you can see an example of this type in Figure 7-3). This second type of sensor will generally not record the sound in question which could be a disadvantage to the smart device you want to build, so understanding the difference between them is important.

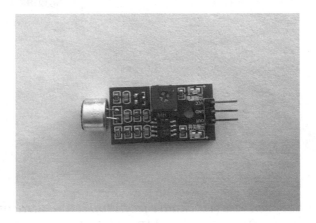

Figure 7-3. *"Hear" sensor – a sound level sensor*

Smell and Taste – The Other Senses

I do not want to trivialize these senses by separating them from the others, and they are important to smart devices, they just don't have the direct analog comparison to human senses in the traditional sense (specific chemical "smell" sensors being the one exception). If we take the same approach we did to defining digital "sight," and accept that smell and taste in the digital sense may not be the same as our own senses, then it is easier to categorize the sensors that make up this category as "taste and smell" sensors. The detection of compounds and molecules in the air is a prime example of the use of this type of sensor and could be classified as either smell or taste.

Some examples of smell/taste sensors could be things like humidity sensors, chemical sensors, and moisture sensors (you can see a chemical sensor in Figure 7-4). The primary types of consumer-grade sensors use a capacitive process that senses the change in the composition of the air by using the capacity of a conductive material and measuring the difference between what it should be and what it is. In the case of a chemical composition sensor, there can be a variety of means used to sense the specific chemical in question; however, the basic gist is that they have a reaction when the specific type of molecule is present in the air. The type commonly used in smart devices has a small amount of reactive material that is tuned for the type of chemical compound they want to sense. When the molecules are present in the air, the compound in the sensor will react with it and trigger the sensor with an electric signal that denotes the presence of the material.

Figure 7-4. *"Smell and taste" sensor – a chemical sensor (front on the left and back on the right)*

Sensor Considerations

Choosing a sensor for your own smart device requires awareness of several things, not the least of which is the type of sensor you need, of course. There are other considerations in deciding the correct sensor for your project, and how the sensor will integrate with your device.

147

Analog vs. Digital

As you will see in the chapter on MCUs, sensor output is the first consideration that you need to make when evaluating which sensor fits your project's needs. This is because both MCU and sensor inputs or outputs are one of two types, analog and digital. The difference is really in the data that the sensor relays and what the sensor can tell your device. A digital sensor is like a switch, when the sensor detects the condition it is designed to detect (such as sound or motion sensors), it completes the circuit and sends the current through to the other end of the circuit. This means that the alert from the sensor is a yes/no value, because there is no variation in the signal that comes from the sensor. This can be incredibly useful for scenarios where just a simple on/off alert mechanism is enough to respond to a change in condition, but it can be a limitation if there is a need to collect detailed information from the sensor, or if the sensor is an analog sensor.

Analog sensors, like digital sensors, react to a condition, and trigger an output response in the same way. The difference is that an analog sensor's output is not the full value of the current through the sensor. The output is a fraction of the current relative to the amount of the thing being sensed. A light sensor is an excellent example of how this works, where the amount of light detected by the sensor is translated into a current value that is a ratio of the amount of light to the amount of current (lower current for less light). A light sensor could also be found in a digital form, where if the light is above a certain threshold, it turns on, and off again when there is not enough light. Several sensors fall into this dual digital/analog category, but it is not a requirement to use both types of outputs, you can use one or the other as your own smart device needs.

It is easy to spot the type of output for your sensor (generally) as the labels on the sensor itself will indicate the output that is expected. You can see the two output types on a sensor in Figure 7-5.

Figure 7-5. *Digital and analog pin image (analog labelled A0 on the left, digital out D0 on the right)*

It is possible to convert a sensor from analog to digital (a common problem for Raspberry Pi users who do not have analog capability as we will see in the next chapter). You need to use an Analog to Digital Converter, or ADC, chip in your circuit which will convert the analog signal, regardless of the voltage, into a signal that can be read by the digital-only Raspberry Pi. Accounting for this requires you to perform some additional math in your code so you can make the conversion from the reported digital information into the analog source data. The chip itself uses a different connection type to transmit the data to the Raspberry Pi, which can show up in other types of sensors as well. (See Figure 7-6.)

Figure 7-6. ADC chip image

Advanced Devices

Often times, sensors and devices will require advanced connectivity to support their operation. This could be because they have requirements for additional data streams, have their own built-in MCU (common in things like displays), or generally have some feature that requires a number of specific features both in the sensor and the MCU. There are two types of this connectivity common in the smart device world, they are I2C and SPI. The MCP3008 pictured in Figure 7-6 uses the SPI interface for example, but many other sensors use I2C.

I2C

I2C was developed in the early 1980s as a basic standard for connecting devices in an MCU circuit. It is also sometimes called a "two wire" protocol, because it uses only two wires for controlling the flow of data to and from the attached devices. Figure 7-7 shows a very basic illustration of a simple I2C bus of devices. When you connect I2C devices, they are given an address that identifies them on the I2C bus. The bus is like a computer IP network, just a very small one, with only a few devices on it. The device's address is how you communicate with the device on the bus to collect its data and to send it commands. Figure 7-7 illustrates the I2C bus data and signalling paths.

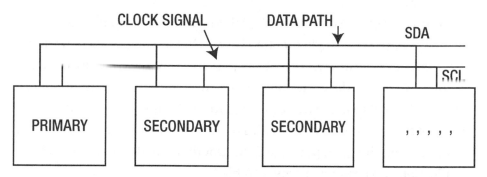

Figure 7-7. I2C bus (Note: Power and ground are omitted)

In the illustration you can see that there is a single primary device on the bus (this would be your MCU that is executing your code), and there can be multiple secondary nodes on the bus. These would be your devices such as the ADC chip I mentioned before or could be any other I2C compatible device (I have a compass module that uses I2C as an example). In order to communicate, the primary node sends a START command and the address of the device onto the bus, and the device responds by sending back its data. There are well maintained standard libraries for using I2C devices in C/C++ and Python, which covers the vast majority of Arduino compatible boards, and the Raspberry Pi. Part of the standard library functionality is the ability to probe the I2C bus and discover the address of the devices on it, which you can then use to issue commands and take readings/receive data from the devices.

I2C and, indeed, any of the advanced protocols are very powerful tools for exchanging data, because they make it possible to have multi-function sensors that can, for example, sense temperature, moisture level, and humidity in a single probe. In doing this, it can greatly simplify the circuit load and wiring needed for a smart device while providing a lot of information in a small package. It is used almost universally for devices that inherently need to send or receive multi-part data packets for their instructions such as position and force sensors, and screens like multi-line LCD displays.

I2C is more involved than the digital on/off signal of a pin, or even the analog output of a single function sensor, but as you advance through your smart device journey, you will undoubtedly come across the need to use an I2C sensor or device at some point. Also, the wiring as mentioned before is different than the basic power/ground/output wiring, requiring the use of special pins on your MCU. The actual pin number is different for every MCU, but the basic pins and their functions are defined by the I2C specification and are shown here in Table 7-1.

Table 7-1. *The pin functions for the I2C protocol*

SDA	Data signaling path – This is the Data channel the device uses for its communications
SCL	Clock signaling path – Used to maintain connection and synchronize transfers
VIN	Power connection
GND	Ground

For more complex sensors, additional hardware clock pins and control frame connections can be required, but the basic requirements of I2C data communications are satisfied by only the Data and Clock pins.

SPI

SPI was developed shortly after I2C in the mid-1980s and is now considered to be a de facto standard for connecting advanced peripheral devices into MCUs. Like I2C, it has a primary node which controls the overall bus, and secondary nodes which are the various connected devices. Unlike I2C, it uses four wires for its communications, and its protocol and addressing are a little more nebulous, which can be both good and bad depending on the application. The primary benefit of SPI is that the data size (called the "word size") is not limited to 8 bits, meaning you can send A LOT of data from an SPI device. Figure 7-8 shows single primary and single secondary SPI bus data paths and their direction.

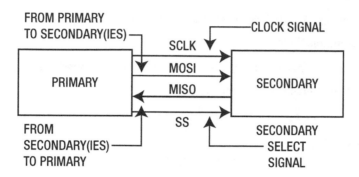

Figure 7-8. *A basic two member SPI bus (note that power and ground connections are omitted)*

As you can see from Figure 7-8, one of the major benefits of SPI is that unlike the two-wire I2C where the data on the data path flows in both directions, SPI has a dedicated path for data going to and from the primary and secondary nodes. This means that communications are isolated to always being out one pin and in on the other. This makes for much simpler software implementations of data signalling and receiving because you do not have to start and stop listening all the time on the same pin. Probably the most impactful downside is just the consumption of connections to your MCU in SPI devices. A basic connection requires the two communications wires for data in and data out, the clock (like I2C, it is used for synchronizing the transmissions), and then the last pin is used to signal the secondary node(s) to perform its respective action(s). The pins and their functions are shown in Table 7-2.

Table 7-2. Pin assignments for SPI

MOSI	Master out secondary in – Signals sent from the primary to the secondary node(s) are on this wire
MISO	Master in secondary out – Signals return from the secondary nodes on this pin
SCLK	Serial clock – Used to synchronize with the secondary node(s) for communications
SS	Secondary select – Used to send the appropriate signal to the secondary node(s) to tell it to start processing
VIN	Power connection
GND	Ground

While a full SPI bus can be wiring and pin heavy (see Figure 7-9), it offers significant simplification of communications in your code, due to the nature of the communication channel carrying multiple data points on a single data read. Also, the data size it is capable of dealing with should not be understated as it makes possible things like proper displays that can show many, many bytes of data at one time as well as things like interfacing with storage devices like an SD card (albeit minimally) from your MCU. As the needs of your project, and most critically your user experience, expand you will find that some advanced devices will naturally come into your design.

To give you some idea of the complexity of SPI in terms of connection load, Figure 7-9 shows the basic RFID sensor that comes with the Eleego starter sensor kit. Even when it is the only device wired to the Raspberry Pi, as in this picture, you can clearly see it is consuming seven pins worth of connections. This is not to deter you from using complex devices in your projects, but more to prepare you for the design considerations of them when they have such a high wiring load. This will become even more important when we talk about building PCBs later on in the book!

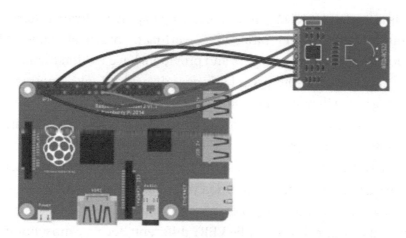

Figure 7-9. *SPI wiring image of a Raspbery Pi and an RFID reader*

To the Library!

Great news for working on your devices though, you don't have to figure all these wiring and connection things out manually, thanks to the concept of code libraries. Thanks to the introduction of libraries built by manufacturers, MCU and operating system providers, and indeed even the passionate members of the various programming language communities, working with the vast majority of sensors in your code is actually pretty straightforward. Libraries are code bits that you can add to your own application and access with a simple line or two of code. By "calling" the library in your code, you can use the tools it provides without writing them yourself from scratch. This means that instead of having to address all the hardware details and understanding all the possible conditions of the sensor, the library handles all that and you can instead use just two quick lines of code like this:

```
mySensor = new(sensor)

MyValue = sensor.Read(mySensor)
```

This is SIGNIFCANTLY easier than trying to poll hardware interrupts inline and wait for data. Libraries are powerful and practical things and I am grateful community members and providers have written them!

For the most part, a library is fairly generic, which is also another VERY good thing as it will make functionality available to a family of sensors vs. an individual sensor. Sensors are usually similar in the same family – sound sensors, light, motion, and others – but not always exactly the same in many cases. A sensor from one manufacturer and one from another may have the same exact appearance when you look at them, but the results from the sensor, the way you get those results, and indeed even the basics of wiring and connections may be VERY different! Because most libraries are purposely written to be fairly generic, this means that you can *probably* get away with using a single library for a type of sensor. This is not always true of course, and I have had numerous occasions where I have swapped a sensor due to lack of available parts or breakage, only to find myself rewriting entire programs because my first library did not support the alternate sensor, and even things as simple as the outputs and basic values get changed.

It is important that you get the libraries you need and "install" them on your MCU with your own code. We will cover this concept in much more detail later on, but the basic concept is that the library gets bundled up with your code and creates a full package that executes. Luckily, both the Arduino IDE and other languages that you may code in (Python and others) have library managers as part of their tooling. In most cases, it is a trivial matter to use a library in your language of choice, unless you are using some really new hardware or cutting-edge sorts of tech which may not have a well-developed library yet. In these cases, you may find yourself doing much more tinkering and tuning than you want, but that's also part of the fun of building smart devices!

Let's look at the two most common types of libraries for the Arduino and Raspberry Pi respectively. Please note this is not a be-all and end-all list, and you can code in Python, C, and about a million other languages on either platform! This exploration is meant to get you from zero to running code quickly, with the resources you are likely to find online within a few clicks. *Generally,* Arduino programs are written in C/C++, and Raspberry Pi device programs are very commonly written in Python. There are myriad reasons for these being the "defaults." The simplest reason is that the Arduino IDE is geared toward C/C++ with most if not all of the included libraries being written in it. With Raspberry Pi, most people coming to the Pi for smart devices are in need of a simple and easily accessible language to do things quickly, and Python fits the bill with its huge number of libraries and extensions.

If we accept these are the most common languages to get started with the two families of devices, then we can look at the specifics of those in the context of the devices and how to use them.

Arduino Libraries

All libraries are a collection of procedures that the application can use, grouped together because the procedures are related to a single concept/idea (in this case a single type of sensor or hardware component). There are literally hundreds of libraries available for Arduino for everything from basic sensors and components to more nuanced things like robotics packages and complete automation solutions. At the core, though, all of these libraries are just a group of functions that expose calls allowing you to take advantage of the library without needing to know every detail of the device it controls.

In a C/C++ context, you "add" a library to a project in the IDE with an #include statement. This tells the program that it will also need the functions included in the referenced library to execute properly. A library is really just a collection of files with the code in them to execute the associated functions. If you look at a library in your filesystem, it will usually be a .cpp file which is the code for the functions and a .h file which is the C/C++ header information. There may also be a keywords file, which helps the IDE with things like syntax highlights. Once you install the library, a simple process in the Arduino IDE as it is a built-in menu option, the programs you write can now use that library with the #include method. If you use an include and the library is not installed, the compiler will give you an error and tell you it is missing. This happens often when you are getting started and copying code online, as it may reference a library you do not have installed! Just install it, and the application will compile.

To install a library in the Arduino IDE (as of this writing), there are three basic ways: import a library that is included in the IDE, download and add a library as a zip file, and manually add one. The first two use the same basic interface, through the IDE itself. Under the "sketch" menu in the IDE there is an option to "Manage libraries" and one to "Add .ZIP library". (You will use this in the lab activity later.) The first one will take you to a list of predefined libraries that are included with the IDE and allow you to select one and install it. If the library you need isn't in there, you can download it as a zip file and use the second option to install the library. If for some reason you need to manually add the library, then you will need to put it in your Arduino/libraries directory and restart the IDE for it to be discovered.

You will be working with a number of libraries in the build labs, and I have included the instructions for the most current versions of them so you can install them and use them in the code in the lab section.

Python Libraries

Library management in Python is built more around the OS than the IDE, meaning that the libraries are installed at the command line and included when you compile the program you are building via the include statement in Python. Python does provide a library manager, but it is done via the command line and does not have a GUI as the Arduino IDE does. Python's library installer is called pip, and if you are developing in Python, you will use it a lot as it is the easiest way to get new libraries installed in Python.

For example, if you need to install the Raspberry Pi Python library for working with the GPIO ports on the Pi, you would type

```
pip3 install rpi.gpio
```

Once the library files have downloaded, now you can simply use the include rpi.gpio statement in your code and access all of the functions of that library to work with the GPIO of the Raspberry Pi.

Summary

Choosing the right sensor for the right job is the builder's eternal challenge. Fortunately, the dizzying array of sensors that are commercially available means that this challenge is getting easier all the time. Imagine those early pioneers who had to build the sensors too, we've come a long way for sure. One last stop before we get to your first smart devices, and that is the MCU itself. Once we get them prepped and loaded, you'll be ready to go for the build lab and your first smart devices and smart system!

CHAPTER 8

The Small Computer

Smart devices can be smart without using a computing device, but they are obviously limited in their functionality without having the computing power to drive the inputs and outputs of the device. As you have seen from our first experiments with circuits, without an MCU to drive them, they can perform some basic functions, and provide a certain level of interaction. Aside from using a preprogrammed sensor or device with some logic already built-in, the ability of a circuit without an MCU to be truly "smart" is obviously heavily stunted. There are many considerations as to which MCU to use for your own projects, and which features and drawbacks will influence the selection most will largely depend on the use case.

It is also difficult to talk about the functions of the MCU fully separate from the sensors themselves, so I have tried to make sure to address the basics of the MCU in this chapter as a means to build from the last where we talked about the sensors themselves. Understanding how your MCU works and the ways to interface to sensors with it will make your projects much easier to design and build than if you figure it all out on the fly!

Small-ish

For a moment, let's break the MCU world for smart devices into two buckets – the haves and the have-nots. What do they have or have not? An operating system and a full-blown CPU (it may not be a powerful CPU, but it is a full CPU nonetheless). More fundamental perhaps is the concept

© Christopher Harrold 2020
C. Harrold, *Practical Smart Device Design and Construction*,
https://doi.org/10.1007/978-1-4842-5614-5_8

of the System on a Chip, or SOC. A SoC is really just a fancy and complex circuit that integrates most of the functions of a standard computer into a really small and simple package. There are three types of SOC, broadly speaking:

- A device that utilizes a microcontroller chip – This means the chip has all the things like the CPU, RAM, and ROM all in a single chip. Examples of this are the Arduino family and the ESP family you can see in Figure 8-2 (the latter of which you will use in the labs).

- Devices that are built around a microprocessor chip – This means the chip only has the CPU functions on board and the remainder are handled by other chips on the system. The prime and most recognizable example of this is the Raspberry Pi – it has peripherals, ports, connections for I/O, and a full CPU and runs a full PC operating system. (See Figure 8-1.)

- Devices that are built for a very specific function and may or may not even have either a microcontroller or a microprocessor – These are called an ASIC, which stands for Application Specific Integrated Circuit. An example of these is found in high-speed networking applications where network communications gear needs extremely high throughput and low latency.

Figure 8-1. *Raspberry Pi 3B*

Figure 8-2. *Node32S (left) and Arduino Nano (right)*

This is a critical distinction between hobby-based solutions and
something that is important for your own consideration as you embark
on the smart device journey. A SoC with a microprocessor offers a lot:
more power, more inputs and outputs, more expansion opportunity,
more processing capability, and so on. With all of that capability comes
some downsides that you can probably guess; they are bigger physically,
they are more complex, and because of the layer of OS abstraction will
have additional overhead. Probably the most impactful issue with a

microprocessor SoC vs. the "all-in-one" types is that microprocessors are generally power hogs, requiring both high current draw at power on and a high sustained current draw as they run.

This is incredibly impactful to you in terms of your projects, because while a full microprocessor SoC may offer more accessibility in terms of tools and programming options, it may be that you cannot meet the needs of your project with the restrictions that it imposes. For example, while running a Raspberry Pi via a solar panel is possible, the size of the panel needed is probably impractical for most applications requiring long duration runtimes, as it would be quite large to generate the 5v needed. The battery likewise would need to be sufficiently large to store enough current to last through the night, and thus makes low-power Raspberry Pi use cases difficult (not impossible, just difficult).

Conversely the family of "all-in-one" SOCs like Arduino, Node, ESP8xxx, and the like are extremely power-light, often able to operate on a single coin battery for extended periods of time with good power management and intelligent coding. This comes with its own restrictions in that these devices are generally limited in what they can do and how expandable they are. There are always ways to expand them, and add in peripherals and expansions, but right out of the box, they might be limiting for your particular project. The other big pro for the "all-in-one" SOC is that with some exceptions, they are SMALL and super lightweight. The standard ESPxxx-based NodeMCU, for example, is only 49 x 24.5 mm and weighs about as much as a couple of coins. Packed into that space is a 32-bit processor, built-in Wi-Fi, a solid amount of GPIO pin options, and enough memory to store even the most complex applications. All of that and it retails for about $12 as of this writing, depending on which version you get.

That last bit is the real catalyst for the explosion of all of the types of SOCs – if you can get a fully functional one for less than $10 in bulk, why wouldn't you put one in everything you make? That cost is for the fully assembled MCU as well; the parts to make one are incredibly inexpensive in volume; fractions of a cent in many cases. Having a low-cost MCU that is easily reprogrammed (no more UV lights!) and can run a variety of external sensor and power management functions means that suddenly the ability to control devices is not just limited to industrial applications anymore. If I can slap an MCU in my projects and get better interfacing and controls out of them, why wouldn't I want to improve the UX? Thus, we come full circle to the whole point of this book. I have devices now that I can embed in practically anything and can easily manage and reprogram over the Wi-Fi that is all over my home and workshop.

All of this power also means when you are designing your smart system, an important consideration is balancing what you are collecting with each individual device. Too many sensors and load on a device may be a bad thing, and when you consider the entirety of the smart system (sensors, collectors, a processing gateway, and the display and action layer), you may really only need one or two sensors for each device. This also allows you to run much lighter code and makes for simpler management in terms of updates, break/fix (parts do wear out or get wet and stop working sometimes), and general maintenance of the system because you can simply swap one relatively inexpensive unit for another, and the system as a whole keeps functioning.

The Magic of GPIO and the Humble Pin

General-purpose input/output, or simply GPIO (pronounced by reading the letters gee-pee-eye-oh), is the single most important capability that an MCU offers the user. There are no MCUs in the mass market that do not have some form of GPIO that you as the designer and programmer control, as they would be too inflexible to support most smart devices. The standard means for these GPIO connections to be made is through a conductive metal rod that is generally soldered in place into one of the corresponding holes on the MCU. Sometimes you will get an MCU that does not have this done already and it will come with the rods to solder yourself in the form of what is called a "header" which is just a group of some number of the metal rods connected with plastic and ready to solder in place. Once they are, they become the conduit for the GPIO and are most commonly referred to as a "pin." You can see a picture of a soldered pin on an ESP8266 MCU in Figure 8-3.

Figure 8-3. *An MCU with GPIO pins clearly visible*

The unassuming pin is the cornerstone of all smart devices, and the ability to tell that pin exactly how to behave (as an input or an output) is the feature that allows us to bridge the divide between software and hardware, combining them into the smart device. GPIO capability is also one of the most important factors in how you choose your MCU, as it determines the total amount of devices you can interface with (sensors and outputs) and will have a very strong correlation with power draw and overall capability.

Fundamentally the common MCU has at its core three types of "pin" or connections to external devices. The two most obvious are the Power and Ground pins which we will use for completing circuits and connecting devices that need continuous power. The third is the true GPIO which can be any number of things depending on both the MCU itself some are defined by the MCU's internal programming and wiring, and the rest of which are up to you the programmer to define. Figure 8-4 shows a common MCU pinout - that is the map of the pins and their functions - (this is an ESP32-based MCU) with its pins defined and labelled.

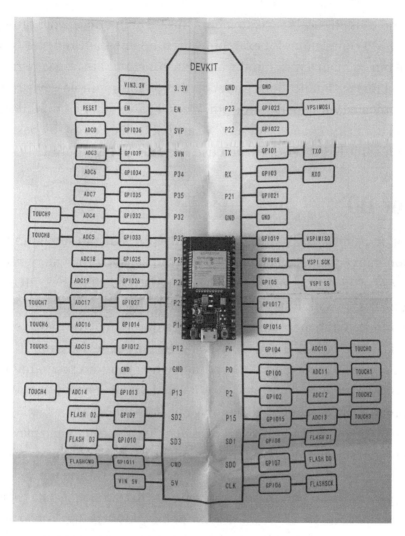

Figure 8-4. *The Node32S MCU pinout diagram and the device*

As you can see in Figure 8-4, the majority of this MCU's GPIO are reserved for the user to decide on what to do with them – essentially everything labeled GPIOXX is yours to do what you want with. You will also notice that there are multiple labels on most of the pins as well, which indicates that they have an alternate function. Alternate functions allow pins to use multiple communications methods without having to dedicate

167

pins, and thus physical space, to them - this is commonly used for things like I2C/SPI connections for example. This fundamentally reduces your overall pin count in a way, but the alternate functions are also generally reserved for communications protocols that enable multiple devices to be communicated with on the same pin. We will cover other communication means later in the chapter. For now we are going to focus on the basic function of the GPIO pins and their use as either input or output.

AO or DO

Analog or digital is the basic question of the GPIO pin and something that you must consider when you choose your sensors. You will notice that some of the pins have a second label of ADCxx next to the GPIOxx in Figure 8-4. This indicates that the pin can be used in either analog or digital mode. At the most basic level this is a question of the data type the pin will relay to the MCU and is driven by the type of device connected to the pin itself. This is critically important when you start programming your software for your smart device as it will determine how you have to interpret the signals coming to or going out from the MCU.

An important analog and digital consideration also comes into play in terms of choosing the MCU platform you will build on. Why is this decision so important? Well, in the case of the Raspberry Pi, there are no **native** analog pins available, only digital. So, if you want to read analog data using a Raspberry Pi, and you likely will at some point, you are going to need to use additional components like Analog to Digital Converters (ADIC), to achieve your desired results. The other side of the Raspberry Pi is that, as a full computer, the Pi is uniquely suited to play the role of hub or gateway system in your smart system. It is capable of running things like Node-RED for data collection and processing, databases for storing data, full web servers for display, and a variety of other nice tools and functions for making a truly smart system on a small scale. As you go through the build lab in Chapter 10, you will build out a simple but full smart system that uses the Raspberry Pi as the hub.

Digital IO

Digital is the easiest to discuss because it is the simplest functional input/ output model for using a GPIO interface. Digital I/O is like a switch; it is either on or off and there is nothing in between. You will see this commonly referred to as "high" and "low" which refers to the voltage of the pin in question being set to either its maximum available voltage (generally 3.3v for most MCUs, although there are exceptions – the Arduino Uno GPIO pins run at 5v) or no voltage at all. In the case of the pin being used as an output, setting the pin high and low generally signals a device on the other end of that pin to start and stop. It is also extremely handy for switching on and off LEDs for things like warnings and diagnostics. Along with the knowledge you have from the previous chapters of wiring an LED to a 3v power source, you can figure out quite easily how to wire that simple circuit up. Figure 8-5 shows a sensor that is digital only.

Figure 8-5. *Digital only sensor – in this case a sound sensor*

For an input device, the digital signal generally indicates that the state-change the device is designed to detect has occurred. We discussed this in greater detail in the previous chapter about sensors, but an example would be if this sound sensor detects a sound above a threshold. If you look closely at the picture, you will see a blue box with a grey-white "x" in it. That is a potentiometer (a type of resistor that can be adjusted) and it sets the value at which the sensor will "trigger." Once that level of sound is reached, the internal logic of the sensor actually turns on its output pin to "high" and thus if your MCU is listening on that pin for that condition, you would be able to register in the code that a sound above the threshold has occurred. Digital signals are basic but are also very common and useful for smart devices since a lot of the functions of smart devices are real-time responses, and identifying an off/on type signal is much faster programmatically than reading in data and computing a result. However, it has very low fidelity, meaning that yes, I know a sound occurred, but I have no real idea of what level it occurred at other than "louder than what I set the threshold to." If you need to know what level the sound is actually occurring at, that's what an analog signal is for.

Analog

Like a digital sensor, an analog sensor also uses a change in voltage to indicate a change in condition. Unlike a digital signal, however, there is much more granularity, and interpretation of the signal is required to understand the output. Generally, the analog signal is a percentage of the maximum voltage, divided into slices. Those slices can be from 0 to 255, 0 to 1023, or whatever the sensor/device is programmed for and is generally published in the usage guidance for the sensor itself. What this means in practical terms is that an analog pin can send and receive fractions of the total voltage to the MCU, which in turn can allow for more fine-grained control over the attached device. Also, analog sensors are generally outputting readings all the time (with some exceptions for sensors that require a start/stop signal), which means that in order to collect those readings you might need to check the readings from the sensor a lot to get the level of fidelity you want. Figure 8-6 shows an example of an analog capable sensor.

Figure 8-6. *Analog sensor – also a sound sensor, but note the presence of an A0 pin*

I have purposely chosen two sensors that do the same basic function – sensing sound. In this case, the analog sensor would potentially offer a much higher level of fidelity to my application, as the presence of an analog sensor indicates that it could output more data. In this case, spoiler alert, it does, allowing me to get a sense of the actual sound level as a fraction of the maximum level (in this case a value somewhere between 0 and 1023 slices of the voltage). This could allow additional functionality in my software, at the cost of additional computation for me to do in code. This is an important consideration for your own devices. If you just need to know that something is or isn't, then programmatically speaking a digital "yes or no" is oftentimes enough to accomplish the purpose.

As an input source to your MCU, this is used for sensors that are detecting the range of a condition. Light sensors, moisture sensors, humidity sensors, and many others use the returned voltage as a means of reflecting the amount of something detected. Generally (but not always), the higher the voltage, the more of whatever the sensor detects is detected. It falls on you to utilize the sensor documentation to determine what the value means, and to provide the associated logic in the software to interpret the voltage result.

The Software of Smart

As you saw in the first chapter of the book, the history of the computing and hardware required for building smart devices was a fractious one, with many companies competing to develop and bring to market all the hardware that drives these smart devices. The software that supports them was, as you can imagine, equally fractured, and it is this fractured landscape that leads us to having so many tools and languages for building smart devices. In some cases, this is limited by the hardware platform itself, as is common with Arduino-style MCUs that default to a C/C++ based application. It is possible to modify this behavior with other tools and libraries that let you build with another language entirely such as Python. In yet other instances, the platform will let you natively build in whatever language you desire provided there are hardware interface libraries available, as is the case with the Raspberry Pi.

In the larger smart system architecture – the place where a collection of smart devices work together to form a smart system – there are many places where one type of device is better suited than another, and this will often influence your choice of device/language/platform as you meet the needs of the system itself. A prime example of this is where real-time collection of sensor data is required – examples would be things like self-driving cars and robotics type situations where you need to sense and respond immediately. In such a scenario, the minimal configuration of the Arduino or ESPx family might be a better choice for collecting this sensor data. This is because it is possible for the sensor data collection to be blocked by the microprocessor-based architecture of the Raspberry Pi. If the hardware is busy with OS processes, the sensor data collection can be delayed. Granted, this delay could be very, very small, well under a second, but in a scenario like a self-driving car that kind of gap could be disastrous. In that scenario, the real-time nature of the Arduino would be a much better choice than the interrupt driven nature of the Raspberry Pi. It is possible to get the Raspberry Pi closer to real time through extensive tweaking and changes to the OS and services, but it may not be worth the effort when you can get that effect with a different MCU "out of the box."

Fortunately, even when you must mix and match devices, you will also have the means to communicate between them with a universal language, which we will come back to. For now, our focus is on getting your devices running and accessible so you can start building your smart device systems.

A Brief Word on Tools

Whatever the platform you choose and whatever language you end up with, at some point you are going to find yourself in need of three basic things to build smart software:

1. An Integrated Development Environment, or IDE

2. A place to store your code

3. A way to get that code on to the device in question

Before I go deeper into the smart software and the architecture of smart device systems, I want to start this section out with a few basic statements of fact:

- You do not explicitly need an IDE to write code, but it is much easier.

- There are many tools for storing code like GitHub, Bitbucket, Pastebin, and others, but you can store it on your local computer as well. I will use GitHub in the labs for some of its more convenient features.

- The way you get code to the device depends on the device, and your personal preferences!

Notepad, VIM, VI, Nano, anything you can type lines of text in will work to write code. An IDE makes writing code *easier*, not possible. IDEs have features like syntax highlighting and inline debugging that tells you if you forgot a ":" or a "!" instead of having to debug it after the fact. They have libraries of different language packs that make writing any language more visually simple by formatting the code in the expected way with proper indents and syntax. They also include simple "nice to haves" like spell check and auto-complete. While you do not NEED an IDE to write code, I would highly recommend you have one if for no other reason than to make life easier on yourself!

There are many IDEs out there that you can use for building your smart application, and all of them offer tools and add-ons that make smart device code in particular more accessible and approachable, with new ones added almost continually. It is this rapid pace of change that makes a timely listing of all the parts and pieces you should include a difficult challenge in a printed form. Instead I am going to focus more on the tooling itself, and the pros and cons of using each one as it relates to a particular platform. It can actually be more difficult to develop against a certain platform if you start off with an IDE that is not well suited to it, and so making this choice up front is worth some thought before you go banging away, only to find that it doesn't have the right libraries you need.

While I will stop short of a full "pros and cons" section here, I will say that my personal preference at the time of this writing at least is for either the "native Arduino IDE" or Visual Studio Code (VSCode) from Microsoft. Both are solid IDEs in their own right, and both will give you the basics without any issues, but it is important to note that with the Arduino IDE, you can write code to execute on other platforms (like an RPi), but you cannot use the IDE to load the code to an RPi, for example.

For programming the Arduino compatible family of MCU, the Arduino IDE has far and away the most library support, a strong community, and is obviously compatible with the MCU. For developing code, for any part of the smart ecosystem, I believe VSCode is a superior choice due to its native multi-language support, extensive add-on support, and general "developer friendly" presentation. Neither of these will be a bad option, and as I said before, an IDE only makes things easier. You do not need one to get going!

One quick side note on the Arduino and compatibles like the NodeMCU/ESP8266 based family of MCUs. Even if you do not use the Arduino IDE for writing your code, you will have to use it, or the command line tooling, for the flashing process. The way you must flash the Arduino compatible presents a downside, not of the Arduino IDE itself, but of the Arduino compatible in general. Because the board is generally programmed for the first time over a USB connection, you will need a computer that supports this. I know you are likely saying that all computers have USB, but not all USB devices are created equal and I can tell you that, at the time of this writing, it is impossible to flash an ESPxxxx-based MCU with a new MacBook Pro using UCB C ports. This is because of the way Apple has chosen to implement their drivers in newer versions of OSx, and a failure of compatibility with the Arduino drivers required to flash this particular device. I have no doubt this will change at some point, and I managed to get it to work exactly once in many hours of trying, but as soon as I unplugged the MCU, it stopped working and never worked again, even with a complete rebuild of my Mac from scratch. I have not experienced this issue with a Windows machine (in fact it was trivially easy to get an older Windows laptop to flash the same MCU reliably and repeatedly). This may have changed by the time this goes to press, but the caution remains that you should always verify you can connect to your hardware!

Regarding some sort of Internet-based code repository? This is the only hard and fast "statement of fact" I will make in recommending something to you - you should absolutely use something to store your code on that is not your local machine. Having your code stored in an external repository that persists if you change laptops, nuke your machine, forget to backup, spill diet Mountain Dew on your key board, and so on is one of those safety nets that you should absolutely have in place. Most of these repository systems are free, spectacularly easy to use, and you should do so. If you do not have an account for one, you should literally put this book down and sign up now. I will wait here until you get back. I have used GitHub myself in both Chapters 9 and 10 for the labs, as I am most familiar with it, but I am not in any way associated with GitHub, other than as a user. I can also tell you it has saved me multiple times already in a number of situations from "didn't I write a loop that did that already?" to "oh heck, there goes my hard drive."

Smart System Basics

With a basic understanding of what is needed to develop your code, let's turn now to what constitutes a smart system. I discussed in the first part of the book that any smart system is fundamentally just sensors collecting data and sending it to a central repository. The basic architecture of all smart systems is fundamentally built on that exact idea: collect data and send it somewhere to see what's going on. Easy right? Of course, as we all know, the "devil is in the details" and it is the specifics of your scenario that makes getting the right pieces in place a challenge. You wouldn't really have much use for a motion sensor if you are monitoring the quality of the soil in your garden or probably care too much about light levels if you are always monitoring something in a closed pipe. The situation enforces obvious choices, but there are many others you will need to consider which we will discuss as we progress further through the book.

For now, let's accept that at this phase, the first prototype, we are focused on one thing; a smart device that collects data and relays it to a central location. We can see the very basic architecture of this system in Figure 8-7. Your smart device will use a messaging method to send data to a central system.

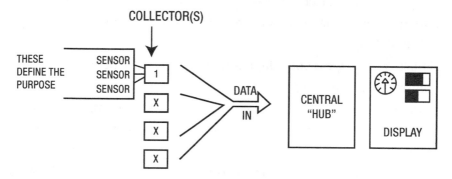

Figure 8-7. *Basic Smart System Architecture*

The thing that makes your smart system "fit for purpose" is the combination of the sensors you employ and the data they collect, combined with what you do with that data on the other end. A smart system that only collects data but performs no actions – alerts, analysis, responses – is not really smart so much as "kind of aware." Intelligence in a system is measured by its ability to detect AND react, not just detect. What makes a smart farm, smart? It is the fact that the sensors and their data are applicable to providing a detailed view of the conditions that are most associated with good farming outcomes (yields, disease/pest controls, growth rates, quality, etc.) and that the data they collect is used to take specific actions to maintain the best conditions for those outcomes. Turning on a sprinkler for dry soil is the most basic and, frankly, the most obvious and illustrative example of this type of outcome-focused system.

In order to build a smart system that provides comprehensive outcomes for the given environment being monitored, it will take a lot of trial and error, research, and just some basic good luck to find the right combination of data points and measures to make things match up to the optimal outcome. It is worth considering at this phase, before you begin the task of building this system, what is your outcome? My example of this is my own garden, where I began simply wanting to know if the soil was too dry for my plants, and I wound up building a complete smart garden. As my system got smarter (and I learned more about what it could do), I expanded my outcome to include new things that were previously not part of my initial design.

Smart systems grow and adapt as technology, uses, people, and capabilities evolve. It is important, as you will see in the discussion later in the book, to always keep this in mind as you start building out your devices. Your expectations and desires for the capabilities of the device will evolve and you can allow for this evolution in your design as you go. In our basic example though, our outcome is clear: dry soil = dead plants. We are going to ensure that scenario does not happen so that our outcome is plants that are alive! Over the rest of this chapter and the build labs that follow, you are going to build out this simple but effective smart system that will illustrate the concepts of all that you have learned up to now.

Let's Get Ready to Rumble!

In order to build a complete smart system, you need to understand the basic architecture of the system, and what part does what. You are going to be building to a pretty standard DIY smart system model, using Arduino-based devices for collecting data from sensors at the source, and then sending that data to a Raspberry Pi acting as the processing hub for that data. You will be using application code for the Arduino, written in C++, and Node-RED as the processing engine on the Raspberry Pi. You will also use MQTT which is a standards-based messaging protocol that allows devices of different types to communicate with basic messaging. I will be introducing you to several concepts all at once during the build, and there will be gaps in what can be fully covered in the realm of this guidance – Node-RED could be an entire book by itself. Just keep in mind that it will all lead up to you putting some of the previous hardware knowledge and the following software knowledge into a system that allows you to collect data from sensors, send it somewhere using messaging, and collect and display it with a processing system. Figure 8-8 shows the exact architecture you will build out in the build lab.

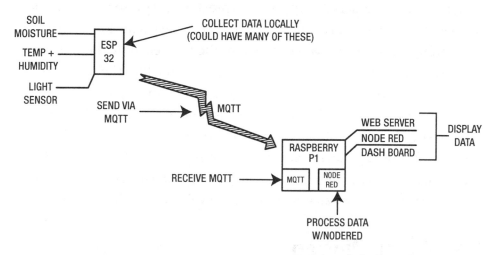

Figure 8-8. *Diagram of the prototype smart system*

A quick note – the "central hub" of the Raspberry Pi can also run on your own computer or laptop. Node-RED and Mosquitto (the MQTT server) can very easily run on a Windows or Mac system, so if you do not have a Raspberry Pi available, that's alright, and you can just install the software onto your local machine as well.

The first step to getting your smart system running is to get your MCUs ready to receive code and perform their functions. I have purposely chosen to use a combination of functionalities, software, and language in the construction phase of this to create both simple devices and a functional smart system. I have provided code libraries that will run as is (via GitHub links provided with the labs in Chapters 9 and 10), if you are using the same devices that I specified in Chapter 2 for building up the workbench to complete the lab section later. Because there are MANY varieties of MCU, it would be impossible to account for every possible means and method of connecting to them and preparing them in a single chapter (or book for that matter!). Instead, I will focus on the same two types of devices (Arduino compatible using an ESP32 made by NodeMCU and the Raspberry Pi) as I have in both Chapters 9 and 10's labs, and give the guidance that for others the instructions provided may also work, but you should of course refer to the documentation that is specific for your device.

Through this process, you will also see the differences in the two platforms come to life as you prep them for functionality. The Raspberry Pi, as a full computer, is significantly more complex to prepare, requiring things like a keyboard and monitor. The Arduino and compatibles are really more of a matter of "plug it into a USB port and you're ready," because the prep applies to getting your computer ready to load code into the device. Because of the contrast, I have not put the instructions "inline," opting instead to have a separate path if you will for each device type.

Raspberry Pi Prep

Getting your Raspberry Pi ready to go is about doing a lot of stuff on the Raspberry Pi itself and very little on your own computer (as opposed to the Arduino which is pretty much the opposite). I will be walking you through using a very "lightweight" RPi operating system called DietPi, that allows you to do the basic things you want and customize as you grow your smart system out. You do not have to use DietPi, as any of the other operating systems available like Raspbian will work fine as well. If your Raspberry Pi was pre-configured you can use that OS so long as it supports Python and Node-RED.

I have used DietPi for simplicity in getting things up and running as fast as possible, and then allowing you to grow your solution without having to do a ton of tedious prep work up front. In order to get your system running though, you will need a few things:

- The SD card that came with your Pi kit (if you ordered the kit online) or some other SD card

- A piece of software on your computer to write SD card images (I recommend something like SD Clone or Balena Etcher – both are really easy and simple to use and can be found with a quick Google search). You can also use the terminal to do this, but having the software is just nicer as it gives you progress and status.

- You will need to download the latest DietPi image to your computer to write to the SD card; go to `https://dietpi.com/` for the download.

- You will need an HDMI cable, a TV or monitor, and a USB keyboard to complete the setup; it is possible to perform a "headless" setup with DietPi, but it has been my experience that this rarely works smoothly, and so it is safe to just assume you will need to plug it in and connect to it directly, and the instructions will assume this.

- Wireless network credentials (also you may want the Raspberry Pi to have a fixed IP – this isn't required, but it will make things easier over time since you will connect to it a lot!).

Once you have those things assembled, you can proceed through the setup steps here and get your Pi ready to go with the OS and Node-Red.

Step 1: Create your OS drive with Etcher:

- Download the DietPi image from dietpi.com.

- Expand the downloaded zip file into a directory and locate the .iso file seen here in Figure 8-9.

▼ 📁 DietPi_RPi-ARMv6-Buster	--	Folder	Today at 4:13 PM
hash.txt	234 bytes	Plain Text Document	Today at 4:13 PM
README.md	9 KB	Markdown Document	Today at 4:13 PM
DietPi_v6.25_RPi-ARMv6-Buster.img	966.8 MB	NDIF Disk Image	Today at 4:13 PM
DietPi_RPi-ARMv6-Buster.7z	110.4 MB	7-Zip Archive	Today at 4:13 PM

Figure 8-9. *Filesystem view of the .iso file you need for the Raspberry Pi*

- Launch Etcher, and choose the image you downloaded, and the SD card from your Raspberry Pi kit as the target, and then simply click "flash" as you see in Figure 8-10.

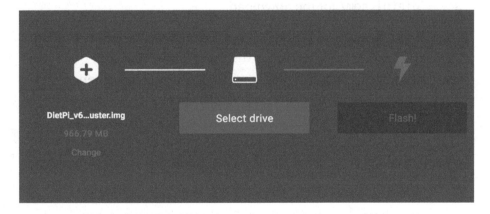

DietPi_v6...uster.img
966.79 MB
Change

Select drive

Flash!

Figure 8-10. *Etcher selection screen*

The process of writing to the SD can take some time, but usually not more than 5 or 10 minutes. Once completed, you can place the SD into the Raspberry Pi, plug it in the keyboard and HDMI, and then the power, and the system will boot up to the screen you see in Figure 8-11.

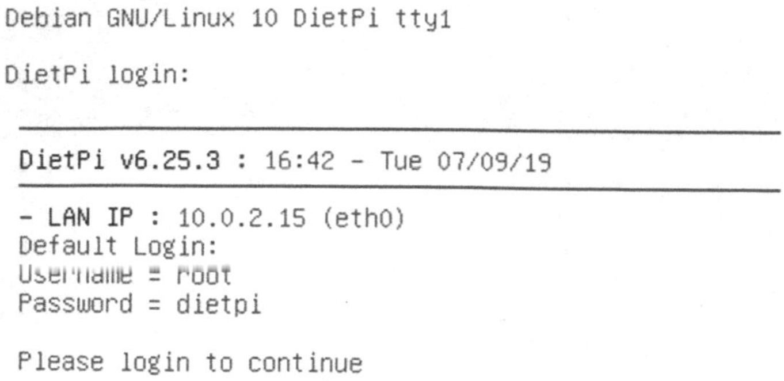

```
Debian GNU/Linux 10 DietPi tty1

DietPi login:
_____

DietPi v6.25.3 : 16:42 - Tue 07/09/19
_____

- LAN IP : 10.0.2.15 (eth0)
Default Login:
Username = root
Password = dietpi

Please login to continue
```

Figure 8-11. *DietPi first boot screen*

Step 2: Install the software you will need to the Raspberry Pi via the DietPi installer. Once you log into the system with the default password and username, and either change them or not (you do not need to for the lab, but strongly recommend you change them for any sort of "real" uses), you will come to the DietPi Software screen seen in Figure 8-12. You are going to want two extra things installed to complete the build lab:

 – Node-RED

 – Mosquitto MQTT server

Also, at this point, feel free to install pretty much whatever else you might want, like a desktop or other tools; as the Pi is VERY flexible, you can use it for many things beyond the scope of this book, and I greatly encourage you to experiment! To install the basics for the lab, follow the steps given here (please note that there may be changes to the process with new versions of the OS – there are new versions released frequently and these steps might be impacted!):

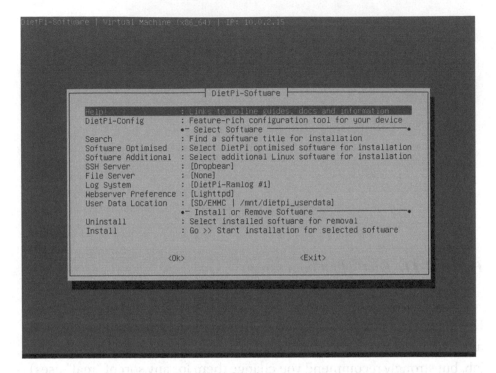

Figure 8-12. *DietPi Software select screen*

1) In the Software screen you should choose the
    "Software Optimized" option with the down-arrow
    key – confirm the selection by pressing "Enter."

2) This will bring you to the list of optimized software.
    There is A LOT of them, which is why I usually
    recommend DietPi to people; the community
    support is amazing and there is so much that is
    "ready to go" for you to use. From this list, choose
    anything you want, but make sure to check the box
    by clicking the spacebar next to Node-Red and
    Mosquitto (numbers 122 and 123 and toward the
    bottom of the list in the Hardware Projects section)
    as you see here in Figure 8-13 and also find and

click the box next to number 69 – Rpi.GPIO as you
will need it for the lab (it is not shown in the picture
but is higher up in the selection list).

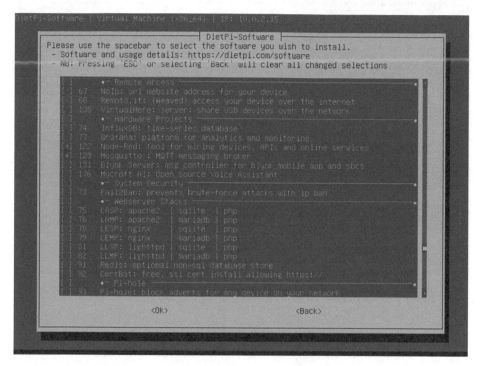

Figure 8-13. *DietPi optimized software list*

3) Pressing "Enter" will take you back to the initial
    software screen. From here just arrow down to
    "Install" to continue by pressing "Enter" as you see
    in Figure 8-14.

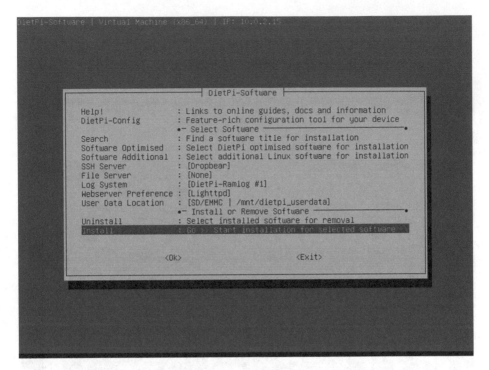

Figure 8-14. *Confirm installation dialog*

4) The software confirmation dialog box you see in
Figure 8-15 will appear and ask if you are good with
the selections. Arrow over to "OK" and then press
"Enter" to start the install.

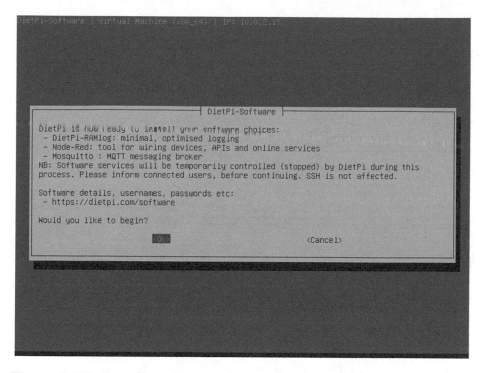

Figure 8-15. *Install confirmation*

5) The software will install (this can take a bit
    depending on your Internet connection and what
    you selected, but generally just takes a moment) and
    you will see the install progress on the screen.

6) You will get one more confirmation as seen in
    Figure 8-16, which is the "data collection" option.
    DietPi uses this to see what bits of software people
    are using and where to ensure their support, so I
    recommend sharing it, but that is a personal choice
    of course! Arrow to your option and press "Enter" to
    continue.

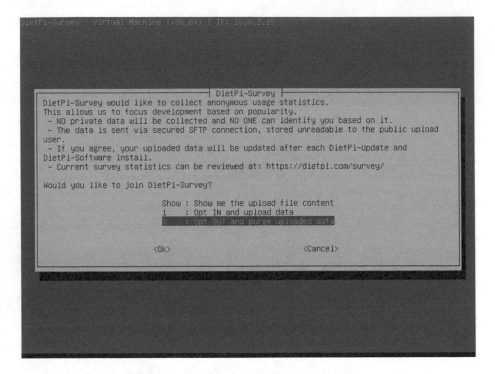

Figure 8-16. Software install reporting screen

7) The system software will complete and prompt
    you to reboot as you see in Figure 8-17 – just press
    "Enter" to reboot and your system to complete the
    install.

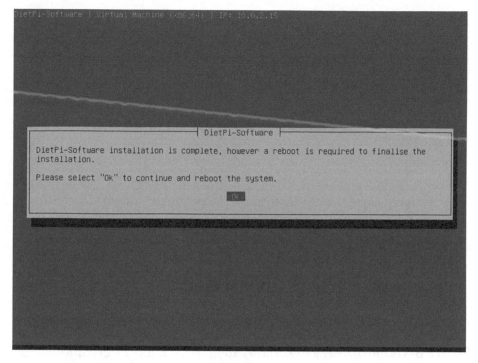

Figure 8-17. All done! Reboot confirmation

8)   When the reboot ends, you will come back up to the
     screen you see in Figure 8-18, which means your
     system is now ready for the lab! You will come back
     and configure the software as you go through the
     smart system build lab.

```
Debian GNU/Linux 10 DietPi tty1

[ OK ] DietPi-Services | Root access verified.

DietPi-Services
────────────────────────────────────────────────
Mode: start

[ OK ] DietPi-Services | start : mosquitto
[ OK ] DietPi-Services | start : node-red
[ OK ] DietPi-Services | start : cron


────────────────────────────────────────────────
DietPi v6.25.3 : 16:21 - Sat 10/12/19
────────────────────────────────────────────────
- LAN IP : 10.0.2.15 (eth0)
Default Login:
Username = root
Password = dietpi

Please login to continue
```

Figure 8-18. Raspberry Pi is ready to go with DietPi – great job!

From here you can proceed to configuring the ESP32 for the lab and then you will be ready to get started on the various builds in the next chapters.

Arduino Prep

Unlike the Raspberry Pi, the Arduino and compatible systems are pretty much "as is" out of the box. Getting ready to use them is much more about the preparation of your computer than of the MCU (which is directly the opposite of the Raspberry Pi). In order to use the Arduino and compatibles like the NodeMCU, you will need the Arduino IDE, and probably most importantly a USB data cable. This is a really important note for the Arduino compatibles – MOST USB cables that you would get to say charge or power a compatible are NOT data cables and you will spend a super long time figuring that out. If you do nothing else to make your life easier, order the USB data cable I listed in Chapter 2 and have a few of them around. Your sanity will appreciate it!

Once that is done, setting up your machine to program your Arduino or compatible is really easy:

- Download the latest Arduino IDE.

- Install the right "boards" from the board manager (boards are what the IDE calls the various type of compatible devices you can program).

- Install any additional libraries.

- Code your code.

- Verify it and then load it to the device.

- Repeat until you have it the way you want!

We will walk through all of these steps to get ready for and perform the labs in Chapters 9 and 10, but it is very simple to get the system ready, and even to try out your first bits of code. With the Arduino and compatibles, the devil is in the details, and the right libraries and the code itself is where all the action is. We will cover some of that in the build outs in Chapters 9 and 10 as much as we can, but a full exploration of all of it would be prohibitive. There are many excellent resources as you go deeper with the Arduino and compatibles, but in the spirit of this book, we will get past the hardware and the basic software so you can grow further with your own research.

1) First, you'll need to download and install the Arduino IDE. The latest version can be found here: https://www.arduino.cc/. Whatever the latest version is will work fine, as they have done a very good job of maintaining the compatibility and structure of the IDE to look and feel the same from version to version. When you are done, you should wind up with a screen that looks like Figure 8-19.

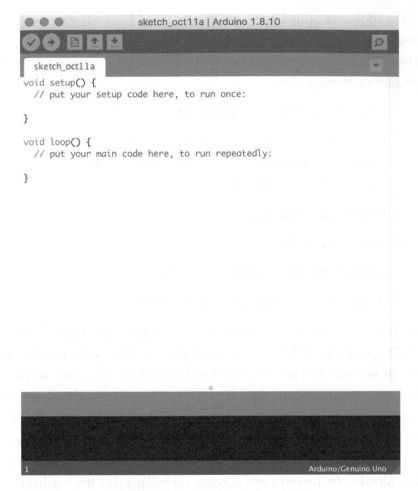

Figure 8-19. *Arduino IDE default sketch screen*

2) Next you need to install the type of MCU you are working with. Luckily the Arduino IDE makes this relatively easy by building the board manager right into the IDE. You will need the exact link that is shown below the image in 8-20 (you can find it online for copy and paste ease):

```
https://raw.githubusercontent.com/espressif/
arduino-esp32/gh-pages/package_esp32_index.json
```

Copy and paste it into something handy, as you will need it to tell the board manager to load additional board interfaces. You do that by choosing Arduino ➤ Preferences from the application menu. You will see the screen in Figure 8-20.

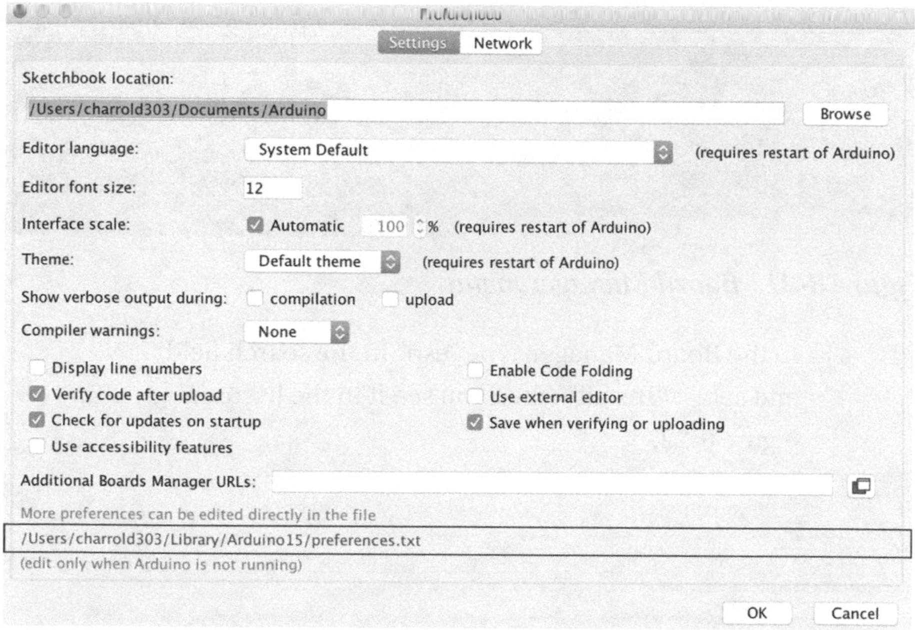

Figure 8-20. *Arduino Preferences screen*

You want to put the URL from above into that field in this screen and click OK.

3) Now back in the main screen, choose Tools ➤ Board "Arduino/Genuino Uno" ➤ Boards Manager... from the menu as seen in Figure 8-21.

Figure 8-21. *Board Manager menu*

4) In the Board Manager, type "esp" in the search field
    and select "Install" when you see it in the list as in
    Figure 8-22.

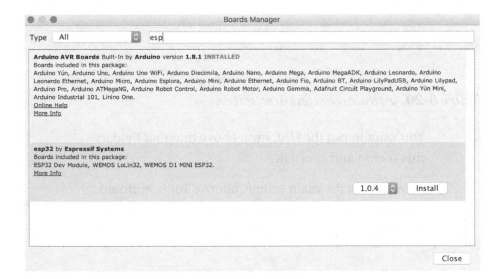

Figure 8-22. *Install ESP32 board into IDE*

This will trigger the board tools and drivers to download to the local cache. When it is done, you will see a screen like Figure 8-23.

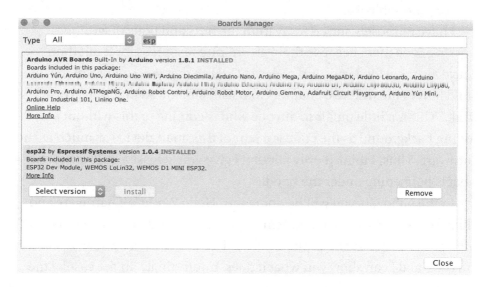

Figure 8-23. *ESP32 installed*

Now the ESP32 is installed and you can program it with the IDE.

Congratulations, your ESP32 is ready to be programmed and you can move on to the build labs in Chapters 9 and 10 with confidence!

A Word on Code

I feel I would be a bit remiss if I did not take a moment and look at the actual code itself. This book is very much focused on hardware, because as I have told you throughout, the hardware presents the bigger challenge. There are endless resources online for hardware and software, but hardware is physical, can go badly wrong, and can cause injury when mishandled. It is just scarier. Software, on the other hand, you copy and paste from an example online and, provided you put the wires in the right place, it just works. Worst case it throws an error, but that's minor, and doesn't result in a painful shock or worse. I hope throughout I have demystified the hardware process and got you to the point where you feel more comfortable with it.

I have purposely stayed away from the nuts and bolts of writing working code then, because there are infinite resources for it out there. I have also provided you with code via GitHub that you can use in the build labs in the next two chapters that will, if followed precisely, "just work." This is a little unfair to anyone who is coming to this without a coding background as the code is a part of the smart device as much as the hardware. Thus, I think it only fair that I give you at least a little overview of what is happening under the hood.

In the build lab, you will be doing the "Hello World" of hardware and blinking an LED. I want to take a moment and show you the code that you will use for the lab for both platforms and dissect it out a bit so you can see the code and I can show you what it does. Interestingly, in the case of the Arduino, the required library to interface with the GPIO pins is actually installed "under the hood" so you do not need an include statement for it. This will change with other sensors later, but unlike the GPIO library for Python on the RPi, you get access to the pins by default in the Arduino world.

Let's first look first at the C++ code for the Arduino in Listing 8-1.

Listing 8-1. C++ code sample for blinking an LED

```cpp
#define LED 2  //instead of remembering which pin this makes it
simpler to reference later in the code
int loops = 0;

void setup() {
    pinMode(LED, OUTPUT);    // LED pin as output.
    Serial.begin(9600);      //turn on the serial output - not
                             explicitly required, but nice to have

}
```

```
void loop() {

    digitalWrite(LED, HIGH);      // turn the LED on
    delay(500);                   // wait for 1/2 second.
    digitalWrite(LED, LOW);       // turn the LED off
    delay(500);                   // wait for 1/2 second.
    loops = loops + 1;            // count the loops
    Serial.print(loops);          // print the loop counter to
                                  the serial output
    Serial.println(" completed.");
```

This very simple program does exactly what it says, turns an LED on and off if correctly wired to the MCU. Let me point out a couple of the more important bits for you to know. This line:

```
#define LED 2
```

This line tells the computer that GPIO pin 2 will be referred to in the code as "LED" and means you do not have to remember what pin 2 is when you go through the code. For this simple program, it's probably no big deal, but for a longer one with lots of pins, having a friendly name is nice.

```
digitalWrite(LED, HIGH);
```

This is a part of the native Arduino library for GPIO interfaces, and tells the MCU to set the voltage output to the LED pin you named to the "HIGH" voltage setting. Remember, digital is on and off, and so this is effectively turning it "on" so the light comes on. Conversely

```
digitalWrite(LED, LOW);
```

turns the LED off again by setting the voltage to the lowest setting. The other variances of this command would be

```
digitalRead(PIN);
analogRead(PIN);
analogWrite(PIN, Level);
```

Digital reads do what you think, they listen to the specified PIN for a signal to come in. This will get used in the build for listening to the sensors and reading the value they are sending. Same with analogRead, although that is a more sensitive measure of the level of the voltage of the pin as we discussed earlier. analogWrite then would allow you to pass the voltage level you want to write at to the pin. There is a nifty variance of the "Hello World" that actually dims and brightens an LED using analogWrite and sending gradually increasing and decreasing voltages.

One last really common tool is the

```
delay(500);
```

lines. Delay is the equivalent to telling the MCU to just wait for xxx milliseconds. This is really, really useful for allowing things to happen or not, and in this case, with no delay between "off" and "on" you would not even see the LED blink at all. It would appear to be on for about half a second or less and then shut off. Side note, I tried it and you see a very faint flutter of the light because it is turning on and off very quickly.

Now to the Python version here in Listing 8-2.

Listing 8-2. Python code sample for blinking an LED

```
import RPi.GPIO as GPIO
import time

#Define the pin we are going to use to power the LED,
# the number of times it will blink,
# and the time between blinks
```

```
pina = 4
iterations = 10
interval = .50

#Turn on the GPIO commands and prepare the ports
GPIO.setmode(GPIO.BCM)
GPIO.setwarnings(False)
GPIO.setup(pina, GPIO.OUT)

#Create our loop to blink the LED based on our iterations value
for x in range(1, iterations+1):

    #Turn on the LED and wait for the sleep interval
    Print("Loop %d: LED on" % (x))
    GPIO.output(pina, GPIO.HIGH)
    time.sleep(interval)

    #Turn off the LED and wait for the sleep interval
    Print("Loop %d: LED off" % (x))
    GPIO.output(pina, GPIO.LOW)
    time.sleep(interval)

#after all the blinks this command is important for resetting
the GPIO board
GPIO.cleanup()
```

Admittedly, I made this bit a little more complex than it needed to be, by specifying variables for the delay and blink factors, but the result is the same. Let's look at the more important bits of the Python code for RPi.

```
import RPi.GPIO as GPIO
import time
```

These two lines tell the Python program to include the libraries for the RPi GPIO pins and a library called "time" which I used for the delays between blinks. The RPi.GPIO library is the one that maps the GPIO header pins to their software functions. Without it, you cannot access the GPIO pins directly without a LOT of extra code. And we need to because, like the C++ code, this line

```
pina = 4
```

tells the program that "pina" (Pin A) is going to be GPIO 4. The program knows this, because later in the code when we want to turn the pin "on," we call

```
GPIO.output(pina, GPIO.HIGH)
```

This command is just like in the C++ where we tell the GPIO function to set the pin (pina which is 4 in this case) to the HIGH setting. There are some other bits of GPIO that we have to do to make that work, which is the following block:

```
#Turn on the GPIO commands and prepare the ports
GPIO.setmode(GPIO.BCM)
GPIO.setwarnings(False)
GPIO.setup(pina, GPIO.OUT)
```

The Raspberry Pi has multiple GPIO modes that support changing the way the GPIO pins are numbered, and here we are telling the software to address the GPIO via the "BCM" mode. This means that the GPIO pin numbers are not the literal pin number on the header, but what the Broadcom Chip that controls them defines them as. There is no right or wrong for this setting, it is just something to be aware of and understand because it will make a difference in your code on the pin address you specify.

The second line is actually something I would not recommend in all but the simplest of projects like this one, because it tells the application to ignore any warnings from the GPIO subsystem. Generally, this is bad, but in this case, there is very little to be impacted by it. The last one is telling the GPIO that the pin we want to use (pina which equals 4) is an OUTput pin and thus will send voltage out, not read it in.

The block that does the work is very much like the one in the C++ code:

```
#Turn on the LED and wait for the sleep interval
    Print("Loop %d: LED on" % (x))
    GPIO.output(pina, GPIO.HIGH)
    time.sleep(interval)

    #Turn off the LED and wait for the sleep interval
    Print("Loop %d: LED off" % (x))
    GPIO.output(pina, GPIO.LOW)
    time.sleep(interval)
```

The Print command is just like the output to the serial console from the C++ command that gives you some debug information. The GPIO commands are the equivalent of the digitalWrite commands in C++ turning on and off the LED by changing the mode of the pin from HIGH to LOW. The last bit is the same as the C++ delay() function and here it tells the code to pause for the duration of the interval defined in the code.

That's the main things to remember for the Python side – forgetting to set the pin mode is a common mistake I still make frequently!

Summary

Whew, that was a lot! I hope that I have not crammed too much into a short space here, but there is just SO MUCH when it comes to all the interconnected disciplines in smart devices. As I said, this book is more about the hardware and so I have tried to stay true to that, but a smart device just isn't without software. There are so many great resources for writing good code and the tools and functions of it that I hope you will forgive me for not going deep into that part of the smart device world. Maybe another book for that someday, but for now I think it is high time you got to building! The two chapters for the Build lab has three total projects: Hello World (aka blinky lights), a simple sound sensor reader, and a full (but simple) smart system with both sensors and outputs. I do hope you enjoy building them as much as I did!

CHAPTER 9

Smart Device Building Lab

The Smart device labs will take you through three builds of increasing complexity and difficulty, culminating in building a modest smart system in the next chapter, that can be used to monitor a house plant and let you know when it needs water. The goal of these labs is to show you the basic interactions of the hardware and allow you to familiarize yourself with prototyping of circuits and sensors with breadboards before you move into the more permanent circuit boards in the final section. It will also, by the very nature of the software needed, begin to expose you to some of the basics of the applications behind the smart device. Because this book is more focused on the hardware, I have provided the code "ready to run" via a download from GitHub, and instead of going line by line through the code, have chosen to focus on a few snippets of the code in the lab to show you key elements and help you understand the code itself, because it is really hard to separate hardware from software when it comes to smart devices.

BEFORE YOU BEGIN – LAB SOFTWARE SET UP

Before you begin, it is worth taking a few moments to prepare your system and getting your devices ready to work with the code from GitHub. In this prep section, I will walk you through

© Christopher Harrold 2020
C. Harrold, *Practical Smart Device Design and Construction*,
https://doi.org/10.1007/978-1-4842-5614-5_9

- Using the SSH command on your computer to connect to the Raspberry Pi

- How to install the git command line tool locally and on your Raspberry Pi

- How to use the git command line tool to clone a repository (specifically the one you need for these labs) locally and on your Raspberry Pi

- How to create your own repository so you can store your own code as you explore

We discussed in the last chapter on the section about setting up your Raspberry Pi that you can hook up a mouse, keyboard, and monitor to the Pi, and use it as you would any other computer. This is 100% fine to continue doing in the labs, but you may find it a little unwieldy and want to work on your laptop/computer directly and connect remotely to the Raspberry Pi. (With the NodeMCU, since you are only using your computer as a vehicle for delivering the code, this is less of an issue as you will 100% work on your computer anyway.) If you followed the instructions previously for installing DietPi on your Raspberry Pi, then you have also installed a tool called SSH (Secure Shell) running on the Pi which allows you to connect to it remotely.

A quick note about finding the IP address of your Raspberry Pi – if you have never done much with your home networking gear, have a router/modem combo from a cable or Internet provider, or otherwise just do not know much about networking, the simplest way to find the IP is to plug the Pi into an HDMI monitor, TV, etc., and just read it off the screen. You can see the IP address in Figure 9-2 of the Raspberry Pi I used for these labs, and this is the simplest and most direct method. The Raspberry Pi *should* reboot with this IP address every time (I say should because there is always a chance it will not, but it is small), meaning you can plug it in, get the IP address off the screen, shut it down and move it somewhere else, and it will reboot with that IP address. You need the IP address, because that is what you will connect to with SSH.

On a Mac, you can use SSH natively from the command line via the Terminal application, but on Windows, you will need a tool to use SSH. I would recommend using a tool called PuTTY for this purpose, which is made for SSH from Windows. I have included images from Mac here, as it is the OS I have the easiest access to, but the putty terminal screen looks very much the same once you make the connection to the Raspberry Pi. The Putty connection wizard can seem a little daunting, as it has many options as you see in Figure 9-1, but you do not need to change anything except typing in the IP address of your Raspberry Pi in the "Host Name (or IP Address)" field. In either case, what will result is a connection window that presents you with a command line prompt from the Raspberry Pi, which will allow you to download the code files and execute them directly on the Raspberry Pi. That looks like Figure 9-2.

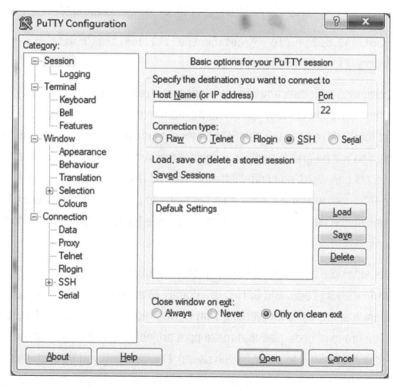

Figure 9-1. PuTTY screen

Figure 9-2. *Terminal screen logged into Raspberry Pi running DietPi*

To connect to your Raspberry Pi from your Mac, use the command:

ssh root@192.168.1.210 (replace the 192.168.1.210 with your
Raspberry Pi's IP address)

This command tells the computer to connect to the IP address you specify, using the username of "root" (which is the admin user for Linux, and the default for DietPi) and to use the SSH protocol to make the connection. Once you do, you will be greeted with a password request. The default password is dietpi (all one word, no capital letters). This will result in the screen in Figure 9-2, from which you can begin the steps to prepare your Raspberry Pi by installing the git command line tools, and clone the repository for the code samples.

Another side note at this point about Git and GitHub. Git is an open source tool for managing code, and GitHub is a commercial product that uses Git. There are multiple tools for working with GitHub repositories (a repository, or repo, is a group of code files that make up a project or application that the developer has shared to other GitHub users). I am walking you through using the command line tool (which is Git), but for Mac and Windows, you could opt to use the GitHub desktop application which is a GUI driven way to work with repos from GitHub on your local machine. I am not walking you through that, because frankly there are entire books about working with Git, GitHub, and the various tools around it, and it would be at least a whole chapter by itself. The Git CLI is fast and easy for what I am showing you, and for this activity, but you should definitely look into the tools that work best for you, and there are numerous resources out there for learning how to use GitHub.

Let me walk you through cloning the repository to your Raspberry Pi by installing Git CLI and running the appropriate commands with you:

1. At the screen in Figure 9-2, type in the command **sudo apt-get update** and hit Enter – this will update the package manager and might take a minute or so depending on your Internet connection.

2. Once that completes, you should be back at the command prompt, and can type in the command **sudo apt-get install git** and hit Enter – this will download and install the Git CLI.

3. You will see the package manager connect to the Internet, look for the libraries, download and install them. When it finishes, you should see something similar to Figure 9-3.

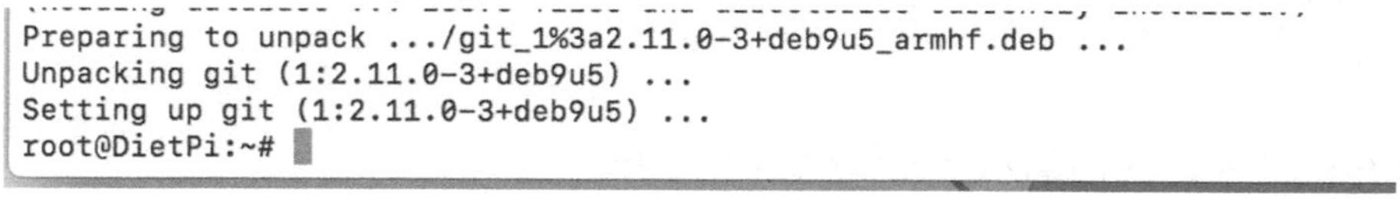

```
Preparing to unpack .../git_1%3a2.11.0-3+deb9u5_armhf.deb ...
Unpacking git (1:2.11.0-3+deb9u5) ...
Setting up git (1:2.11.0-3+deb9u5) ...
root@DietPi:~#
```

Figure 9-3. *Completed install of git command line tools*

4. You can confirm that git is installed by typing **git** at the prompt which should return what you see in Figure 9-4.

```
[root@DietPi:~# git
usage: git [--version] [--help] [-C <path>] [-c name=value]
           [--exec-path[=<path>]] [--html-path] [--man-path] [--info-path]
           [-p | --paginate | --no-pager] [--no-replace-objects] [--bare]
           [--git-dir=<path>] [--work-tree=<path>] [--namespace=<name>]
           <command> [<args>]

These are common Git commands used in various situations:

start a working area (see also: git help tutorial)
   clone      Clone a repository into a new directory
   init       Create an empty Git repository or reinitialize an existing one

work on the current change (see also: git help everyday)
   add        Add file contents to the index
   mv         Move or rename a file, a directory, or a symlink
   reset      Reset current HEAD to the specified state
   rm         Remove files from the working tree and from the index

examine the history and state (see also: git help revisions)
   bisect     Use binary search to find the commit that introduced a bug
   grep       Print lines matching a pattern
   log        Show commit logs
   show       Show various types of objects
   status     Show the working tree status

grow, mark and tweak your common history
   branch     List, create, or delete branches
   checkout   Switch branches or restore working tree files
   commit     Record changes to the repository
   diff       Show changes between commits, commit and working tree, etc
   merge      Join two or more development histories together
   rebase     Reapply commits on top of another base tip
   tag        Create, list, delete or verify a tag object signed with GPG

collaborate (see also: git help workflows)
   fetch      Download objects and refs from another repository
   pull       Fetch from and integrate with another repository or a local branch
   push       Update remote refs along with associated objects

'git help -a' and 'git help -g' list available subcommands and some
concept guides. See 'git help <command>' or 'git help <concept>'
to read about a specific subcommand or concept.
root@DietPi:~# ▮
```

Figure 9-4. *Confirmed git tools installed*

5. If you are familiar with Linux and file systems, you can ignore the following steps and create a directory wherever you want for the repo files to be cloned to, but these steps will help you create a directory in the /temp folder in the root of the Raspberry Pi's file system so it is easy to get to again:

    a. Type the command **cd /** and hit Enter – you will see the command prompt change as in Figure 9-5.

```
[root@DietPi:~# cd /
 root@DietPi:/# █
```

Figure 9-5. *Change directories to the "/" (root) directory*

b. Now type the command **mkdir temp** and hit Enter. This will
    create a dirootory, called "temp" in the root (the /) of your
    Raspberry Pi's filesystem. If you type the command **ls** and hit
    Enter, you will see it in the list of directories as in Figure 9-6.

```
[root@DietPi:/# ls
 bin  boot  dev  DietPi  etc  github  home  lib  lost+found  mnt  opt  proc  root  run  sbin  srv  sys  tmp  usr  var
[root@DietPi:/# mkdir temp
[root@DietPi:/# ls
 bin  boot  dev  DietPi  etc  github  home  lib  lost+found  mnt  opt  proc  root  run  sbin  srv  sys  temp  tmp  usr  var
 root@DietPi:/# █
```

Figure 9-6. *Make a directory (mkdir) to create the "temp" directory confirmed with "ls"*

c. Now type the command **cd temp** and hit Enter. This
    will change directory (cd) to the temp directory you just
    created. Your prompt will change as in Figure 9-7 to show
    you are working in this directory now. Whenever you want
    to work with the code, you will clone from now on in the
    lab, it will always be in this /temp directory.

```
[root@DietPi:/# cd temp
 root@DietPi:/temp# █
```

Figure 9-7. *Changing to the "temp" directory*

6. Now that you have a directory and are working in it, you can clone
    the repository for the book to your Raspberry Pi. (This will include all
    the code for the NodeMCU as well, but it is all quite small so it will
    not waste a lot of space.) Just follow the steps here to clone the repo:

    a. In your regular web browser on your computer, go to: (The
        capital C and H are intentional and required)

        https://github.com/ChrisHarrold/smartdevicebook

    b.   The git hub page will open the repository of code files for this book, and you will see the screen as in Figure 9-8.

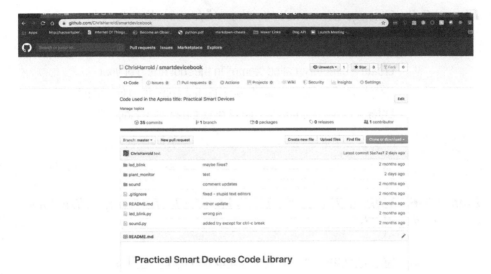

Practical Smart Devices Code Library

Figure 9-8. *The GitHub repository for this book in a browser window*

    c.   Notice the green button on the right side that says "Clone or download"; click on it. You will see the prompt appear as in Figure 9-9. Highlight the URL displayed in the field, and copy it.

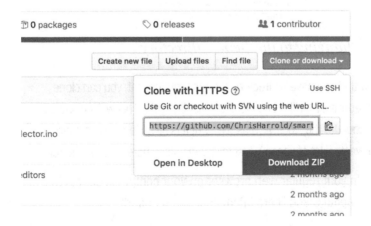

Figure 9-9. *Clone or download prompt*

d. Back in your terminal or putty window, type the command
    git clone and then paste in the URL you just copied – the
    full command should be

```
git clone https://github.com/ChrisHarrold/
smartdevicebook.git
```

Once done press Enter.

e. You will see the git command process and download the
    files from the repository on GitHub, into a folder called
    "smartdevicebook." As the files are quite small, it should
    not take very long, and you should see the screen as in
    Figure 9-10 when it finishes (I typed in an "ls" command to
    confirm the folder was created).

```
[root@DietPi:/temp# git clone https://github.com/ChrisHarrold/smartdevicebook.git
Cloning into 'smartdevicebook'...
remote: Enumerating objects: 84, done.
remote: Counting objects: 100% (84/84), done.
remote: Compressing objects: 100% (60/60), done.
remote: Total 84 (delta 29), reused 57 (delta 13), pack-reused 0
Unpacking objects: 100% (84/84), done.
[root@DietPi:/temp# ls
smartdevicebook
root@DietPi:/temp# ▊
```

Figure 9-10. *Cloning the smartdevicebook repo to your Raspberry Pi*

f. If you type the command **cd smartdevicebook** and hit
    Enter, you will now be in the working directory for the
    remainder of the labs on the Raspberry Pi. (If you type **ls** and
    hit Enter you should see something similar to Figure 9-11
    to confirm you are in the right place and the clone was
    successful.)

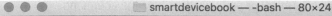

```
● ● ●                    ▥ smartdevicebook — -bash — 80×24
[Chriss-MacBook-Pro-3:smartdevicebook charrold303$ ls
README.md          led_blink.py      sound
led_blink          plant_monitor     sound.py
Chriss-MacBook-Pro-3:smartdevicebook charrold303$ ▮
```

Figure 9-11. *What your directory should look like after cloning and running "ls"*

7. Now that you have the clone downloaded on your Raspberry Pi, you will also need a local copy of the files for your NodeMCU and for the later Node-Red parts of the labs. For this I am going to show you an alternate method for downloading repos from GitHub that might be more simple for something like this where you just need the files.

    a. In your regular web browser on your computer, go to

        https://github.com/ChrisHarrold/smartdevicebook

    b. The GitHub page will open the repository of code files for this book, and you will see the screen as you did back in Figure 9-8 again.

    c. Again, click the green button on the right side that says "Clone or download." And you will see the prompt appear as it did in Figure 9-9. This time, however, click the "Download Zip" button as highlighted in Figure 9-12, which will download a zip file to your local machine, containing all the files.

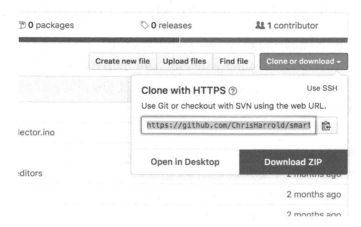

Figure 9-12. *Download as ZIP button*

    d.   Browse to where you saved the download, and simply double-click the zipped file and it will expand into a "smartdevicebook-master" folder as in Figure 9-13. Feel free to rename this folder to whatever you want or leave it as is, just remember where it is so you can find it later in the labs!

Figure 9-13. *Downloaded compressed file, and then after expanding into its own directory*

    8.   That's it! You now have a copy of all the code files you need to complete the labs and get started on the physical builds.

What Are You Going to Make in These Labs?

The first lab is the classic HELLO WORLD for hardware, of making an LED blink with your MCU. Instructions are included for both Raspberry Pi and the Node MCU. You can, of course, use another MCU, just make sure your pinouts are correct and the code may need to be modified to work on your MCU.

Next you will wire up a basic sensor and use the digital signal it provides to alert to changing conditions (in this case, sounds). This basic sound sensor build will let you see the basics of the wiring and connections for a sensor, and for controlling multiple LEDs with your MCU for the purposes of signaling.

Lastly, in Chapter 10, you will build a small but complete smart system. This system is meant to monitor a plant to see what the moisture level is, send updates to the central hub, and provide a display from which you can see the status of the plant. It will use both a Raspberry Pi and a NodeMCU to serve the different functions and show you how hardware that is fit for purpose can be tied into a full system to perform a broader task. This is a launchpad to expand into larger and more complex systems that can either monitor many more plants (I use an expansion of this in my own garden), or indeed, with other sensors as part of the device, could be used to do something entirely new altogether.

LET'S BUILD IT – HELLO WORLD

First up for our smart device build lab, we are going to revisit the basic LED circuit we built in the first section, and I will walk you through building out that most time-honored tradition of "Hello World" for hardware projects – the blinking LED!

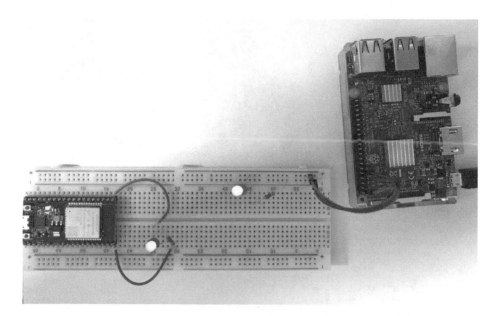

Figure 9-14. *Node and R-Pi circuits on breadboard for the "HELLO WORLD" build*

In Figure 9-14 you can see the two circuits that this lab will help you construct. (If you only have one or the other MCU, you can skip to the lab with your MCU in it, but I have included both here.) In this picture I am using the "power only" pins from the MCU for convenience of taking a picture with the LED not blinking, but you will use a GPIO pin, and you will define in the software which pin and how long the light should blink on and off.

Raspberry Pi Circuit Build

Building your LED circuit with the Raspberry Pi is really just a matter of replacing the battery used in the previous lab with the Raspberry Pi itself. This is fundamentally the role of the MCU in the smart device, a really, really smart battery that you control with software.

Figure 9-15. *RPI close-up with the LED lit*

In order to make this circuit, you need the parts you can see in Figure 9-16.

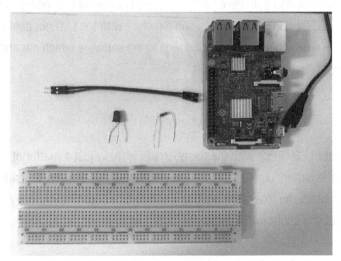

Figure 9-16. *Picture of basic circuit parts for Raspberry Pi*

216

- Raspberry Pi and power cord

- Breadboard

- 68Ohm resistor minimum – I have used a 100 Ohm resistor here

- LED

- Two M-F wires (the color doesn't matter, just that you have two)

To assemble the hardware circuit, follow these steps:

1) Connect one of your two wires' male ends to the breadboard by inserting the bare end into one of the connections in the "–" rail. (See Figure 9-17.)

Figure 9-17. *Step 1 – Wires plugged in to breadboard*

2) Connect the other wires' male end to the "+" rail on the breadboard. See Figure 9-17.

3) Connect one side of the resistor to the "−" rail, and put the other end into any of the pins in the grid. The exact number isn't important, just that you know where it is. See Figure 9-18.

Figure 9-18. *Step 3 – Resistor connected to breadboard*

4) Connect the short "leg" of the LED into the same column in the field as you placed the resistor and place the other leg into the "+" rail. See Figure 9-19.

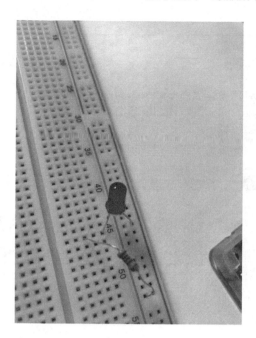

Figure 9-19. *Step 4 – LED connected to breadboard*

5) Your circuit is now wired and you can "turn it on" by completing the circuit and plugging in the female ends of the wire to the right pins on your Raspberry Pi. Here is where understanding pinouts becomes critical to not making things broken. See Figure 9-20 for the Raspberry Pi 3B+ pinout. You will use pin 7 (labelled as GPIO4) and pin 9 (labelled as GND) for this lab. This is important because the code is written for that GPIO pin. If you change pins, you have to change the code too.

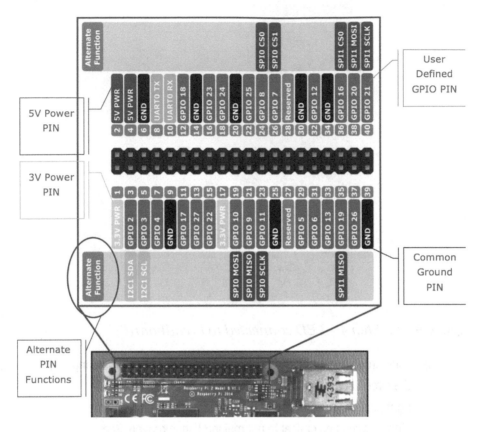

Figure 9-20. *Standard Raspberry Pi pinout*

6) Plug in the end of the "–" rail wires' female end to pin 9 of your Raspberry Pi. (See Figure 9-21.)

Figure 9-21. *Ground pin connected*

7) Now to complete the circuit, plug in your other wire's Female end to the pin 4 on the Raspberry Pi. (See Figure 9-22.)

Figure 9-22. *Everything connected*

8) The last step is to plug in your Raspberry Pi and allow it to boot. Now you will need to execute the code to make the LED blink.

If you have not done it already, make sure you go back to the last chapter and prepare you Raspberry Pi and complete the earlier steps in this chapter on preparing your Raspberry Pi for the labs. If you don't you will not be able to follow the steps for easy access to the code.

Provided you have completed the steps to prepare the Raspberry Pi, via the SSH command, execute the following commands:

1) Type **cd /temp/smartdevicebook** and hit Enter. This will make sure you are in the directory that contains the code to actually make the LED blink.

2) Type **python led_blink.py** and hit Enter. This command tells the RPi to execute the led_blink.py file using the Python interpreter, which will now make your LED blink. You will see the output on the screen as in Figure 9-23 that shows the command running on the RPi.

```
[root@DietPi:/temp/smartdevicebook# python led_blink.py
Loop 1: LED on
Loop 1: LED off
Loop 2: LED on
Loop 2: LED off
Loop 3: LED on
Loop 3: LED off
Loop 4: LED on
Loop 4: LED off
Loop 5: LED on
Loop 5: LED off
Loop 6: LED on
Loop 6: LED off
Loop 7: LED on
Loop 7: LED off
Loop 8: LED on
Loop 8: LED off
Loop 9: LED on
Loop 9: LED off
Loop 10: LED on
Loop 10: LED off
root@DietPi:/temp/smartdevicebook# █
```

Figure 9-23. *Executing the python "led_blink" application*

And as you watch, your LED should blink 10 times with a 1/2 second interval. Let's take a quick look at the code in Python:

```
import RPi.GPIO as GPIO
import time
```

These two lines tell the application to include the libraries for accessing the Raspberry Pi's GPIO pins, and the "time" library which is a common library for things like intervals, delays, and other "wait:" conditions as well as time keeping.

```
#Define the pin we are going to use to power the LED
# the number of times it will blink
# and the time between blinks
pina = 4
iterations = 10
interval = .50
```

The lines that start with a "#" are comments. Comments are a way that your past self can leave a note for your future self so that you have a prayer in Hades of understanding what the heck you were doing. I am a HUGE proponent of commenting as much as possible and I like to include many many comments to remind myself of what I was doing! As the comments in the code tell you, the three lines of comments here are for:

- The pin we will use (I have called it "pina" and assigned it to GPIO pin 4 – the reason for this is instead of having to remember what pin number I am using for a pin in a complex application, I can give it a more memorable name that I can reference in the code as you will see in a moment.)

- The number of "interations" or loops that the application will run. In this case, for this simple program it is equal to the number of times the LED will blink.

- The space in between on and off commands – or the "interval"

Importantly, these variables allow you to tweak an application by changing one or two values, without rewriting many lines of code. For example, you can draw out the length of time the LED blinks by changing the interval to be longer (1 or 2 or 10 or whatever you need/want), or make it blink 100 or 1000 times by changing the iterations value. Please note that the variable names are somewhat arbitrary BUT there are two things I advise you to keep in mind:

-   There are "reserved words" in all languages that you cannot use for variable names.
-   You should make the variable names something meaningful to you (and use comments liberally to remind you what they meant!).

```
#Turn on the GPIO commands and prepare the ports
GPIO.setmode(GPIO.BCM)
GPIO.setwarnings(False)
GPIO.setup(pina, GPIO.OUT)
```

These lines set up the GPIO interface and enable the pin for the LED as an output (current flowing out, not in). I won't dig into this a lot, but the modes for the RPi vary and there is lots of information out online about what to use and why.

```
#Create our loop to blink the LED based on our iterations value
for x in range(1, iterations+1):

    #Turn on the LED and wait for the sleep interval
    print "Loop %d: LED on" % (x)
    GPIO.output(pina, GPIO.HIGH)
    time.sleep(interval)

    #Turn off the LED and wait for the sleep interval
    print "Loop %d: LED off" % (x)
    GPIO.output(pina, GPIO.LOW)
    time.sleep(interval)
```

This section is where all the "work" happens. It uses a construct called a "for" loop, which could have been any number of loops, but a for loop was what I chose (mostly so you would see one). What this says in English is

- For x in range(1, iterations+1) is the same as "Keep running everything below here, starting at x = 1, until x (an arbitrary placeholder value) is equal to the number in 'Iterations' plus 1 more."

  - Print a line to the console, turn the LED on (GPIO.HIGH), and then wait (sleep) for the "interval" value.

  - Print a line to the console, turn the LED off (GPIO.LOW), and then wait (sleep) for the "interval" value.

    ```
    #after all the blinks this command is important for
    resetting the GPIO board
    GPIO.cleanup()
    ```

This last bit just "turns off" the GPIO pins on the Raspberry Pi and cleans up the connections we used. You do not explicitly *have* to do this, but it is definitely a best practice for programming on the PI.

Note   If your LED did not light, there are three likely culprits:

1. Did you connect the wires the right way to the Raspberry Pi and on the right pins to match the code?

2. Pull the LED off and spin it around.

3. Check that the Resistor and LED are in the same column on the breadboard.

A Node MCU Circuit

The Node Circuit is similar to the Raspberry Pi Circuit, except that you need MM wires instead of MF. Unlike the Raspberry Pi, the Node-based MCUs are designed to be mounted to a PCB or breadboard instead of a freestanding device. This makes it important that you mount it into the breadboard used in the lab. You can see how to do that in Figure 9-24. **Special note:** DO NOT press down on the big metal part in the middle – this is the chip and Wi-Fi shielding and you can damage the components underneath. It is better to press on the sides to push it into the breadboard. It will take a firm push to get it to sit fully down on the board. Do not be afraid to wiggle it and apply firm pressure!

Figure 9-24. *Node on Breadboard – note the orientation of the power connector*

Once your NodeMCU is mounted, you can proceed to follow the build instructions and create your NodeMCU LED circuit as you see in Figure 9-25:

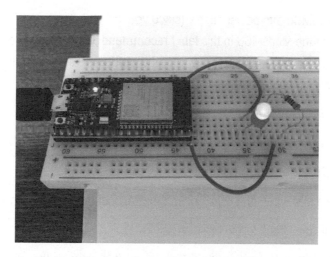

Figure 9-25. *NodeMCU picture with LED lit (this picture used the 3v power pin so the light would stay on)*

In order to make this circuit, you need the parts you can see in Figure 9-26.

Figure 9-26. *Picture of basic circuit parts for NodeMCU build*

- NodeMCU and power supply (since you will be loading code onto the ModeMCU in this lab, I recommend just using the data transfer cable to supply power to the MCU while connected to your laptop or computer)

- Breadboard

- 68Ohm resistor minimum – I have used a 100Ohm resistor here

- LED

- Two MM wires (the color doesn't matter, just that you have two)

To assemble the circuit follow these steps:

1) You will undoubtedly notice after you get it in place on the breadboard that you only have one free slot on each side of the node MCU in which to connect wires to the breadboard. When working with these particular MCUs, we will skip wiring the power and ground rails and go directly to the corresponding pins. See Figure 9-27 for the pinout of the Node32S used in the lab. We will use the GND pin furthest from the power connector, and P22 (also labelled GPIO22 in the picture).

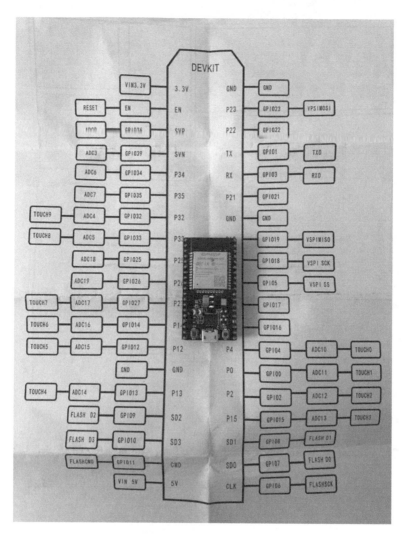

Figure 9-27. *NodeMCU 32s pinout*

2) Connect one of your two wires' male ends to the breadboard by inserting the bare end into the connection next to the GND pin on your NodeMCU. Connect the other end to any column on the breadboard. See Figure 9-28.

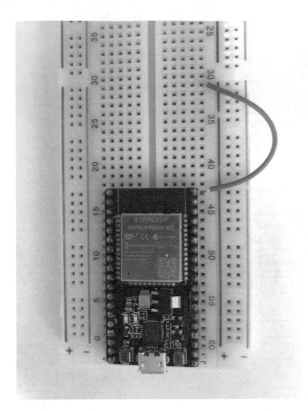

Figure 9-28. *Ground Pin connected*

3) Connect one end of the other wire to the breadboard next to pin 22 (the third pin down) on your MCU. Put the other end into any free column on your breadboard (somewhat close to the other wire). See Figure 9-29.

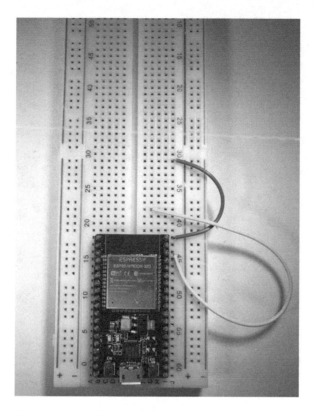

Figure 9-29. *GPIO pin connected*

4) Connect one side of the resistor to the same column as the wire
    that comes from the GND pin. Connect the other end into any
    OPEN column on the breadboard. See Figure 9-30.

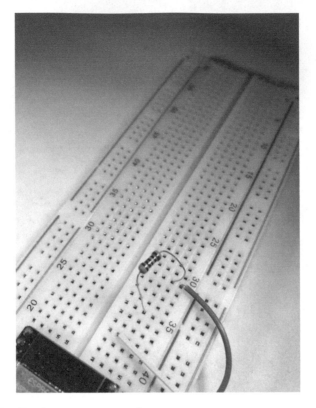

Figure 9-30. *Resistor connected*

5)   Connect the short "leg" of the LED into the same column in the
     field as you placed the "open" leg of the resistor. Place the other
     leg into the same column with the wire from the GPIO pin on
     your MCU. See Figure 9-31.

Figure 9-31. *LED placement closeup*

6) The last bit to do is to upload the code to the MCU from the Arduino IDE. Provided you followed the download instructions earlier in the chapter, you are ready to go! If not, you will need to go back and follow the steps to clone/download the repository, and in it you can find the led_blink folder with the led_blink.ino file inside. Open it with the Arduino IDE. (You can see it open on the screen in Figure 9-33.)

7) In the IDE, click the Arrow in the top of the IDE – this is the "upload to MCU" button. See Figure 9-32.

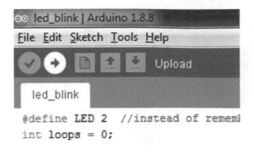

Figure 9-32. *Arduino IDE*

8) This will start the upload process. You will see it happening in the bottom part of the IDE screen as in Figure 9-33.

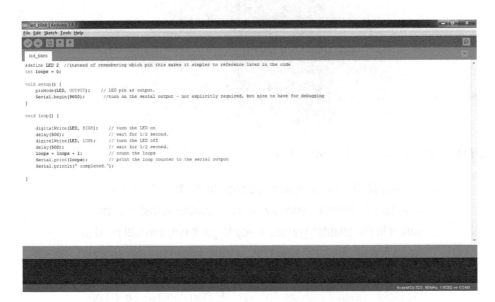

Figure 9-33. *IDE Screen – the black area in the bottom will display the upload messages*

9) When you see the message in the message area that says "Connecting" and starts a pattern of alternating dots and underscores as in Figure 9-34, you will need to press the I00

button on the ESP32 and hold it down until the upload continues in your IDE screen. The image in Figure 9-35 is the button location, and Figure 9-36 shows the message you will see when the upload has started. Once it does, you can let go of the button.

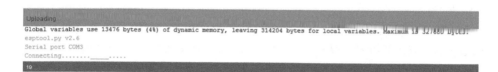

```
Uploading
Global variables use 13476 bytes (4%) of dynamic memory, leaving 314204 bytes for local variables. Maximum is 327680 bytes.
esptool.py v2.6
Serial port COM3
Connecting........_____.....
10
```

Figure 9-34. *The "waiting to upload" pattern in the IDE window*

Figure 9-35. *Press and release this button*

```
Uploading...
Compressed 15328 bytes to 9994...

Writing at 0x00001000... (100 %)
Wrote 15328 bytes (9994 compressed) at 0x00001000 in 0.9 seconds (effective 135.0 kbit/s)...
Hash of data verified.
Compressed 199248 bytes to 100565...

Writing at 0x00010000... (14 %)

12
```

Figure 9-36. *You did it correctly, and the upload has started!*

10) Once the upload completes, the IDE sends a reset command, and
the LED should now begin to blink. It will do this until you either
reset the board or unplug it as the code instructs it to never stop
looping. If you open the Serial monitor in the IDE, by selecting
Tools ➤ Serial Monitor from the menu, you will see the output
from the loop counter as shown in Figure 9-37.

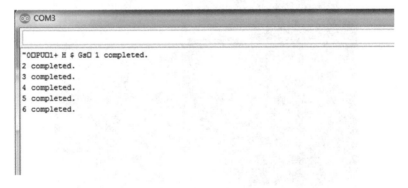

```
COM3


"0⊡P⊔⊡1+ H $ Gs⊡ 1 completed.
2 completed.
3 completed.
4 completed.
5 completed.
6 completed.
```

Figure 9-37. *Serial monitor output of the loop running*

Note   If your LED did not light, there are three likely culprits:

1. Did you connect the wires the right way to the breadboard and to the righ MCU pins? Check Figure 9-31 again to verify.

2. Pull the LED off and spin it around.

3. Check that the Resistor and LED are in the same column on the breadboard.

Let's Take a Quick Look at That Code

Much like the code for the Raspberry Pi, the one for the NodeMCU, while written in C++, is incredibly simple. I will take you through the key parts briefly so you have a sense for what's going on.

```
#define LED 2  //instead of remembering which pin this makes it
                  simpler to reference later in the code
int loops = 0;
void setup() {
    pinMode(LED, OUTPUT);    // LED pin as output.
    Serial.begin(9600);      // turn on the serial output – not
                               explicitly required, but nice to
                               have for debugging
}
```

Minus my comments (comments in C++ world start with the "//" indicator), this first section is much like on the RPi. We do not need any extra libraries for this, as they are all native to the code, but I do define my pin number and a variable called "loops" which is the counter you saw displayed in the serial monitor. The second part, starting with "void setup() {", that is how you define a function in C++ and in particular for programming on Arduino and compatibles, this section is exactly what it says – the "setup" of the environment. Mine is simple, as it is just setting the LED mode, but I also have a line there for the serial console. This is what allows the serial monitor to work later on when the code is running. "Serial.begin(9600);" tells the program to open the serial port with a 9600 baud connection rate.

```
void loop() {
    digitalWrite(LED, HIGH);    // turn the LED on
    delay(500);                 // wait for 1/2 second.
    digitalWrite(LED, LOW);     // turn the LED off
    delay(500);                 // wait for 1/2 second.
    loops = loops + 1;          // count the loops
    Serial.print(loops);        // print the loop counter to the
                                   serial output
    Serial.println(" completed.");

}
```

Again, in the next part I am defining a function called loop. For all intents and purposes, this is the "main" part of the program. I can call other functions and do other things here, but this runs as a loop forever, or unless I have a programmed stop somewhere in my code. If you looked at the RPi code, it should be pretty easy to spot the similarities here with C++ and working with GPIO. digitalWrite HIGH and LOW for on and off again, and a delay(500) much like the sleep command in the Python code. Instead of the for loop in Python, I am using a straight loop here that will repeat forever, but that counts itself. That is what gets displayed into the serial console via the Serial.print and .println commands – the difference in those is a Serial.print appends to the existing line in the console, and the .println puts a new line command in the end. This is super useful for formatting serial output later.

So that's it for the MCU version. Again, I picked a slightly simpler method (without a for loop) just to give you an idea of the options, but this basic loop is all you need to control an LED. You can even remove the logging to the console, and really shrink this down to a VERY tiny program of just a few kilobytes. That is the power of good, lightweight code – and very important on a device like the NodeMCU that does not have endless terrabytes of storage for that code!

Hello World Recap

Congratulations! You have completed the Hello World for hardware, and have seen the code basics to perform this most time-honored rite of passage into the big world of building smart devices. This is obviously a trivial bit of both hardware and code, but it is massively important in your understanding of how to assemble circuits and use the MCU to control them. There is hardly a device or object you will make or work with that does not have this exact simple circuit on it, and uses the exact same loop methods and commands for controlling LEDs. I often come back to reference these steps in my other projects because they are so deeply ingrained in all smart devices.

Next, let's get serious and actually use some sensors!

LET'S BUILD IT! BASIC SENSOR BUILD

For your first real smart device I'm going to show you how to build both the Raspberry Pi and MCU versions of a classic, the simple sound detector. This was my first smart device build and the story behind it is that I was trying to let my kids know when they were getting a little too loud. I built this and put a big red light on when the sound level got too high so they would know and quiet down. Better living through smart devices!

This first build is meant to get you comfortable with the working of a sensor and will allow you to read the output from a sensor and work with multiple LED indicators. It could be used to control the LED itself a-la a sound-activated light switch, or just to detect loud noises like mine did for my kids, or if your dog barks during the day at home.

239

Raspberry Pi Build

This is a more complex unit than you have built previously and so our parts list has grown accordingly. Figure 9-38 shows the Raspberry Pi version of the completed device, and Figure 9-39 is the needed parts.

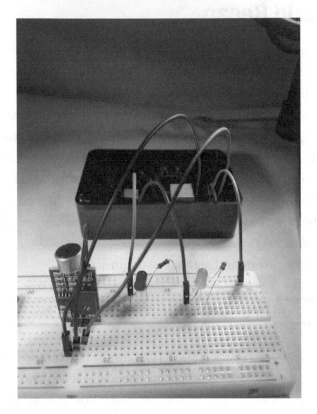

Figure 9-38. *Completed sound sensor*

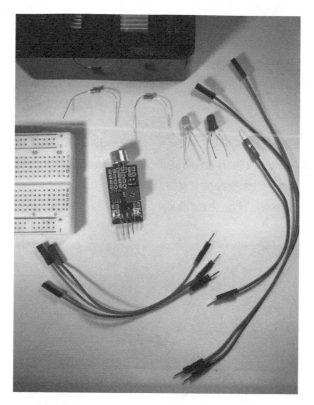

Figure 9-39. *Required parts*

For the build you will need

- One digital sound sensor – I am using a version of the LM393 sensor

- Your Raspberry Pi

- A breadboard

- Five M-F wires (I used a mix of lengths for convenience, but any length will suffice)

- One M-M wire

- Two 68Ohm resistors minimum (I used 100 Ohm)

- Two LEDs – I used a Red and Green, but any color will work

241

Assembly is pretty straightforward and follows the next set of steps. As always, if you change any of the pins you plug into on the Raspberry Pi, you will need to update the code accordingly. If you follow these exactly, the code in the repository you cloned will run without modification.

Assembly steps:

1)   First find a spot up against the IC ravine where the Sound sensor will sit cleanly into three parallel columns as in Figure 9-40. This is not always as easy as it sounds, and can result in bent pins, so make sure you choose carefully!

Figure 9-40. *Sensor in place*

2) Next, connect the ends of two M-F wires to the breadboard in the
    same column as VCC and OUT as in Figure 9-41.

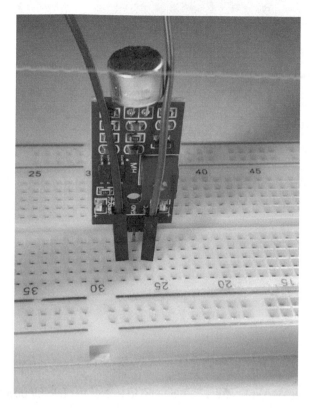

Figure 9-41. *Power and signal wires connected to the breadboard for
the sensor*

3) Connect a M-M wire to the breadboard in the same column as
    the GND pin and connect the other end of the wire to one of the
    holes in the "–" rail on the breadboard as in Figure 9-42.

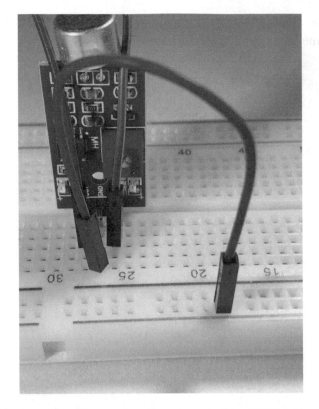

Figure 9-42. *Step 3 – Ground rail connected to GND pin*

4)   Connect the VCC wire's Female end to one of the two 5V power
     pins on your Raspberry PI as in Figure 9-43.

Figure 9-43. *Power connected to RPi*

5)   Connect another M-F wire to the same "–" rail you put the GND
     wire into as in Figure 9-44.

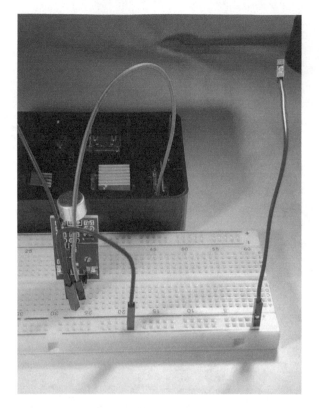

Figure 9-44. *MF wire in the "–" rail*

6)   Connect the Female end of that wire to any pin labelled GND on
the Raspberry Pi GPIO header as in Figure 9-45.

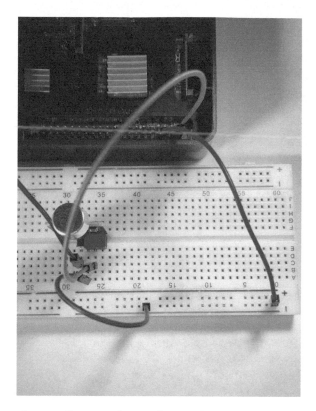

Figure 9-45. *Ground wire plugged into the RPi GPIO header*

7) At this point I am going to break from the build for just a moment, and have you perform a little tuning exercise on the sound sensor. This sensor is meant to detect sound above a certain level, but that level isn't something it actually has preprogramed, because it needs to be set by you. To do so is very easy, and the sensor I have used has built-in LED indicators to tell you when you've found the level. This quick detour will make sure that the sensor works as expected later when you run the code. For now, follow these sub-steps to tune the sensor:

a) Plug in your Raspberry Pi and wait for the indicator light on the front of the sensor to come on indicating it has power as in Figure 9-46.

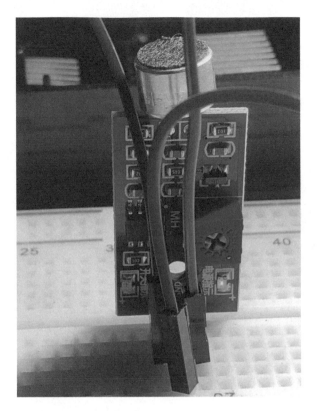

Figure 9-46. *Power light is on*

b) See the big "X" shape on the front of the sensor above
the power light? That is a potentiometer, or variable resistor,
and it is that dial that changes the sensitivity of the sensor.
You may see the second LED on the front also lights when
your sensor powers on, and that is because the sensitivity is
too high as in Figure 9-47. To adjust it, use a small Phillips
head screwdriver and turn the dial until the light *just barely*
goes out. It might even flicker a bit when you move away
and that's perfect because it is detecting the sound of your
movement.

Figure 9-47. *Detection LED on (it is the one on the left in this picture)*

c) To confirm, rub the microphone or clap/snap/yell at it, and the detection light will light up and go out as the noise occurs as you can see in the set of images in Figure 9-48.

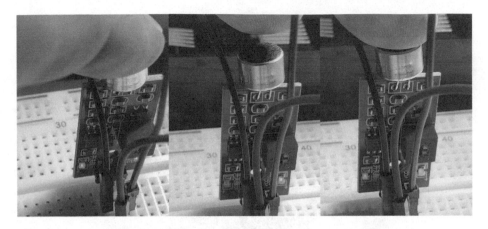

Figure 9-48. *Light going on and off with sound – touching the mic is a really effective test*

You have dialed in the sensor now and can proceed with the rest of the build. **Unplug your RPi again before you go forward!**

8) Connect each of the two resistors from the "−" rail to an open column on the breadboard as you see in Figure 9-49.

Figure 9-49. *Resistors connected to "-" rail and to the field*

9) Plug the RED LED in with the short leg in the same column as
    one of the resistors, and the long leg into an open column as you
    see in Figure 9-50.

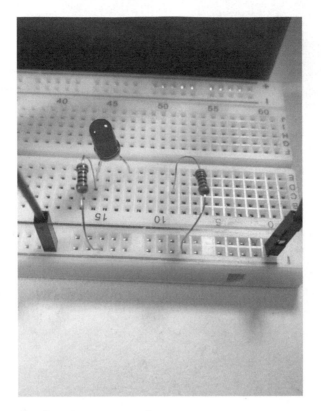

Figure 9-50. *Red LED connected*

10)   Repeat with the GREEN LED – short leg in the same column as
the other resistor, and the long leg into an open column as you
see in Figure 9-51.

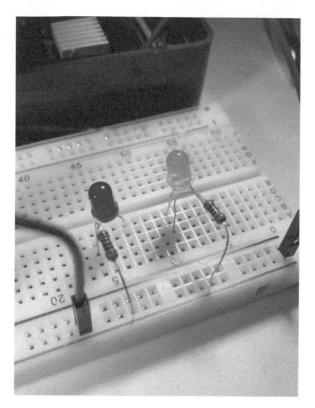

Figure 9-51. *Green LED connected to the breadboard*

11) The reason the LEDs cannot share the power rail is because you are going to control them in software with a GPIO pin. The last two connections will be the power from those GPIOs to the LEDs – start with connecting the male end of one of the remaining M-F wire to the same column as the long leg of the red LED as seen in Figure 9-52.

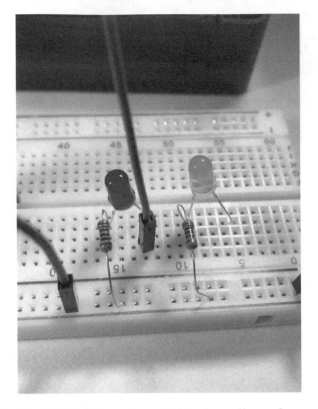

Figure 9-52. *Red LED wire connected to breadboard*

12) Connect the other Male end of the last M-F wire to the column with the long leg of the green LED as in Figure 9-53.

Figure 9-53. *Green LED wire connected to breadboard*

13) Now connect the Female end from the red LED to pin 21 on the Raspberry PI as you see in Figure 9-54.

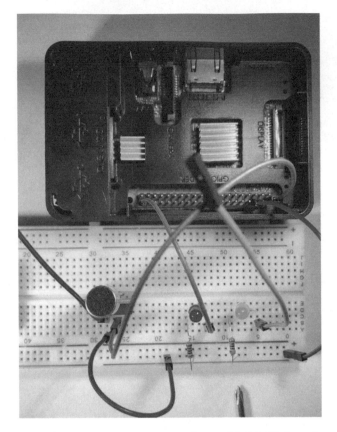

Figure 9-54. *Red LED Wire connected to RPi GPIO header*

14)   And then the same with the green LED to PIN 20 as in Figure 9-55.

Figure 9-55. *Green LED wire connected to RPi GPIO header*

15) Lastly you need to connect the sensor's output wire to the pin
    that will listen for its signal, pin 18 as in Figure 9-56.

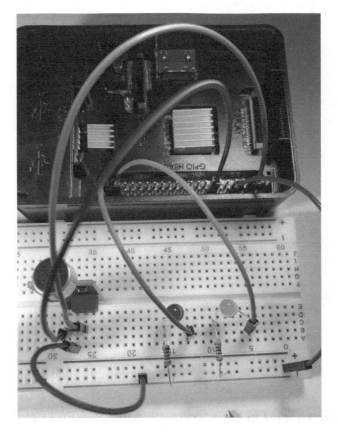

Figure 9-56. *Sensor signal wire plugged in*

That's it! You can plug the Raspberry Pi back in and as before with the blinking LED code, if you cloned the GitHub repository to your Raspberry Pi you can execute the sound sensor code from an SSH session with the command

```
python sound.py
```

Make sure you are working in the /temp/smartdevicebook directory first (cd /temp/smartdevicebook is the command)

Once you hit Enter on the command, you should see it echo out the start-up of the program to the console, and then it will start listening as indicated by the green LED being on as in Figure 9-57. You can trigger the red light on and off by making sounds like clapping or whistling or even talking as you see in Figure 9-58. You can exit the program at any time by pressing Ctrl-C on the keyboard in the terminal window. If it spams a million "Sound Detected" alerts to the console, you may need to tighten up the sensitivity a little bit more. Mine did while doing the photos for the lab and I had to dial it down again, so don't be afraid to adjust it until it is where you need it.

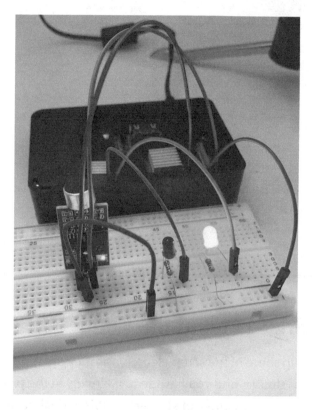

Figure 9-57. *Green Light on as program is running*

Figure 9-58. *Red light on because sound is too loud!*

A VERY Brief Look at the Code

I am going to skip some of the setup elements as they are repetitive, and the
loop construct is simple, and you have seen it already in the previous code,
and focus right in on the couple of key parts of this code that you can see
here:

```
try:
    # Define a listener on the sound sensor to wait for a
    signal - this will cycle the LED as sound comes in
    def callback(sensor_in):
```

```
if GPIO.input(sensor_in):
        print "Sound detected - turn on"
        GPIO.output(red_led, GPIO.HIGH)
else:
        print "Sound detected - turn off"
        GPIO.output(red_led, GPIO.LOW)
```

```
GPIO.add_event_detect(sensor_in, GPIO.BOTH,
bouncetime=300)  # let us know when the pin goes HIGH or LOW
GPIO.add_event_callback(sensor_in, callback)  # assign
function to GPIO PIN, Run function on change
```

```
# infinite loop
while True:
        time.sleep(1)
```

This is the part that counts in this lab, and it is using a callback function which is semi-unique to the RPi and Python. (The functionality is called different things in different hardware worlds and they work similarly, but use the functionality of the underlying hardware which is, of course, somewhat different from chip to chip and for various GPIO systems.) What this section is doing:

- First I am choosing to use the try: except: format for this loop. In Python, this allows you to handle errors better than just running a "naked" loop as it will handle exceptions that you define. What this means is "try this bunch of code here, and if there is anything wrong go to the exception block related to that. We will look at those in a moment.

- Next, I am defining a callback on my sensor pin. This is a native function in the RPI GPIO package that essentially "listens" for a set of conditions I specify on that particular GPIO pin and then does what I tell it to in the next part (turn on and off the Red LED using the GPIO. output HIGH and LOW you already know).

- Then I define my callback conditions:

  - GPIO.add_event_detect(sensor_in, GPIO.BOTH, bouncetime=300) – In English this is: add an event listener to the pin (sensor_in) and tell me if it changes (GPIO.BOTH means to look for a HIGH or LOW state since it could be either). Bouncetime is like the "wait at least this long between checks" and is in milliseconds. 300 is a good sweet spot for this sensor (found with trial and error).

  - GPIO.add_event_callback(sensor_in, callback) – In English this is: "did you detect the thing I told you in the last line, on that pin (sensor_in)? Do the callback function that is defined earlier in the code.

So, to be perfectly honest, this is not an ideal method for this, but it illustrates two really important tools – the listener and the response function (the "callback" in this case). Why is it not great? Because with the delays and the loop resets, this is pretty far from real time, and effectively the sound detected LED locks on and off with sounds. HOWEVER, for what I wanted, this would be just right, because the red LED would stay on when a sound was detected, until another sound turns it off. This is great for a "clapper" style light switch as well, so while not explicitly "real-time" it is a good analogue for it, and a good example of how to interact with the GPIO listener function on the Raspberry Pi.

ESP32-BASED BUILD

The ESP32 build is very similar to the RPi, with a few minor exceptions to the wires and connections (mostly due to the space limitations of the ESP32 when it is on a breadboard. Figure 9-59 shows the ESP32 version of the completed device, and Figure 9-60 is the needed parts.

Figure 9-59. *Completed sound sensor*

Figure 9-60. *Required parts*

For the build you will need

- One digital sound sensor – I am using a version of the LM393 sensor

- Your ESP32

- A breadboard

- Six M-M Wires (again I used a variety of lengths for convenience, but any length will work)

- Two 68 Ohm resistors minimum (I used 100 Ohm)

- Two LEDs – I used a Red and Green, but any color will work

Assembly is pretty straightforward and follows the next set of steps. As always, if you change any of the pins you plug into on the ESP32, you will need to update the code accordingly. If you follow these exactly, the code in the repository you clone will run without modification.

Assembly steps:

1) If your Node MCU is not already on the breadboard, you can see how it should be oriented in the image in Figure 9-60. I am assuming it is already there from the previous lab, but if not, you should seat it to the breadboard now.

2) First find a spot up against the IC ravine where the Sound sensor will sit cleanly into three parallel columns as in Figure 9-61. This is not always as easy as it sounds, and can result in bent pins, so make sure you choose carefully!

Figure 9-61. *Sensor on breadboard*

1) Next, connect the ends of two M-F wires to the breadboard in the same column as VCC and OUT as in Figure 9-62.

Figure 9-62. *Power and signal wires connected to the breadboard for the sensor*

2)   Connect a M-M wire to the breadboard in the same column as the GND pin and connect the other end of the wire to one of the holes in the "–" rail on the breadboard as in Figure 9-63.

Figure 9-63. *Ground rail connected to GND pin*

3) Connect the VCC wire's Female end to the 5V power pin on your ESP32 as in Figure 9-64.

Figure 9-64. *VCC pin wired to ESP32 5v pin*

4) Connect another M-M wire to the same "–" rail you put the GND
    wire into as in Figure 9-65.

Figure 9-65. *MM wire in "–" rail*

5) Connect the other end of that wire to any pin labelled GND on the ESP32 as in Figure 9-66.

Figure 9-66. *Ground wire connected to ESP32 GND pin*

6) Connect each of the two resistors from the "−" rail to an open
    column on the breadboard as you see in Figure 9-67.

Figure 9-67. *Resistors connected to "−" rail*

7) Plug the Red LED in with the short leg in the same column as one of the resistors, and the long leg into an open column as you see in Figure 9-68.

Figure 9-68. *Red LED connected*

8) Repeat with the Green LED – short leg in the same column as
the other resistor, and the long leg into an open column as you
see in Figure 9-69.

Figure 9-69. *Green LED connected*

9) The reason the LEDs cannot share the power rail is because you are going to control them in software with a GPIO pin. The last two connections will be the power from those GPIOs to the LEDs – start with connecting one end of a remaining M-M wire to the same column as the long leg of the RED LED as seen in Figure 9-70.

Figure 9-70. *Red GPIO Cable in breadboard with LED*

10) Connect one end of the last M-M wire to the column with the long leg of the GREEN LED as in Figure 9-71.

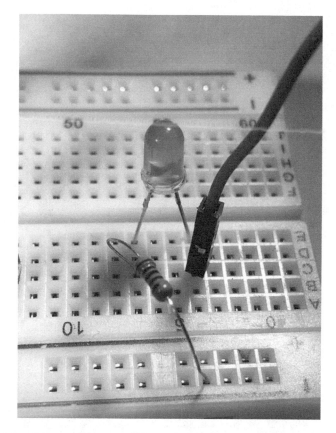

Figure 9-71. *Green GPIO Cable in breadboard with LED*

11) Now connect the other end from the RED LED to pin 21 on the ESP32 as you see in Figure 9-72.

Figure 9-72. *Red LED wire connected to GPIO 21*

12) And then the same with the GREEN LED to PIN 22 as in Figure 9-73.

Figure 9-73. *Green LED connected to GPIO 22*

13) Lastly you need to connect the sensor's output wire to the pin that will listen for its signal, pin 23 as in Figure 9-74.

Figure 9-74. *Sensor signaling wire to GPIO 23*

That's it! You can now plug the ESP32 in to get flashed from the Arduino IDE. Open the sketch in the "Sound" folder (sound.ino is the filename) and click the upload button as you did before. Follow the steps from the previous exercise we took to upload the sketch to the device. Once it is uploaded, the device will reboot and it will start running the program automatically.

You should see it echo out the start-up of the program to the serial monitor, and then it will start listening as indicated by the green LED being on.

Now remember the tuning exercise I had you do for the Raspberry Pi version? You need to revisit that here, because probably your RED LED is pegged on as well. Remember also how I told you that the NodeMCU is "faster" than the Raspberry Pi in terms of real-time sensing? This is that functionality in action, and where the sensor might have worked fine for the Pi, it is likely too sensitive for the ESP32 and it is triggered on and fixed.

THIS IS SLIGHTLY DIFFERENT FROM THE RPI TUNING, SO PLEASE DO THIS PART!

---

1) Plug in your MCU and wait for the indicator light on the front of the sensor to come on indicating it has power as in Figure 9-75 (this will happen instantly really).

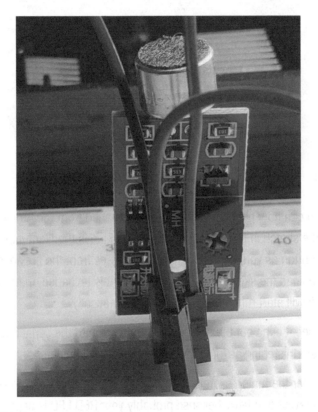

Figure 9-75. Sensor powered on

2) See the big "X" shape on the front of the sensor above the power light? That is a potentiometer, or variable resistor, and it is that dial that changes the sensitivity of the sensor. You may see two lights when your sensor powers on, and that is because the sensitivity

is too high as in Figure 9-76. To adjust it, use a small Phillips head screwdriver and turn the dial until the light *just barely* stays on with a flicker. If you have already flashed the code, this should make the RED LED flicker as well. Because of the higher fidelity of the GPIO on the NodeMCU, it is operating closer to real time, and so the RED LED will essentially mimic the onboard LED now.

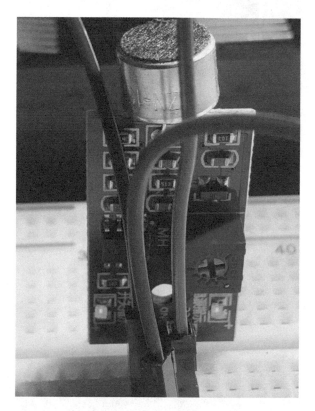

Figure 9-76. *Sensor pegged "high"*

3) To confirm, rub the microphone or clap/snap/yell at it, and the detection light will light up and go out as the noise occurs as you can see in the set of images in Figure 9-77. Now the sensor is dialled in for the much more high-speed reads of the ESP32 chip!

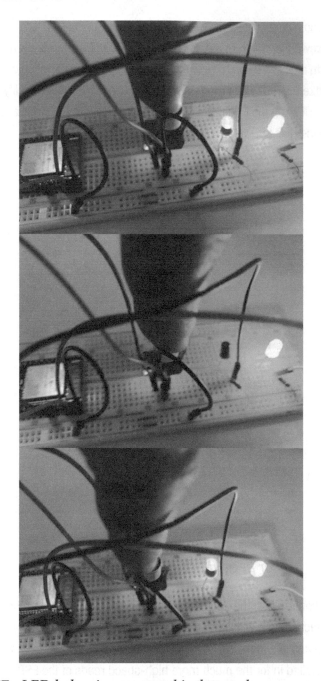

Figure 9-77. *LED behavior as sound is detected*

I just want to chime in here dear reader and note that I literally had to muck with this last ESP32 bit for a good solid 2 hours to get not just the code doing what I wanted, but the hardware and the tuning exercise above. DO NOT despair if it takes you a bit to get it all dialled in, even those of us who do this a lot have to mess with things a bit to get them to work right. This is the beauty and the challenge of smart devices in a nutshell, phenomenal power to build anything, endless messing with it to make it work the way you want!

Again, a VERY Brief Code Recap

What does this code do and how? Here is a brief look at the important bits for you – as in the RPi section I have skipped the setup and basic parts as it is just a minor expansion of what you already know (more LED pin definitions and turning on the LED and defining the sensor pin). The main loop is what counts, so let's look at that here:

```
void loop() {

  int SensorData=digitalRead(soundSensor);
  if(SensorData==1){

    if(LEDStatus==false){
        LEDStatus=true;
        digitalWrite(REDLED,HIGH); // this turns on the LED when
                                   sound it detected
    }
    else{
        LEDStatus=false;
        digitalWrite(REDLED,LOW); //when the sound stops the LED
                                  will turn off
    }
  }
}
```

This loop may look a little daunting with all those if conditions, but it is REALLY simple as I will show you.

- First step: int SensorData=digitalRead(soundSensor); In English: create a value that is an integer (int SensorData) and assign it to the result of a digitalRead of the sound sensor pin (soundSensor).

- Evaluate the value I just read off the pin: if(SensorData==1){ – and if it does have data, then I would execute the resulting code block. If not, then I just loop up and start again. (This process is sub-millisecond time to process so the loop could run many times per second if there is no sound.) This could also be written as if(SensorData).

- The next part is a "nested if" statement that checks the value of a variable called LEDStatus. That variable is Boolean or "true/false" and so the statement if(LEDStatus==false){ means that if the LEDStatus is currently "false" it will change that and turn on the red LED. This is because new sound detection has occurred. This can also be written as if(!LEDStatus).

- The "else{" part of the nested if says that if the LEDStatus is currently True, it will change it, and turn off the light.

So, can you spot the logic fault in this loop? The program will actually turn off the LED if sound is detected again. This results in the "flutter" effect you see on the Red LED, because it is actually getting cycled by every *other* sound detected. The better way to do this loop would be to ONLY match on the SensorData value and change the LED based on that. The Red LED would almost certainly still flutter but would more closely mirror the LED on the sensor itself since this is effectively what the onboard logic on the sensor does. Again, I chose this construct to provide some additional loop type examples and evaluation tests, and to show you that even an imperfect logic loop can generate the desired outcome. The challenge to us as the builder and creator is to make sure that outcome is indeed the desired result, and not a false positive or negative!

Basic Sensor Recap

WOOT TO YOU! Your first smart device. Yes, it doesn't do anything amazing per se, but it is a device that responds to external stimuli and reacts. That is a smart device and you built it and that is AWESOME! From here it is now time to bring together all of your skills and the things you have learned to assemble your first smart system.

CHAPTER 10

Smart System Building Lab

So now it is time for the big end-cap assembly project, the smart system! This will be a collector, sender, and receiver that will show you all the workings of a complete smart system, and how to assemble it. You will be working with technologies we have mentioned earlier in the book as well as the various hardware techniques for building this smart system prototype.

Before you begin the build, let's look at the system you are going to build, and the parts that are involved in a little more detail. You are going to construct a system that consists of three main parts (and lots of little components):

- The collector – This is the smart device itself really, which consists of the sensor(s) and the MCU to collect the data itself.

- The network that allows you to send messages and data from point to point using a messaging software.

- The central hub – This is just the name I am using, not a formal convention so you can call it the hub, or the central system, or whatever you like, but its function is to take the data coming in from the collector(s) and to translate it into something human readable. (We will use Node-RED for this.)

© Christopher Harrold 2020
C. Harrold, *Practical Smart Device Design and Construction*,
https://doi.org/10.1007/978-1-4842-5614-5_10

The software in this case is going to take on a much more important role. While I could just build a collector and use LEDs to alert me to changes in conditions, that is not nearly as useful in all applications as being able to collect and store historical data or displaying it in a more visually pleasing manner. Dashboards are the way that a lot of smart devices communicate with users, and they provide an effective visual representation of what's going on, so they make sense in any application where you want to present data in a simple and meaningful way. Node-RED, in addition to being able to collect and process inputs from both hardware and software sources, also has a really nice and simple dashboard component which if you are not great at web sites (like me) provides a "click button, get graphs" way of creating dashboards.

We will also introduce the use of a messaging software for allowing data packages to be sent and received in a standard format. Mosquitto is a free software implementation of the popular MQTT protocol for messaging and allows you to do a lot of really cool things as you expand your smart device horizons. It is built on the concept of publishers (things that send messages) and subscribers (things that read messages). In the case of this smart system, the Collector is the publisher, and the Hub is the subscriber. The messages themselves can be further classified and categorized through the use of queues, called topics (which look like directories in the file system) and allow you to provide some levels of routing and separation of messages should you need it.

The messages in this case will be sent using the JSON format. JSON stands for JavaScript Object Notation, and what it is, is a series of key:value pairs that provides for sending data in very small packages. Unlike the olden days of having to use a big SQL query or other really "heavy" process, JSON objects can be very small, but contain a lot of information. The messages your collector will send in this exercise are on the order of a few kilobytes in size, but even a very large message would be very small. It is worth noting that there is a maximum message size for MQTT and Node-RED both (you will not experience it here in this lab). I tell you this because as you expand, you may want to send data from, say, a handful of sensors. That would require maybe a very long string of JSON keys and values. You could exceed the message size, but you can surmount this easily by breaking it up and sending more than one message, another very nice feature of the technologies we are using!

LET'S BUILD IT! SMART SYSTEM BUILD

This lab will require you to have both MCU options to complete it "as built" in these steps, but you absolutely can use your personal computer as a replacement for the Raspberry Pi in this lab, and it will function more or less the same. The purpose of using the Raspberry Pi for the hub in this smart system is twofold:

- It is a very cheap option as a home automation hub, as it is capable of running multiple tools for simplifying your own automation projects

- It removes the need for you to use your own computer/laptop as the hub. You can 100% do that, but that also means that if you shut off your laptop or leave the house with it, your system stops working.

Note   You can run Mosquitto and Node-RED on all major OS platforms and the code provided will work for any implementation with essentially the same networking changes that are called out in the lab. Also, the instructions in the lab will generally work for any OS that you might be running, but on Windows you may have some minor changes to make – the reason I do not have those 100% documented is the Windows machine I used for the Arduino IDE is woefully underpowered, and I could not get Mosquitto and Node-Red to run reliably enough to test it all out. There are great install guides out there on the Internet and can be found in an easy search for either Node-RED or Mosquitto for Windows.

Depending on what you use for the Hub, Raspberry Pi or your own system, your finished smart system will look like one of the following in Figure 10-1.

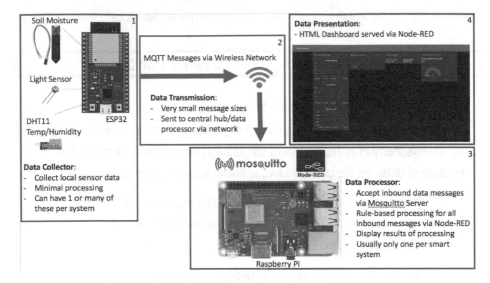

Figure 10-1. *Architecture diagram for options 1 and 2*

No matter what you choose, you will need to use a web browser to access Node-RED during the lab, which I recommend doing from your computer/laptop.

The first thing you are going to build is the Collector. You will be wiring up the sensors and lights on a breadboard as you can see in Figure 10-2.

Figure 10-2. *The complete smart system set of hardware*

Note   This lab will also include a LOT more software than you have used before now. I have provided you "ready to run" code *mostly*. The mostly here is that you will be using a network now, and because of that you will need to change some things in the code to match your environment. I have called them out and show you where they are, but if you have issues later on, it is highly likely that you have an error in one of those changes to a setting that is causing the network environment to be off.

Part 1 – The Collector Hardware

First, you are going to wire up a few sensors and lights to the collection unit. You will use the ESP32 NodeMCU for this part of the lab and the Raspberry Pi (or your own computer) for the central unit for data collection and display. For the collector you will be creating a monitoring device that uses three sensors:

- Temperature/humidity sensor – DHT11 style sensor with a digital output (it has real digital data, not just on and off!)

- Light sensor – Standard photo-resistant diode that will record the light level and works using a voltage divider circuit!

- Soil moisture sensor – I used the Gikfun Capacitive style sensor for a lot of reasons, but the main one is they are just better. If you want to use this for any length of time, I recommend them over the cheap "two metal prongs" versions that come with a lot of starter kits. Those kinds degrade very quickly and are not as reliable, BUT they do work just fine with the appropriate wiring changes during the build. Also, this is a straight up analogue sensor, so you will be reading a raw voltage and making it make sense with software!

These three sensors are what make the collection unit "fit for purpose" and determine the type of smart system this will be. In this case, it is a way to monitor conditions for a plant to grow in and track that information over time. The latter part is done through the dashboard feature of Node-RED, which will be configured in a later part of the lab. For now, let's focus on building our collector hardware, and wiring up the sensors to the NodeMCU.

BEFORE YOU BEGIN – If you have not prepped your computer, Raspberry Pi, and cloned the GitHub repository companion for the book, go back to the beginning of Chapter 9 and do so. It will make things so much easier for you later on, as the code is going to be a major factor in this build.

In order to build the collector, you will need the parts seen in Figure 10-3.

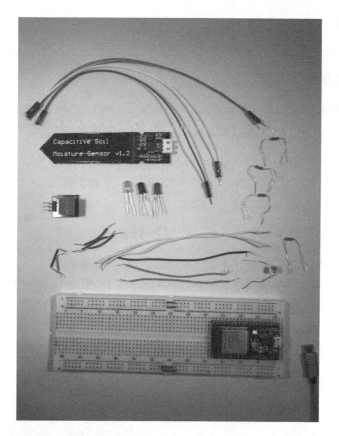

Figure 10-3. *Complete parts for the collector*

- NodeMCU

- Breadboard

- Three 68 Ohm Resistor Minimum – I have used a 100 Ohm
  Resistor here

- Three LEDs – Any color is fine, but I used Red, Green, and Blue.

- Three M-F wires – The color doesn't matter; I do recommend
  long ones here if you have them

- 10 MM Wires – Color is not an issue, but this is one place I will say
  that a variety of lengths will make things nicer for you as you build.

291

- One photoresistor

- One 10k Ohm resistor for the voltage divider!

- A DHT11 temp/humidity sensor

- Again, I used the capacitive soil sensor, but the other "metal legs" one will work too.

- Small glass of water (or a plant) – Optional but makes for interesting readings of the sensor, without it you will get roughly the same reading all the time.

To assemble the hardware circuit, follow these steps:

1) Start by putting the Node MCU onto the breadboard (if it wasn't there already from previous labs). You can see clearly in Figure 10-4 how it should be oriented if you did not already do so.

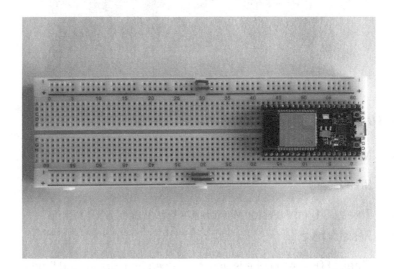

Figure 10-4. *MCU on Breadboard*

2) Next take the DHT11 sensor module, and place it up against the IC ravine like you did with the sound sensor in the previous lab and shown in Figure 10-5.

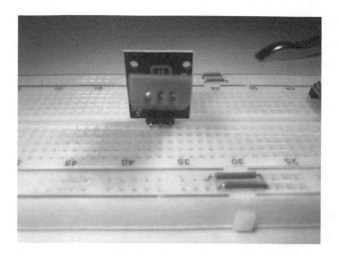

Figure 10-5. *DHT11 on the board*

3) You are going to wire up your breadboard with a 3v and a 5v power rail – one on either side. You are going to choose which is which now, by putting the photoresistor with one leg in the "+" rail and one leg in the breadboard field anywhere that isn't occupied as in Figure 10-6.

Figure 10-6. *Photoresistor in its power rail and breadboard column*

4) Now we will put the LEDs into the breadboard. Again, as before, these will be controlled by a GPIO pin so they do not share the power rail. Place them across multiple columns, and not in the same column as anything else, as in Figure 10-7. Note that in the image, my anode "leg" is to the right on all of them. This will help me remember where the wire from the GPIO plugs into.

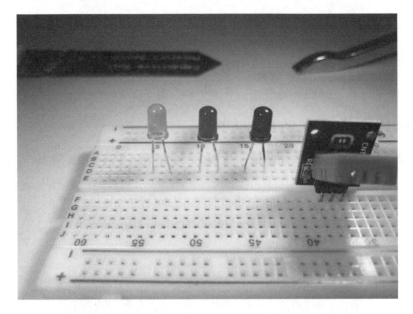

Figure 10-7. *LEDs on the breadboard*

5) Now we can also plug in the three 68 Ohm (I used 100 Ohm) resistors for each of the three LEDs. Place one leg into the breadboard with the cathode leg, and the other into the "–" rail of the breadboard on the 3v side as in Figure 10-8.

Note   I rotated the board 180 degrees for the image for clarity, so the change in orientation doesn't throw you off!

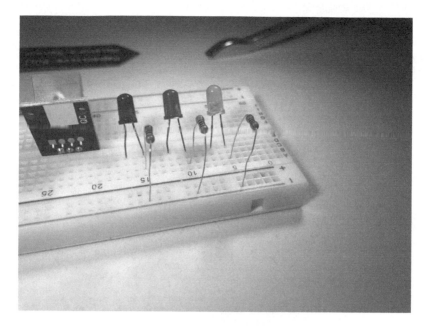

Figure 10-8. *Resistors for the LEDs plugged in*

6) Now you will plug in the 10k Ohm resistor for the voltage
    divider circuit on the photoresistor. This will go from the same
    column as the photoresistor to the "–" rail on the 5v side of the
    breadboard as in Figure 10-9 (again – rotated the breadboard
    back to its original orientation for clarity in the image).

Figure 10-9. *10K resistor on the breadboard for the voltage divider*

7) Now you will connect the MF wires to the soil moisture sensor.
If you did not use the same sensor I have, but the other type
you will need to do this as well but the connection is slightly
different. Just pay attention to the labels on the small PCB for
the sensor and the rest should be the same. Plug the Female
end of the three wires into the socket on the sensor body. (It
comes with a wire, but this is a more convenient arrangement
for the breadboard and doesn't impact functionality at all). See
Figure 10-10 for the end result.

Figure 10-10. *Wires in the soil moisture sensor*

8) Now you will make all the remaining wire connections to get
the system ready to work. You will start with the power and
ground rails. Plug in one end of a MM wire to the "−" rail on
each side of the breadboard as in Figure 10-11. I chose the
spot I did as it is relatively close to a GND pin on the MCU.

Figure 10-11. *Both ground rails with MM wires in*

9) Next plug those wires into the GND pin that you have chosen.
    See Figure 10-12 for the end result.

Figure 10-12. *Ground wires connected to ground pins*

10) Now you will connect the 5V "+" rail – we won't need a 3V
     rail, as only one sensor (the soil moisture) uses that voltage.
     You can save a wire this way which in a complex prototype is
     sometimes a nice thing! As before, start with one end of the
     MM into the "+" rail on the 5V side as in Figure 10-13.

Figure 10-13. *MM wire in 5v power rail*

11) Then plug the other end into the 5v pin on the Node32 as in
     Figure 10-14. Notice that I chose this location for proximity to
     that pin.

Figure 10-14. *5v pin connected to power rail*

12) Now you can plug in the DHT11 to the power and ground rails using MM wires. The DHT11 pinout can vary depending on your sensor, so check yours carefully. The one used in the lab is shown in Figure 10-15 and goes "Signal, Voltage, GND" from left to right as you look at the front.

Figure 10-15. *DHT11 pinout*

13)   Start with two MM wire, one in each column with the middle
and rightmost pin on the DHT11 as in Figure 10-16.

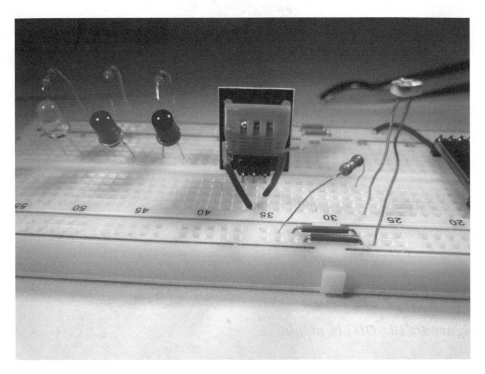

Figure 10-16. *DHT11 wires in place*

14) Take the other end of the corresponding wire and plug it into the "−" and "+" rail as shown in Figure 10-17. Middle wire to the "+" and right pin to the "−" rail.

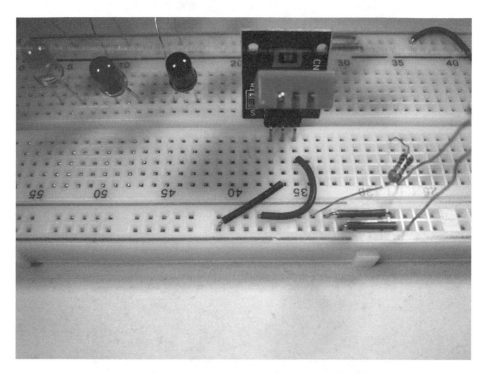

Figure 10-17. Power and ground from DHT11 plugged in

15)   Now plug in a MM wire to the column that corresponds to the left pin of the DHT 21 as in Figure 10-18.

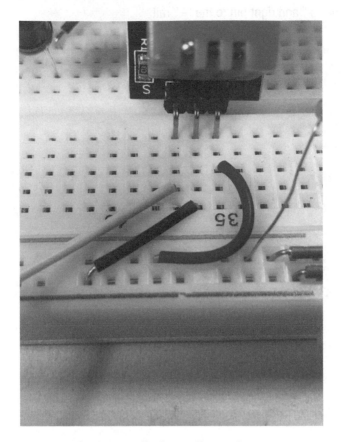

Figure 10-18.   *Signal wire in the breadboard*

16)   The other end will go to pin 17 on the ESP32. How do you know that? It is determined in the code as the "DHT" pin number (17). If you change this, you need to update the code, but if not, it will work as is as you can see in Figure 10-19. Things are starting to get complex with wires crossing over, but it will all come together!

Figure 10-19. *DHT11 plugged into pin 17 on MCU*

17) You can also finish off the voltage divider circuit for the
photoresistor by connecting a MM wire in the same column as
the photoresistor and one of the legs of the 10k Ohm resistor as
in Figure 10-20.

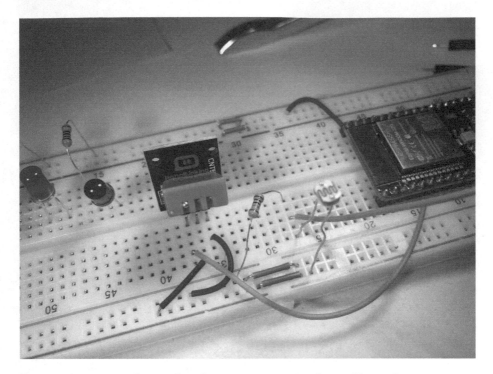

Figure 10-20. *Voltage divider circuit wire in breadboard*

18) Then connect the other end into the "light" pin which is pin 36 – again, this is determined by the code so if you change this, you will need to change the code as well. Figure 10-21 shows it plugged in to the right pin on the breadboard.

Figure 10-21. *Analogue signal wire from the voltage divider circuit to the MCU*

19) Now you can finalize the LEDs for the indication of Power, Execution, and Network connectivity. (Green, Red, and Blue respectively. A MM Wire in the same column as the anode (long) leg of the LED to start as in Figure 10-22. Again, I've rotated the board for clarity in the image.

Figure 10-22. *MM wires for the LEDs in the breadboard*

20)   Now you will plug them in to the appropriate pin for the
       program, again, determined by the settings in the code – they
       are plugged in in Figure 10-23:

       –   Green LED wire goes to pin 22

       –   Red LED wire goes to pin 21

       –   Blue LED wire goes to pin 16

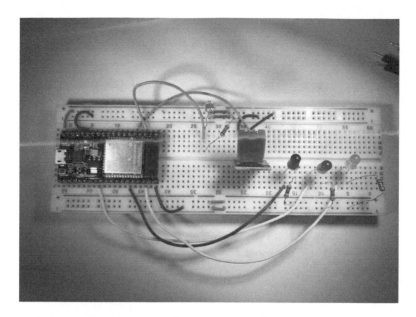

Figure 10-23. *LED wires in the corresponding pins on the MCU*

21)   Last part to connect is the moisture probe. You will need to connect the power, ground, and signal wire to the right pins. Start with power and ground by connecting the GND wire to the "−" rail on the 3v side of the breadboard, and the VCC wire directly to the 3v pin on the ESP32 as in Figure 10-24.

Figure 10-24. *Moisture probe power and ground in place on board*

22) The last connection that completes the connector is to plug the signal wire from the probe into the pin as determined by the code. As with the other GPIO pins, if you change this you have to change the code. In this case pin 34 is the pin for the sensor to use and it will look like Figure 10-25 when connected.

Figure 10-25. *Moisture probe sensor in place on the MCU*

That's it for the collector – it is now ready to run and collect readings. However, there is something missing from our smart system; someplace to send the data to! This collector is predicated on the central hub existing and without it, it will just keep pinging away at trying to connect forever. Now you will need to move on to make the required software changes to make the collector and hub talk and to finalize the software that supports the hardware you just created.

There are two parts to this change – the collector end of things, where your sensors are, and the hub end where your dashboard and display waits to collect the data and show you what it says. You will start by updating the settings on the collector and making sure it can connect to your wireless network, and then update the hub to ensure that it is ready and waiting to receive data and display it out. You will be working with some C++ code on the collector, and with Node-Red that I mentioned before for the hub and dashboard.

The collector code is written in C++ and is significantly more complex than anything you will have worked with to this point. I will dig a little deeper into the dissection of the key parts, because they are things you will trip over as you grow your knowledge, and they are important parts of building more complex devices. You will also need to install a couple of libraries that are not default in the Arduino IDE to support the networking, MQTT, and the DHT11 sensor, and I will walk you through that part first.

Part 2 – The Collector Code

This part will take place in the Arduino IDE, and when complete you will have done the following:

- Installed the supporting libraries for the DHT11, Networking, and MQTT

- Changed the network settings to match your network

A quick networking side note for you. Wireless networking equipment comes in many sizes, shapes, and flavors. The current standard is starting to be more commonly in the 5GHz spectrum, which is faster and more reliable. Unfortunately, none of the stuff you are using for these labs works with 5GHz; it uses the older 2.4 GHz standard. MOST wireless routers broadcast both frequencies, but if yours does not you are going to have a hard time working with any of these MCUs as they do not support the 5GHz standard.

You will want to browse to the smartdevicebook folder, and find the plant_monitor directory. Inside is the plant_monitor.ino file, which is the standard file extension for Arduino files. This file has the code in it that will drive the collector and is meant to be opened in the Arduino IDE. I made sure to really clearly comment the part you care about in the code for the collector, right at the top under the libraries that are required. You can see it here in Figure 10-26.

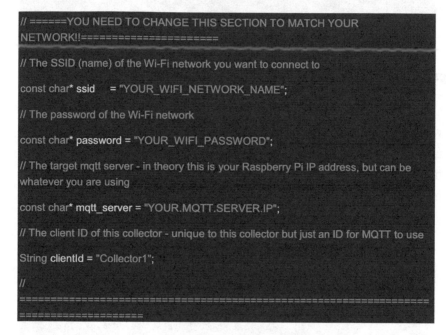

```
// ======YOU NEED TO CHANGE THIS SECTION TO MATCH YOUR
NETWORK!!==========================

// The SSID (name) of the Wi-Fi network you want to connect to

const char* ssid    = "YOUR_WIFI_NETWORK_NAME";

// The password of the Wi-Fi network

const char* password = "YOUR_WIFI_PASSWORD";

// The target mqtt server - in theory this is your Raspberry Pi IP address, but can be
whatever you are using

const char* mqtt_server = "YOUR.MQTT.SERVER.IP";

// The client ID of this collector - unique to this collector but just an ID for MQTT to use

String clientId = "Collector1";

//

==========================================================
====================
```

Figure 10-26. *The network settings section of the collector code*

As you can see, you need to change the YOURXXXXX to match your home network setup in the file and save it **BEFORE** you upload it to the collector MCU. If you upload it without changing those settings, it will try to connect, literally, to the YOUR_WIFI_NETWORK_NAME wireless network, which, unless that is your network (that's totally hilarious, btw) nothing will happen.

Once you have made the changes, it is a good opportunity to take a browse through the rest of the code too. It will not compile in its current state because we have not installed the requisite libraries into the IDE, but you can look at it and see what it is going to do. I have put in a lot of comments to guide you to what is happening but let me highlight a couple of the more interesting parts here for you as well.

```
#include <DHT.h>

#include <DHT_U.h>

#include <time.h>

#include <WiFi.h>

#include <PubSubClient.h>
```

Figure 10-27. *The libraries required for the collector*

Libraries, as I said, are the backbone of smart devices, allowing you to interact with sensors and devices in a snap. Figure 10-27 shows the libraries in this application from the top of the code. Time you know from previous builds, but the new ones here are for the DHT11 sensor, and the networking/MQTT elements. (WiFi.h and PubSubClient.h) I will walk you through installing these in the Arduino IDE momentarily, as the code will not compile without them!

```
// define the wait time between readings (milliseconds) - the max value for this is
2147483647 which is roughly 25 days

// realistically a reading every 4 hours (14400000) for an outdoor garden

// or 8 hours (28800000) for a potted plant is probably fine - by default the interval is 10
seconds. This is far too short

// and once you are satisfied with the readings you should for sure change it.

const int timer_value = 10000;
```

Figure 10-28. *Time Between readings setting and comments*

Figure 10-28 is the time between readings, and the comment pretty much says it all, but it is worth pointing out. Every 10 seconds is excessive for checking on a plant, but I have left it like that for the lab because otherwise you wait for hours for a reading, and that's not as exciting. The timer_value controls the time in between readings. For my outdoor garden I checked at 4-hour intervals (Denver's climate is hot and dry in the summer and it was not abnormal for water levels to fluctuate by 50% or more during a day). Indoor plants an 8-hour reading is OK. Obviously, this is a "you choose" setting, so I only offer guidance for you based on my experience; there is no right or wrong here!

```
// declare our Wifi and MQTT connections
WiFiClient espClient;
PubSubClient client(espClient);
```

Figure 10-29. *The Wi-Fi and MQTT settings in the application*

Just because this is new to you, the commands you see in Figure 10-29 use the libraries you imported to establish a new Wi-Fi connection and the connection to the MQTT server. You will use the "client" to make publishing requests later and control the connection to MQTT. "espClient" is the wireless connection and is how you will use the wireless network.

```
// These Options control the precision of the analog reading, and the voltage reduction
capability of the ESP32
// Attenuation number 3 is 11DB and is the widely recommended setting
analogSetWidth(10);
analogSetAttenuation((adc_attenuation_t)3);
```

Figure 10-30. *Analogue tuning on the ESP32 analogue inputs*

Analogue readings are finicky things sometimes, and this code bit in Figure 10-30 controls the accuracy of the analogue readings on the analogue inputs. It is not required, but always good to have, and these settings are the recommended for best results with the sensors in use.

```
// publish the sensor value. the sprintf is also a string formatting tool in C++ - in this
case allowing you to insert

// a variable into a string. The string looks complex because it has to be JSON at the
other end for NodeRed

// there are other (perhaps more elegant) ways to skin this cat as it were, but this one
works solidly

placeholder_value=sprintf(data0, "{\"Message\":\"Sensor1\", \"Sensors\":
{\"S1\":\"%s\"}}", s1);

Serial.println("Publishing message 1:");

while (!client.publish("garden1", data0)) {

Serial.print(".");

}
```

Figure 10-31. *MQTT Publishing command with JSON String Formatting*

This is the actual MQTT publishing command (there are a few in the code, I have chosen this one toward the end of the code). This little blob here does three things:

- Formats up a nice JSON string to send off to the hub using the C++ inbuilt function "sprintf" which lets you have a bit more control over strings. I find C++ is frankly unwieldly for working with strings of text, but sprintf takes a bit of the load off. The JSON is important, because that's what Node-RED expects and we will look at that shortly as well.

- Next it lets the console know it is going to publish (Serial.println again).

- Then it calls the client.publish method to push the string present in the data0 array off to the MQTT server with the message topic of "garden1" (this could be anything really, and if you had, say, multiple gardens, you might want to change that "garden1" value). In our simple system, the MQTT broker on the other end doesn't care about having different topics, so anything here will work.

Obviously, there is a heck of a lot more going on in there, but those are some of the more interesting bits. In order for this to run though, you will need the right libraries in the Arduino IDE. Installing them is pretty simple, just a search and button click effort really thanks to the nice library manager built into the IDE. You will be installing three libraries:

- DHT11 Sensor library

- ESP32 Wireless library

- MQTT Client library

Follow these steps to get them installed so you can compile the code:

1) In the Arduino IDE, select the Tools ➤ Manage Libraries option as in Figure 10-32.

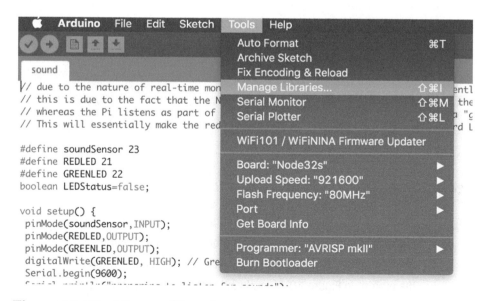

Figure 10-32. Manage libraries menu

2) In the library manager, click into the "Search" field on the upper
right as in figure and type in "DHT-11" as in Figure 10-33 and
hit Enter.

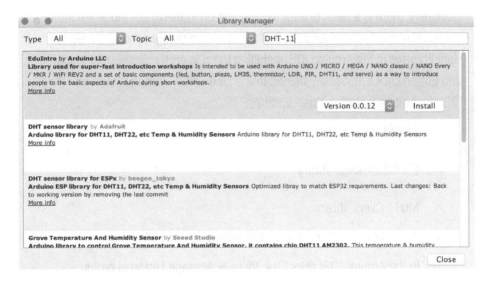

Figure 10-33. *DHT11 search*

3) The library we want is by the fine folks at Adafruit, and should
be the second one in the list, as highlighted in Figure 10-34.

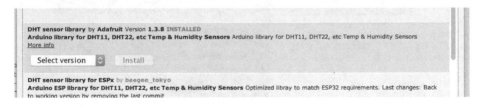

Figure 10-34. *DHT11 Library to install*

4) Click the install button next to the version box as in
Figure 10-35. You will likely be prompted to also install the
Adafruit unified sensor library, so click the "Install All" button on
the prompt in Figure 10-36 and wait for the install to complete.
(It should only take a few seconds.)

Figure 10-35. *Install button to start installation*

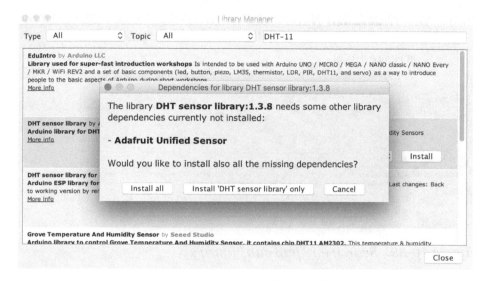

Figure 10-36. *Install supporting libraries prompt*

5)   It will now say "Installed" next to the library as in Figure 10-37.

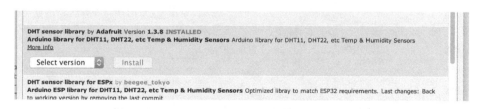

Figure 10-37. *Library installed*

6)   Now in the search field type "esp32 wifi" and hit Enter.

7)   Scroll down the list and select the ConfigManager library from the list and install it, as you did with the other library by clicking the Install button, as shown in Figure 10-38.

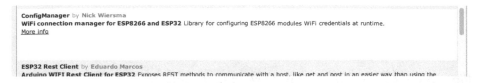

Figure 10-38. *Install this library for Wi-Fi*

8) Last, replace "esp32 wifi" in the search bar with "pub sub" as in Figure 10-39.

Figure 10-39. *Search for "pub-sub" library*

9) Scroll down and find the PubSubClient by Nick O'Leary in the list that you can see in Figure 10-40,

10) and again, install by clicking the Install button.

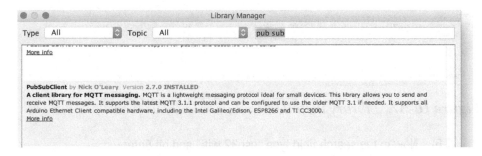

Figure 10-40. *Install this library*

Now you have the libraries you need to make the IDE compile and test the code for deployment onto your collector. You can validate this by closing the library manager and clicking the Checkmark in the upper left of the IDE. This is the "validate" button, and it will test the code and ensure there are no errors. You can see the button highlighted in Figure 10-41 and the result when all the code is right in Figure 10-42.

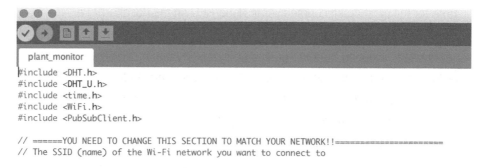

Figure 10-41. *The "Validate Code" button*

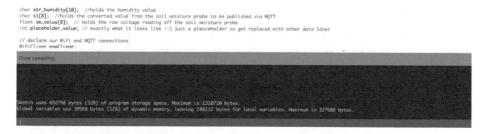

Figure 10-42. *Code validated success!*

At this point you can flash the code to your ESP32 as you did with the other applications in the other builds, and it will run, but it will not see the result of this, because you have to get the hub ready to receive and display the information. If you are watching the serial monitor, you will see the application attempting to connect to the hub, and retrying this behaviour in a loop forever. This is expected behavior for the collector at this point, but I do not want you to be disappointed you've done something wrong. This is now part of a smart system, and in order for it to work, all the parts need to be up and running, and if one is not, then the system doesn't work the way it's meant to. I will walk you through getting the hub ready in the next part, so you can get everything up and running.

Part 3 – The Hub

Time for the most crash course ever in Node-RED on the Raspberry Pi! Node-RED is a phenomenally accessible language, built on top of Java and pretty much designed from the ground up to make working with smart devices WAY simpler. It uses a drag-and-drop model of programming that takes all the formatting and syntax and structure away and replaces it with "nodes" that get dropped onto a canvas and "wired" together to form a "flow." The flow is essentially an application that starts and ends based on inputs.

As with the other code in the book I have taken the liberty of building out the Node-RED flow for you for the lab. If you did not follow the instructions in Chapter 8 around the configuration of the Raspberry Pi (or are using your local machine), you will need to install Node-RED and Mosquitto before you can proceed to the directions for configuring the Hub. You can run these on Mac, Windows, and Raspberry Pi, so if you do not have the Raspberry Pi for this and are using your own computer to act as the hub, I won't spell out the instructions here, as there are lots and lots of resources online to guide you on the installation of both.

There is also the possibility that I could have used some hardware on the hub, the Pi does have a GPIO header, and Node-RED will interact with it to control the GPIO outputs which can turn on lights and read sensors and all of that. For the smart system, the strength of the Raspberry Pi lies in the fact that it is a computer and can act as the central hub for our smart system. The hardware access it has is a bonus then that you could explore to expand its capability beyond "just the hub." Also, because I do not want to exclude anyone who does not have a Raspberry Pi to work with, hardware would have meant missing part of the function of the lab if you have to use your own computer as the hub.

So why does that matter? It only matters because in this exercise the hub is 100% software and from here on out, everything is done in a web browser on your own computer or laptop, as Node-RED is all driven out of a web-based UI. I will be taking screen shots from Chrome on a Mac, and connecting to a Raspberry Pi, but it will look identical on any platform and browser (minus the browser menus which you will not use). You do need the IP address of the Hub (your computer/laptop or the Raspberry Pi) for this, as that is how you will connect to both the UI and connect Node-RED to your MQTT server. Now let's get your Node-RED Flow ready to run, and you can finally see your smart system in action!

1) In order for this part to work, you need at a minimum the following:

   a. Your Hub (Raspberry Pi or your own Computer/Laptop) needs to be running and on your network.

   b. You need Mosquitto and Node-RED installed on your Raspberry Pi as we covered in the setup section earlier, OR on your own computer laptop if you do not have a Raspberry Pi.

2) Regardless whether you have used the Raspberry Pi, or your own Computer/Laptop, in your regular web browser on your laptop or computer, type in the IP address of your hub (Raspberry Pi or computer) and add :1880 to the end of the IP address (the ":" matters). This will open the Node-RED canvas to the default flow as you see in Figure 10-43.

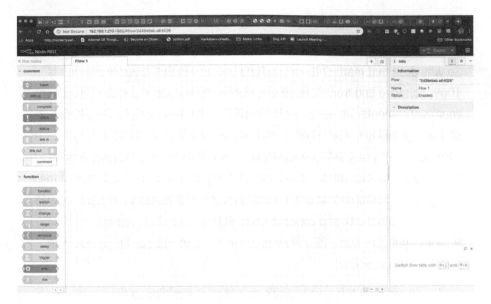

Figure 10-43. *The default Node-RED canvas*

3) This is the pure, default canvas for building Node-RED flows.
    The flow that you will import from the code repository requires
    some extra add-in nodes, which are like libraries for Python or
    C++. They are very easy to install, with these steps.

    a. First click on the "hamburger" menu on the far right of the
        UI (the three lines stacked horizontally) and you will see the
        menu as in Figure 10-44.

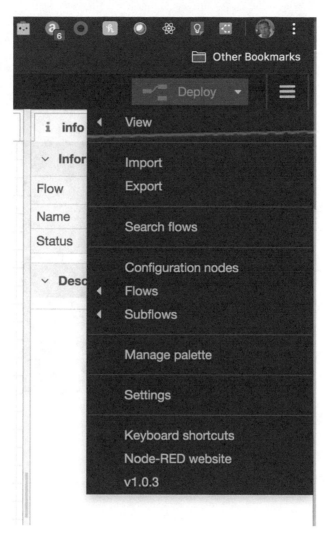

Figure 10-44. *The hamburger menu in the Node-RED*

b. From the menu click the "Manage palette" option as in
    Figure 10-45.

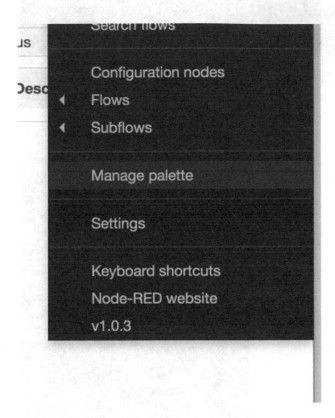

Figure 10-45. *Manage palette menu option*

c. The Palette Menu will pop up. Click on the "Install" tab at
    the top as in Figure 10-46.

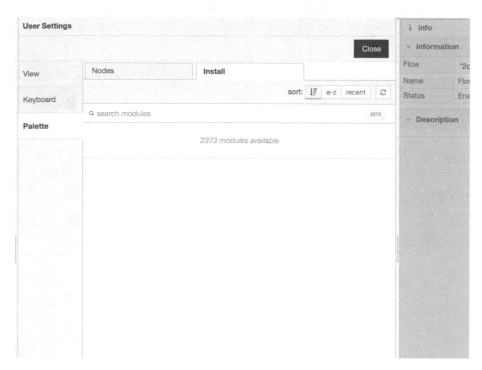

Figure 10-46. *Install tab in Palette Manager*

d. Type in "dash" and the search results will fill in. You are
    looking for the second one in the list as in Figure 10-47.
    (Highlight added for clarity – it will not be highlighted in the
    list.)

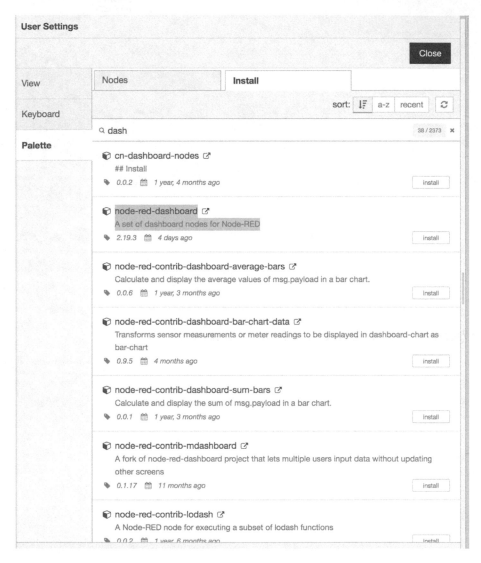

Figure 10-47. *Dashboard library to install*

e. Click the Install button to the right of the package name in the list as in Figure 10-48.

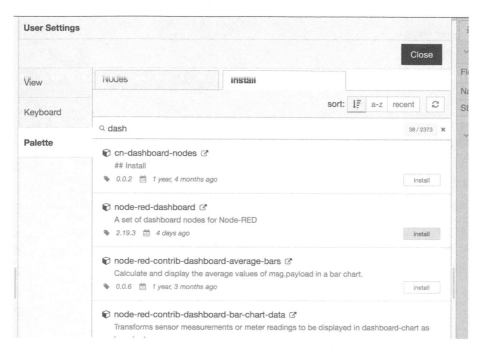

Figure 10-48. Install button for installing libraries

f. A popup will appear as in Figure 10-49, and you may click the Install button on the lower right.

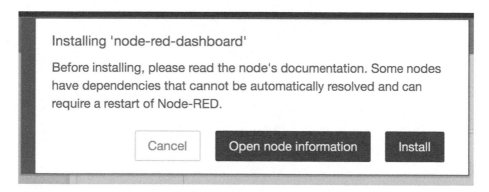

Figure 10-49. Confirmation popup

g. The install will begin and the package will change to the
    progress bar seen in Figure 10-50.

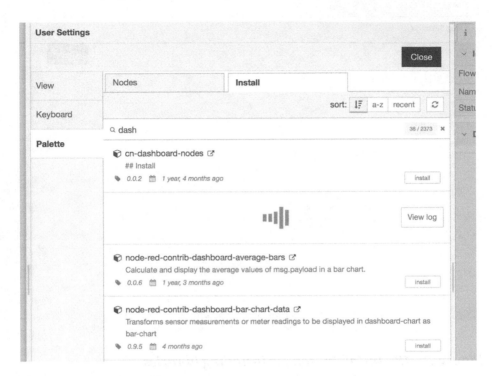

Figure 10-50. Install progress

h.   When it finishes, you will see the button changes to say "Installed" and is grayed out as in Figure 10-51.

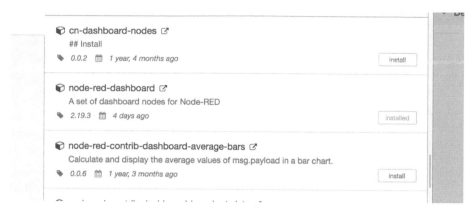

Figure 10-51. *Install complete*

i.   You need to install two other sets of nodes by repeating the same steps. First type "moment" into the search bar, and choose the highlighted package as in Figure 10-52 by clicking "Install" – follow the previous steps for any prompts.

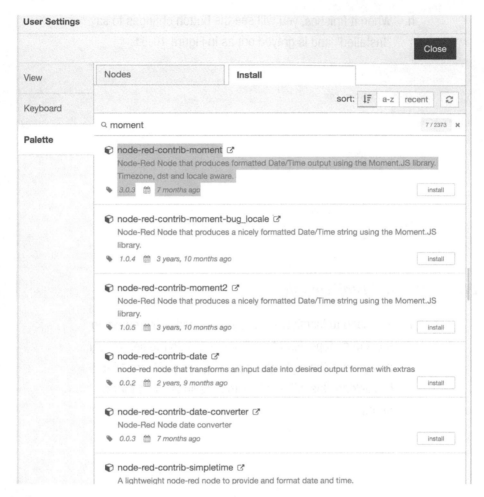

Figure 10-52. *Moment library to be installed – highlight added for clarity*

j. Then change the search to "message count" and install the
    package highlighted (it should be the only one in the list) as
    in Figure 10-53.

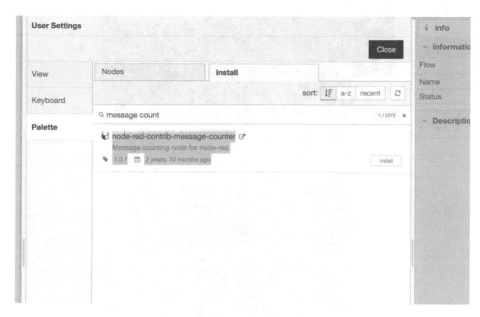

Figure 10-53. *Message count library to install – highlight added for clarity*

   k.   You can now click "Close" in the upper right, and the
        needed packages will be ready for use.

4)   Next step is to import the flow that was created for you and
     is in the repository for the book you cloned/downloaded from
     GitHub. In your web browser, click on the "hamburger menu"
     in the upper right of the UI, and select the "Import" menu as
     shown in Figure 10-54.

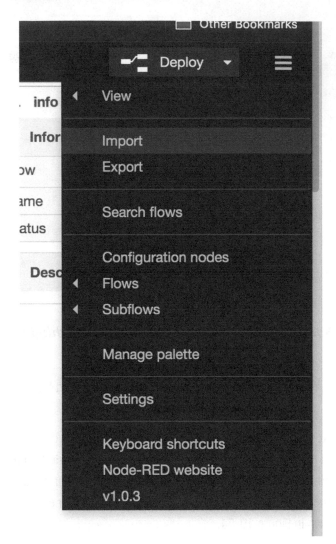

Figure 10-54. *Import menu*

5) The "Import Nodes" dialog box will open as you see in
Figure 10-55.

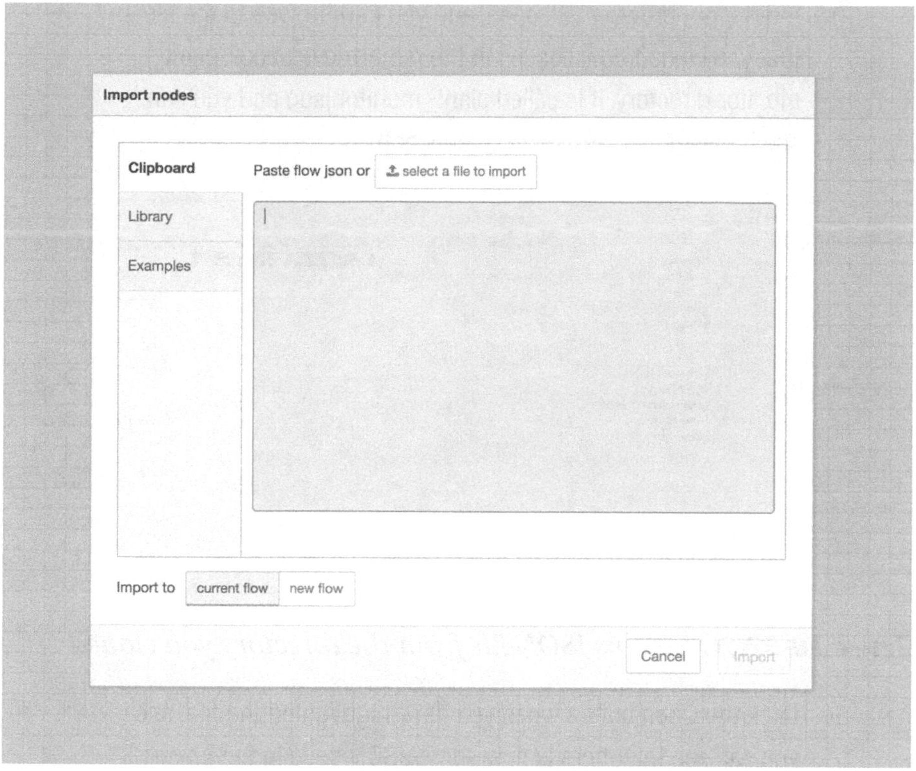

Figure 10-55. *Import nodes dialog*

6) Click the "Import from File" button at the top of the box that you
    can see in Figure 10-56.

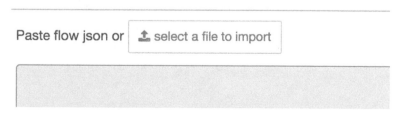

Figure 10-56. *Import from File button*

7) A directory browser will open, and you can browse to the file that you cloned/downloaded in the /smartdevicebook/plant_monitor directory. It is called plant_monitor.json and you can see it in Figure 10-57 (Mac screenshot).

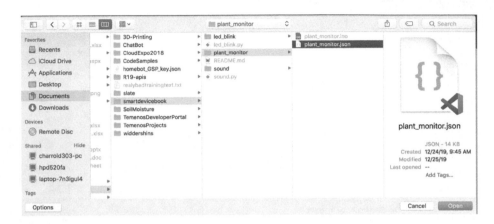

Figure 10-57. *Open this JSON file from the directory you cloned*

8) Click the Open button when you have highlighted the file, and you will see that there is now some JSON code in the import screen as in Figure 10-58.

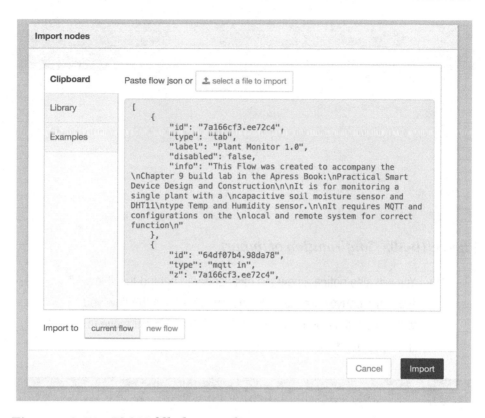

Figure 10-58. *JSON filled in ready to import*

9) Click the "Import" button at the lower right of the dialog,
    and a confirmation will appear at the top of the screen as in
    Figure 10-59.

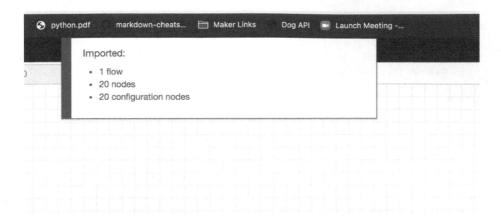

Figure 10-59. *Confirmation of import*

10) You will also notice a new tab has appeared behind the "Flow 1" tab in the canvas area as in Figure 10-60. This is the flow you will work with so you can click on that tab and it will move to the foreground.

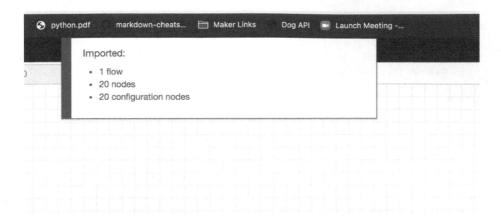

Figure 10-60. *New tab in the UI*

11)   The flow should look like the image in Figure 10-61 – if you have any errors about missing nodes, or nodes that are not right looking (dashed border line, or orange text), make sure you installed all three needed libraries from the preceding steps!

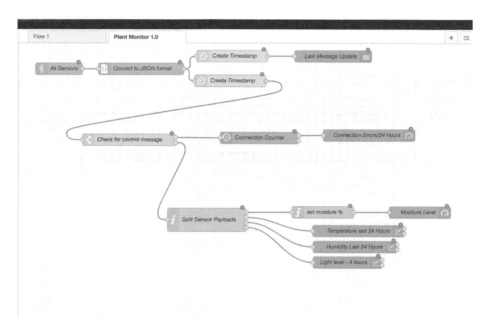

Figure 10-61. *The imported flow*

12)   There are a couple of settings that you will need to change to make the flow work, but they are very easy. Start by double-clicking the node at the far upper left that is highlighted orange, called "All Sensors" as you see in Figure 10-62 – this is the first node of the flow, and it is an MQTT input node type. It reads the MQTT message queue and if a new message appears it will process it based on the rules in the flow.

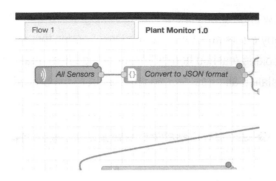

Figure 10-62. *The "all sensors" node to be edited*

13) The node configuration dialog will pop in from the right side of the UI as in Figure 10-63. This is how nodes are configured to do what you want them. The MQTT Node requires five settings:

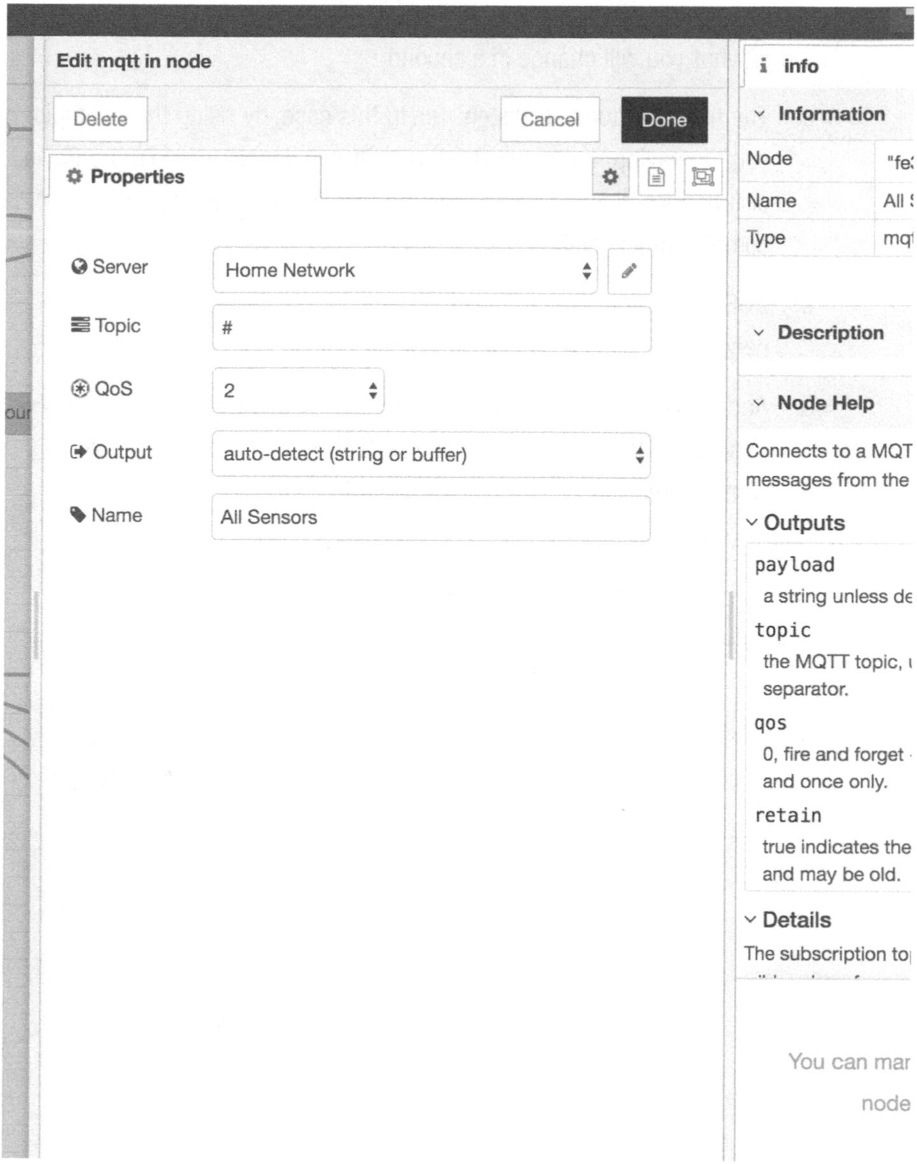

Edit mqtt in node

Delete   Cancel   Done

⚙ **Properties**   ⚙ 📄 🖾

🌐 Server   Home Network   ↕   ✏

⚏ Topic   #

✴ QoS   2   ↕

↪ Output   auto-detect (string or buffer)   ↕

🏷 Name   All Sensors

ℹ **info**

˅ **Information**

Node   "fe?

Name   All §

Type   mq

˅ **Description**

˅ **Node Help**

Connects to a MQT
messages from the

˅ **Outputs**

payload
  a string unless de
topic
  the MQTT topic, ι
  separator.
qos
  0, fire and forget
  and once only.
retain
  true indicates the
  and may be old.

˅ **Details**

The subscription to

You can mar

node

Figure 10-63. *The MQTT settings in the node configuration screen*

a.   The network to connect to (called "Home Network" in this flow) – This is what you will change in a second.

b.   The message topic to "listen" for. In this case, by using the "#" topic you are saying "listen to everything". If you decide to add more flows or functions, this can be changed to just listen to the messages that come from a specific sensor collector.

c.   QOS and Output are defaults but could be changed based on your needs – They are not usually required though.

d.   And lastly the Name – This is literally what appears in the flow on the node itself. In this case I named it "All Sensors", but you can call it what makes sense for you if you want to change it.

14) Click on the little pencil icon next to the Server field where it says "Home Network" in Figure 10-64. This will open the server configuration node.

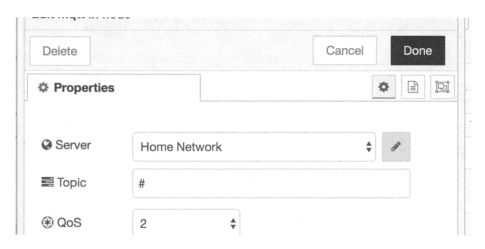

Figure 10-64. *Modify configuration button*

15)   There is only one field you must change in this config, and that
       is the IP of the MQTT server. This should match the IP of your
       Raspberry Pi or computer depending on what you are using as
       the hub, as you can see in Figure 10-65 mine matches the IP I
       connected to for the Node-RED UI.

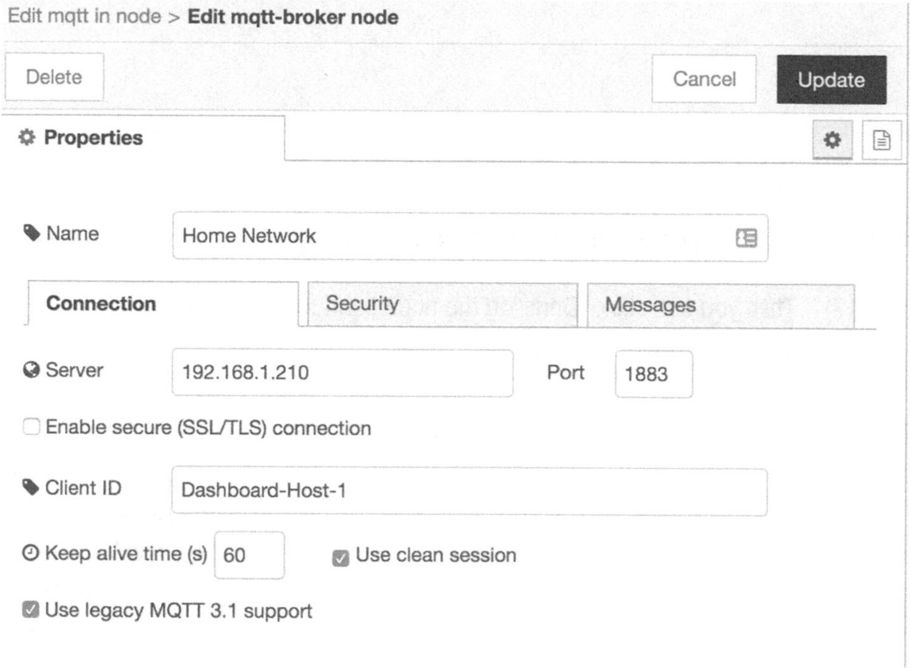

Edit mqtt in node > **Edit mqtt-broker node**

| Delete | | Cancel | Update |

⚙ **Properties**

🏷 Name   Home Network

| **Connection** | Security | Messages |

🌐 Server   192.168.1.210   Port   1883

☐ Enable secure (SSL/TLS) connection

🏷 Client ID   Dashboard-Host-1

🕐 Keep alive time (s) 60   ☑ Use clean session

☑ Use legacy MQTT 3.1 support

Figure 10-65. *MQTT server configuration – change IP field to match
your MQTT server IP*

16) Once you've entered it in, click the "Update" button at the upper right to update that configuration as in Figure 10-66.

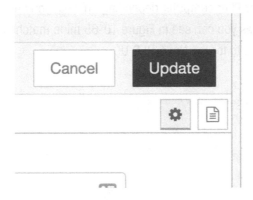

Figure 10-66. *Update button to confirm changes*

17) Then you can click "Done" in the node configuration screen as in Figure 10-67.

Figure 10-67. *Click Done to confirm settings*

18) Back in the canvas, notice the small blue pip on the tops of all your nodes (same as in Figure 10-68)? That means that while the node is present, it is not actually running. Node-RED requires you to Deploy the flow before it executes (like flashing your ESP32 or executing the code on the Pi from before).

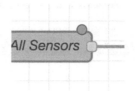

Figure 10-68. *Undeployed updates pip on a node*

19) To deploy the flow, click on the big red "Deploy" button on the upper left, as in Figure 10-69.

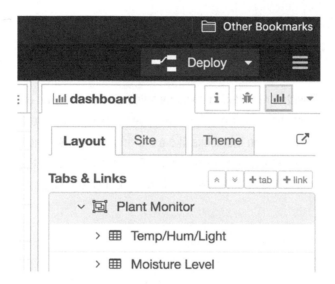

Figure 10-69. *To deploy your flow to active – click the Deploy button*

20) You will see a confirmation pop in from the top of the browser, confirming the deployment as in Figure 10-70. The unused configuration nodes notice is an erratum from my prepping for the book and you can ignore it.

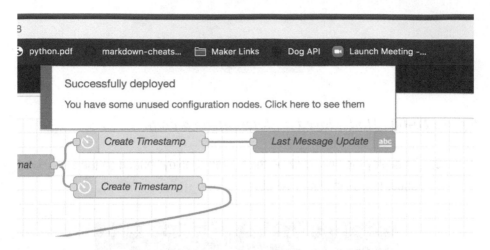

Figure 10-70. *Confirmation of deployment popup*

21) The Dashboard nodes that you installed earlier are what drives
     the UI for the sensor data. On the upper right of the UI, you will
     see a little button that looks like a bar graph and if you hover
     over it, it will say "Dashboard" as in Figure 10-71. Click the
     button to bring up the dashboard configuration options.

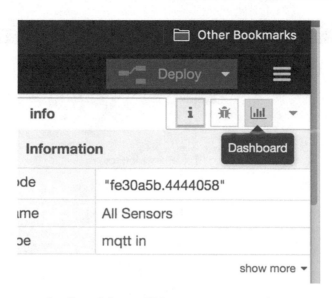

Figure 10-71. *The "Dashboard" button to open the dashboard config*

22) Another strange erratum of my prep work appears when you
     do this, showing what would appear to be three duplicate
     dashboards under the configuration, but when it opens there is
     only one. I tried to eliminate this, but since it isn't broken, I left
     it. Just do not be surprised when you see Figure 10-72, it is not
     broken!

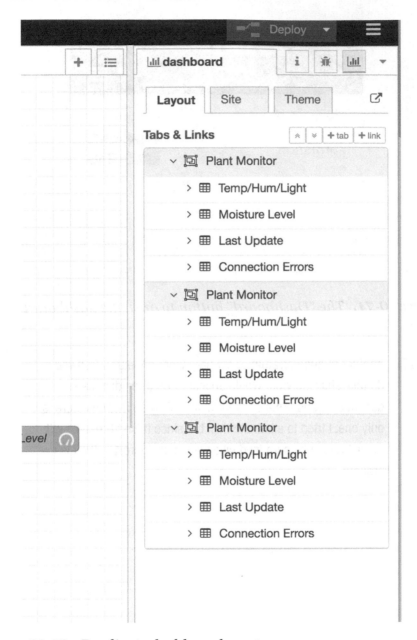

Figure 10-72. *Duplicate dashboard erratum*

23) The dashboard UI is accessible from the tiny "go to" link on the upper right side of the configuration menus just below the bar graph button as you see in Figure 10-73. Clicking this will open the dashboard for your sensors.

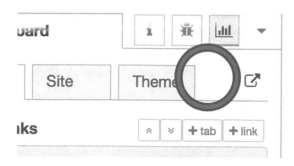

Figure 10-73. *Click this "go to" link to open the dashboard in a new tab*

24) The default dashboard shows up as in Figure 10-74.

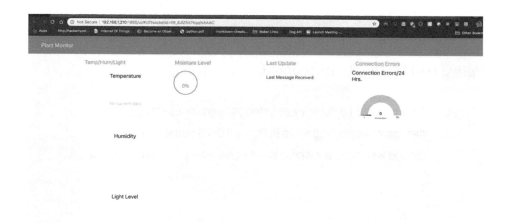

Figure 10-74. *The default dashboard*

25) Now, I personally do not like the "Light" color scheme as I find it hard to read. If you want to change it, click back on the tab in your browser for the Node-RED editor, and click the "Theme" tab in the dashboard config menu, seen in Figure 10-75.

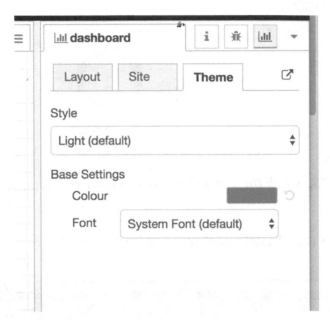

Figure 10-75. *The theme configuration tab*

26) Click on the drop down there at the top and choose "Dark" and then click "Deploy" again as in Figure 10-76 (remember, no change you make anywhere in the editor exists until you deploy it!).

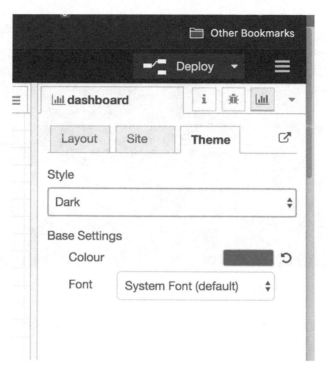

Figure 10-76. *Deploy the Dark!*

27) Now if you click back, the dashboard will be in dark mode and a lot friendlier on the eyes as in Figure 10-77. Notice also, there is not data there. That is because your sensors are still sitting cold and dark on the workbench, waiting to be fired up!

Figure 10-77.   *The dark themed dashboard*

With the hub up and ready, the last step is to turn on the collector and watch the data flow in!

Part 4 – The Whole System

Time for the grand finale! Depending on where you stopped with the collector, you probably have a contraption sitting next to you that looks like Figure 10-78, and has been happily turning LEDs on and off (if you left it turned on, if not you can plug it in now) and sending messages to the Mosquitto server on your hub. Up until now though, you have not had a way to see what that looks like, because the Node-RED piece had been missing. Now that the hub is configured, if you start up your collector, you will start seeing the data arrive on the dashboard. It will change from the empty one you started with to one that looks more like Figure 10-79.

Figure 10-78. *Your sensor pack looking ready to do something!*

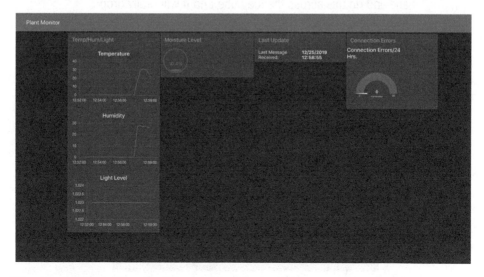

Figure 10-79. *The dashboard in Node-RED – now with actual information!*

For some fun and to make the readings more interesting, there are a few little things you can do to make the graphs move around.

— Cover the light sensor with your hand (like I did here in Figure 10-80) which should make the light reading drop considerably. Make sure to really cover it well, as it is actually quite sensitive.

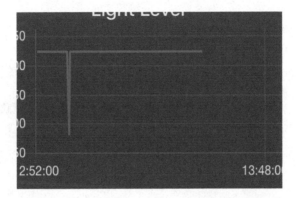

Figure 10-80. *Covering the light sensor makes it drop its reading*

— Blow on the DHT11 sensor (you can put an ice cube in your hand and do this across the ice cube and it will really drop measurably). The DHT11 is not supersensitive, but you should see a downward spike like in Figure 10-81.

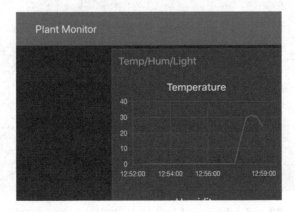

Figure 10-81. *DHT11 temp drop thanks to some ice cold "wind"*

- My personal favorite, stick the moisture sensor in a glass of water (careful not to submerge the electronics!) or in a plant! Figure 10-82 shows the result when the water level bounces up.

Figure 10-82. *Moisture reading in a glass of water*

Smart System Recap

Your first smart system fully functioning and collecting data, sharing it visually, and otherwise improving something. That is a fully functioning smart system and you built it and that is AWESOME!

Some things to point out at this moment of triumph. You have reached the point where you are taking default, **uncalibrated** readings from your sensors. EVERY mass market sensor has variance and frankly some of them are a lot worse than others. You will need to do some tuning to figure out the right ranges and variances for your sensors/environment/needs. Commonly I see people complain about sensors throwing seemingly "bad" data and I wonder how much of that is trusting it to be perfect out of the box. If you look at the reading from the soil moisture sensor in Figure 10-82, it says roughly 50% – meaning 50% water present, but it is LITERALLY IN A GLASS OF WATER! That is 100% water. How do I fix that? Well I need to take wet and dry readings, and then figure out what the real range the sensor can read is and do my math from that. For example, in my own garden, I had to divide my sensors' readings by around 920 instead of 1024, because that was about the highest raw value reading they would register, even in a glass of water. This tuning of your devices is really critical to the performance of your system, and something all builders go through.

We have also come to the big turning point in the smart device builder's path, where you have something functional, that works and does what you intended. The thing about this is you can expand it, add more sensors, more collectors, and so on and really scale it out! BUT, all those wires, and the breadboard are fragile. Seriously, go move it around a bunch. I will wait here. Did wires come loose? Kind of a pain, right? Prototypes like this are critical to making things work, and they are fun! They just aren't permanent, and that's where we go next. On to making this prototype something that will last and stand the test of time (or at least being moved across the room).

PART IV

Permanence

We come now to the end, but not the end of your process! Just the end of my ability to teach you more. From here, the process is the teacher, and using all you have learned you can move forward on building new and fantastic things as yet undreamt of. You will try new sensors, expand your skills developing software, and build new and interesting devices that do new and interesting thing and all through that you can use the concepts you have learned in the chapters of this book.

Before you embark on that journey, I want to leave you with one last set of skills and tools that will take you beyond the prototype you just built in the last chapter. That is the concept and skills of designing for "permanence." Now I put that in quotes because, as you will see, nothing is permanent, but it is definitely more permanent than the prototype you built, and this is the last thing you need to really seriously build your smart devices and integrate them into your life.

We will touch on a number of topics and ideas in the last chapter, but the end result is that "permanence" is more attainable and more important than ever, and you can build something that can stand up to regular use with ease. You just need the right tools.

CHAPTER 11

Your First Circuit Board

Congratulations on completing the prototype labs and building out your first functioning smart device(s). Getting to the point where you have working sensors, actual data, and can start to really see how all these things work together is a huge step on the smart device journey. At this point, you have also probably figured out the reason why building on a breadboard is good for prototypes and not a lot else. If you aren't sure why, move your device around a bunch, drop it for good measure (from a low altitude!), and otherwise use it. It will not take long for one of your wires to come out, a connection to get bent wrong and short out, or have some other sort of trauma that causes it to stop working. I, for one, am a HUGE fan of the "caught a wire with my finger when moving" disconnection which results in a lively game of "what the heck did this connect?!" (see Figure 11-1).

© Christopher Harrold 2020
C. Harrold, *Practical Smart Device Design and Construction*,
https://doi.org/10.1007/978-1-4842-5614-5_11

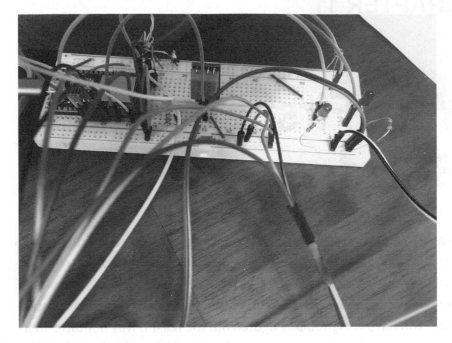

Figure 11-1. *Complex prototype missing a single wire*

Now of course you can fix these issues with your prototype; just reconnect, replace, fiddle, and so on, and it will be back and working in no time. Remember, way back in the first part of the book I said the key thing that smart devices do is enable functionality without babysitting? That's why breadboards are lousy for "production", because they need to either never be touched or require constant babysitting. So how do you fix this issue and move beyond prototype into something more permanent? The great news is there are lots of ways you can do this, and we will discuss the most simple and likely solutions in the next couple of chapters on the way to permanence.

Locking It Down

One of the simplest and easiest ways to start building more rugged prototypes for more rigorous conditions is to use a simple solderable breadboard or protoboard. Figure 11-2 shows a picture of some of them, and they are exactly as they sound, a breadboard that you can solder connections to. There are A LOT of varieties out there and you can spend some pretty good money on them easily, so make sure that the one you choose works for you. The ones in the picture are a simple, two-sided protoboard that you will find readily online, and that I will use in the builds. If you are using something different, please adjust accordingly.

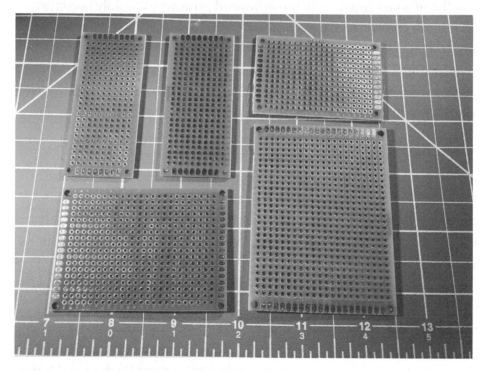

Figure 11-2. *Solderable breadboards*

You can solder your jumper wires, chips, MCU, really anything with a through-hole mount, which is pretty much everything you are likely to encounter unless you are getting into some of the more exotic, circuit board–specific components, and we will talk about that in the next chapter. This attachment provides a semi-permanent (it can be removed) connection that won't fall apart the second you pick it up or drop it. It can even be mounted to another surface with standoffs through those holes in the corners and made something akin to a permanent device. As you get into testing a prototype this is a great way to be able to test devices "in the field" without spending money on PCBs upfront.

This of course indicates that you will need to solder, and soldering is a skill that when you want to move beyond prototypes rapidly becomes mandatory. Soldering is one of those "barrier to entry" skills that is VERY daunting to people, as there is heat, and multiple parts, and lots of things to learn about it as a discipline by itself. The thing I will tell you is that soldering is actually really a great skill to have, fun to do, and is not as hard as it seems at first with some good prep and proper tools to make things smoother.

The most important thing to remember is, of course, soldering irons get HOT, and they burn. I have several nicks and scars from mine, and it stings like the dickens. That said, I have soldered many thousands of connections with my trusty pen soldering iron, and I rarely give myself any mementos of the experience anymore. Just have a little respect for your kit and the heat, and soldering can be a great experience.

Really the first thing you need is your soldering kit. A good, reliable soldering iron can be had for very little, and a complete and functional soldering "kit" can be put together for well under $50 that will last you a long time and be perfectly functional. I recommended some of them in Chapter 2 on building your workbench, but let's review the basic soldering components you should not be without. See Figure 11-3 for pictures of the parts:

1. Soldering iron with a temp control – You will want to control temperatures! In the olden days, only very high-end machines had this, but now even basic ones have a little dial that gets the job done.

2. Desoldering tool – This is a nifty little vacuum tool that plucks hot solder off your parts. You WILL need this; you will mess up and put too much solder on and this is how you remove it.

3. Tip tinner and cleaning "pod" – Tip tinner is like "non-stick coating" for the soldering iron, and the cleaner "pod" is a metal pod with a steel wool–like bundle in it that is made of brass. This is for cleaning off excess solder from the tip of your iron.

4. Soldering tips – Like paintbrushes for the artists out there, solder tips come in specific shapes for specific sorts of tasks, fine point, wedge, big fat tips, and others. You won't always use all of them, but having a variety is super helpful.

5. "Helping hands" aka the part holder – This little (or big – there are some crazy complex versions out there!) is invaluable. Soldering is hard when you are trying to hold four things at once, and the helping hands (and magnifying glass) make holding and seeing what you are soldering MUCH easier.

6. Soldering stand – A simple little coil of wire on a metal base that is literally hugely important and useful. It means you can set the iron down without setting your workspace on fire!

7. Solder – Here's the great news, a big ole spool of
    this costs a few bucks and lasts forever if you are not
    at commercial scale. Readily available at big box
    hardware stores and online.

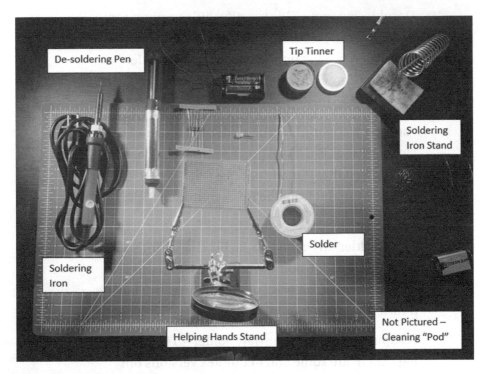

Figure 11-3. *Soldering kit parts*

Soldering is such a core competency that learning how to do it is pretty
much a basic requirement for making. There is no way a wearable for
something like a cosplay prop or a costume, or something that moves like a
drone or robot is ever going to hold up without more permanent means of
making connections. Breadboards are way too finicky and the connections
to fragile for something that needs that level of security in its connections.

As you move beyond prototype, and get into making your own circuit
boards, it just is as simple as you HAVE to be able to solder. Soldering really
well is another matter, and something that really only comes with practice.

I still make mistakes when soldering, and have to clean up things, but that's part of mastery. Don't be afraid to make mistakes and learn the right technique for you. As well as practice, there are many, many resources and tips, tricks, and things you should know for soldering available online, but I have collected some of the most important and relevant as you are starting out for you here:

- Soldering tips wear out, no matter how much you baby them. They are meant to and will eventually need replacement. They are inexpensive to replace but doing so will save you a huge amount of headache, as they can make soldering very difficult when badly worn.

- I recommend the brass "sponge" cleaning pod over the damp sponge that comes with most kits. The interaction of the hot and cold will cause the tip to wear out faster. It is worth the few extra bucks to keep things operating smoothly.

- Soldering stations are COOL, and you might need one eventually. A pen-style soldering iron is ready to go in a few seconds and will get the job done unless you are soldering many thousands of connections – a really nice kit is available online for around $30. Way better for getting started than a $300 station that you might not use a lot!

- Always have a soldering iron stand, always. It looks so simple, but it is so important. You will need to set the iron down and it WILL burn the heck out of everything!

- DO NOT BUY/USE COPPER PIPE SOLDER BY MISTAKE – I have a "friend" who did this once. That friend is me, I did it, and it destroyed the tip and the component and the board, and there was great sadness.

- DO get lead-free solder with a rosin core (this is what you will find most readily online and in stores if you are not looking in the pipe solder section).

- Make sure you solder in a well-ventilated area – you don't need a big air mover and all that, but do step away for a few minutes as the fumes and smoke can have nasty stuff in them. A small fan isn't a terrible companion to your bench while soldering.

- Clean up your workspace and yourself after soldering – wash your hands really well with soap and water as solder can leave residue.

- Lay down some paper or other disposable covering on your workspace – solder will spatter here and there, and the rosin and other coating materials from boards can also drip and it will damage desks and benches

- Tin the tip before you start a new soldering session, and frequently during your sessions. You will have a much better soldering experience as it will keep solder flowing cleanly and also gives you a chance to examine the tip for damage.

The basic point of soldering is to put the two things you want to solder next to each other, and then apply solder to connect them. The solder flows as a liquid while hot, and cools (very quickly) to form a solid bond. Any metal-on-metal connection can be soldered from components and parts to a solderable board, to bonding two or more wires together. Figure 11-4 shows the basic gist of soldering. By filling in the "gap" between the element and the board, you make a nice, strong connection that also conducts electrical current. In this way, the solder becomes a part of the circuit and helps to complete the flow of electricity.

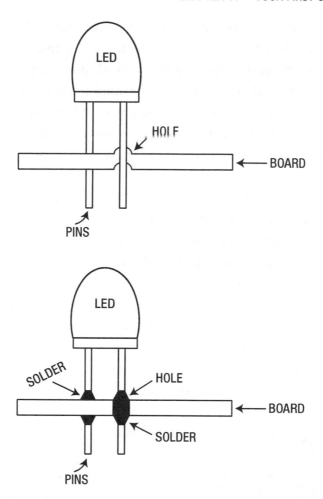

Figure 11-4. *A soldered connection – the top is before soldering and the bottom is after*

Functionally, there isn't a "right" or "wrong" way to solder such as "only touch the pad" or "only touch the wires." You will undoubtedly read in other places that one way or the other is better, but in the spirit of just making this easy for everyone, the right way to solder is the one that you are comfortable with and makes nice connections!

I generally prefer to almost "paint" with the solder, by touching the iron to the solder and then flowing it into where I want it like paint on a brush. You can also heat the connection pad where the solder will go, and then touch the solder to that area, but I find this to be unwieldy for me, and doesn't always give me the connection I want. Ultimately, you should take a solderable board and a few "disposable" components and just practice by soldering and removing them. You can always pull the solder out and remove the component, and in doing so you won't ruin it. Then you can just use it again, and this will help you get the feel for what technique lets you make good connections.

What makes a good vs. bad solder joint? That is not open for debate, and there is only one "right way" that solder connections are "good." Figure 11-5 shows what a good, through-hole component connection should look like, and what a bad one looks like. Notice the nice "cone" around the pin, and that the connection is clearly not touching any other connections in the good image. This connection is solid, fills in the full space of the pad around the pin, and does not contact other connections or pads. In the bad one, you can see that there is too much solder and it has bled into the pad next door. This can cause a short and create very bad things depending on the component connected.

Figure 11-5. *Good vs. bad solder joints*

Solder makes a strong and lasting connection, but not really a "permanent" one in the truest sense of the word. Simply heating up the joint with the soldering iron and applying the solder remover and you can clean it up easily. Figure 11-6 shows the after picture of the "bad" connection once I removed the overage and cleaned it up. The solder remover vacuum is the pen-shaped device with the plunger, and using it is so easy! You just press the plunger down, heat the solder, and then put the tip of the "pen" next to it and push the release button. The resulting vacuum inside the remover's chamber sucks up the hot solder and instantly cools it to a little blob. I generally have a few of these blobs on the workspace after soldering. Notice in the image that I hold the pen fairly close to this iron. The white tip of the pen is a silicon material and so does not melt easily, and the closer it is to the heated blob, the more it will pull away. To clean out the hole itself, I would set the board vertically with the pen on one side and the iron on the other, and it will pull all the solder out of the hole.

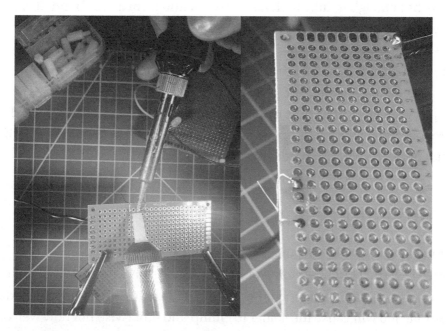

Figure 11-6. *Cleanup of bad connection on the left and after image on the right*

The other common thing that can happen is scorching of the circuit board surface. This happens and it is OK! No real damage is done there, other than the discoloring of the surface of the board. (You can see it on the right-hand side of Figure 11-6, around the spot I cleaned up) There isn't really anything you can do to clean this up, but again, no damage really done, so it's fine to just leave it. Really the only thing that makes a solder joint "bad" is just that it has too much solder and has bled into something next to it, and those are the ones you need to clean up. Now it is possible that you can overdo it and burn through the PCB material and affect the traces inside on a manufactured board. This is obviously BAD, and you may have damaged the board to the point of being unusable, but you generally need to really leave the iron on it a long time for this. Just double check that you've not melted away the material from anything.

It is worth mentioning the other type of solder mistake here that can occur, which is the "cold solder" joint. This occurs when the solder is not really hot enough to fully melt into the joint and form a nice bond. It is very hard to see these types of joints, because the surface will often look like a good solder joint, but underneath it will not have melted and flowed into place. These types of joints can be cleaned up in the same way as my messy solder job earlier, and replaced with a fresh joint, but in a larger project they may cause unintended damage if they fail. The key is to make sure that if you allow your tip to cool for any reason, that you make sure it is hot enough for good solder flow before you start again.

Maintaining Good Iron

"Tinning the tip" of your soldering iron is another important thing to do both when you start a session and during the session when you notice the tip turning black. This happens because of oxidization of the tip and solder material and will cause the solder to clump and otherwise not flow well off the iron. The tin that you apply is like non-stick spray for solder and also coats the iron to delay the oxidizing effect so that you can work longer.

You can solder without it, but it will be painful. Figure 11-7 shows a series of steps for tinning your soldering iron tip.

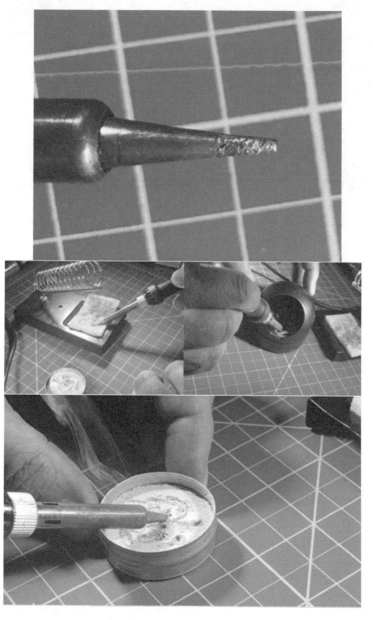

Figure 11-7. *Tip tinning steps*

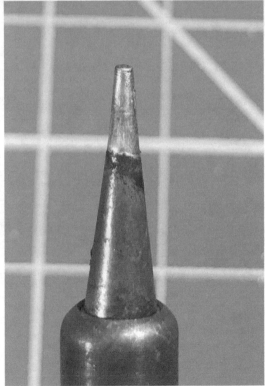

Figure 11-7. (continued)

- First picture – A "bad" tip. Notice how pitted and scored it is; it needs to be cleaned up and tinned again to work better.

- Second picture (left) – Prep the tip for tinning by giving it a nice wipe-off with your wet sponge.

- Third picture (right) – A pass through the bronze pad in your cleaning pod removes old tin and gets the tip ready for the tinning.

- Fourth picture – Into the tinning material; you don't need it in here too long, as soon as I see some "smoke" rising I pull it out.

- Fifth picture – One more solid wipe with the sponge to remove excess tinning material (you can see the little blob on the sponge).

- Last picture – A nice cleaned and tinned tip; notice how all the scoring and roughness is now smoothed and the tip looks much better; that is a good tip!

Cleaning the iron is also important, and you will find that even with a good tin coating, there are still clumps and excess. The default for this is to use the little sponge (get it wet with cool water) that comes with the iron holder usually. I recommend against this for frequent cleanings, as it can accelerate the tip's degrading because of the expansion and contraction with hot and cold. The brass sponge cleaning pod is much better as it will not cause the tip to change temp, and also more efficiently scrapes off the excess solder. When you find you have clumps, just stab and drag – stab the tip into the brass sponge and drag it out while twisting, and it will scrape off the excess. The only time I generally favor the wet sponge is when I am going to re-tin the tip, because it takes more of the oxidization off than the brass does. Having both is never a bad thing, and you will find the one that gives you the best result as you practice.

Replacing your tip is iron specific, but MOST pen-style irons work the same way. Unscrewing the retainer on the end of the iron and removing the tip. (LET IT COOL OFF ALL THE WAY FIRST – I say that because I have done exactly what you think, and it hurts.) Inside you will see a ceramic element which is the actual hot-end of the iron. The tips slide over this element and are held in place by the retainer sleeve. Be careful not to drop or otherwise bash the ceramic element while exposed as they can break and render the iron useless. Figure 11-8 shows my iron with the (fully cold) tip off.

Figure 11-8. *Iron with tip removed*

In the lab later I have a couple of practice soldering exercises that will give you a chance to solder, remove, and refine your technique a bit. I highly recommend doing them a few times as they will give you the chance to refine your skills a little before you tackle making your first circuit board using the protoboards. Once you have the hang of it, soldering will be like Ohm's law, just another part of the process that you are comfortable with and ready to use. This is important, because it's almost time to make your first circuit board!

Semi-permanent

Circuit boards are EVERYWHERE in our modern life and for good reason; light, easy to make, and reliable, the printed circuit board, or PCB, is the standard means for permanently wiring up devices that have multiple components and need to be held together permanently. They are relatively rugged, enduring in harsh temperatures and tight spaces, and providing a reliable surface to permanently connect things together. It is that word, permanent, that makes PCBs the final step in building a smart device from prototype to "ready to go." That's because unlike our breadboard, and even the solderable breadboard or protoboard we will use for this first circuit board, the real, fully manufactured PCB is 100% fixed. What's there is there, and unless you have planned for expansion or changes, they are not easily or reliably possible. Figure 11-9 shows a few PCB examples from my own collection of PCBs.

Figure 11-9. *Some PCBs I have designed*

Instead of leaping directly to a fully manufactured PCB, there is a nice interim which is to essentially make your own using solderable breadboards. It is because of the permanence and what it means that I have opted to even take this path with you to build what is essentially another prototype. This "middle ground" lets you validate your prototype with solid connections that won't accidentally get removed through use, and to make sure that nothing in your design is wrong before it's all made up of permanent connections. This will let you test your device in a more stand-alone way as the last step before going to a full PCB, which we will in the next chapter.

In fact, this is often the stopping point for many devices that you might make for your own use. The reality is that once it has solid connections, and the ability to be put into a more rugged container such as an electrical box or even something you may have 3D printed, the reality is that you have made a permanent device. A full PCB isn't a requirement of *functionality*, it is a convenience ultimately, and something that makes mass replication possible at all really, but isn't strictly required for a device to be considered "field ready" as it were. The protoboard or solderable breadboard is a more than functional means of making something work for a prototype or even a few devices that you are using to validate concepts without the inconvenience of the fragile breadboard. These solderable boards are an effective platform in their own right for this type of prototype exercise and you may only wish to move on to a full PCB when you get to the point of mass replication.

The best part of the protoboard? It works EXACTLY like a breadboard, but with solder. This means you can almost literally lift your circuits and devices off a breadboard and put them onto a protoboard (with some modifications of course, depending on your protoboard). This is exceptionally handy since as I said before, it means you don't have to reinterpret your wiring diagrams and layouts. For example, Figure 11-10 is a simple circuit that you will build, side by side with its breadboarded counterpart. On the surface, they are identical, which means that translating is pretty easy.

Figure 11-10. *Side-by-side of protoboard and breadboard for the same circuit*

For something more complex, or just bulkier, you may find it easier to break parts up into smaller boards. Protoboards come in so many possible sizes that this is also relatively easy to accomplish by selecting the right size protoboard. For example, you might choose to put the sensor on a small board along with any resistors or other small components that need to connect to support the sensor. Then you can connect that via a wire to the board with the MCU on it to conserve some space on that board for connecting devices. Our multi-sensor I2C chip, for example, would be good to mount on its own board with connections to the MCU via the surface pads. This would also make it more "portable" if you decided to swap MCUs, for example.

The nicest element of using the protoboard for your first PCB is undoubtedly that while it is permanently connected up, it can be removed. You can heat up the solder to liquid again and remove the component and move it around or change it all together. This semi-permanence is really important because once you move beyond the prototype to a full PCB, you are now bound by the board. I and many I know have had to replace entire boards, make very ugly patch jobs, or simply start again because of a design flaw with a PCB. Prototyping on the solderable just gives you one more way to make sure it's all right before you take the leap into the PCB itself.

There are many types of solderable prototyping boards available for your prototypes. I have chosen to use a solderable protoboard for the purposes of the book; however, there are other options such as stripboard where the points on the board are connected in strips (thus the name). There are also solderable breadboards that look exactly like your prototype breadboard, with the same labels and colors even, and having the same types of connections. All of these and more exist and vary widely in cost, but the basic solderable breadboard is a good option for simple prototypes, as it is so inexpensive as to be almost disposable. Let's take a closer look at the solderable breadboard and talk about the ways you can turn that blank canvas into a functional, semi-permanent circuit board. Figure 11-11 is a close-up of one of the larger solderable breadboards I have. There are two types of connection points or "pads" on the board: the "through hole" pad and the edge pads, which are surface pads only. Through hole mounts are the standard for connecting devices to a breadboard. You will also find these on your permanent circuit board in the next chapter as they form the basis of all PCB connections. The "pins" from the device (LED, sensor, component, even the MCU) poke through the breadboard, and can be soldered to make the connection permanent (they can be removed, but for our intent they are "permanent").

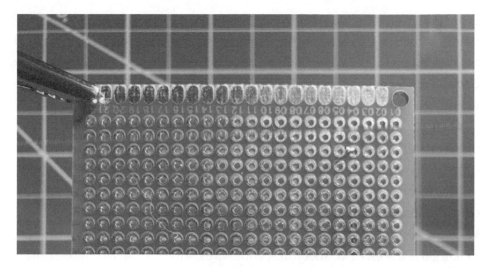

Figure 11-11. *Close-up of solderable breadboard*

The surface pads are a nice way to connect external things like our battery packs from previous chapters to the board or even other boards to one another. This particular protoboard is "two sided"; it means that the metal on the "top" and "bottom" of the board does not connect through the board. This is important because of two reasons: this gives you "layers" and is incredibly important when you get to the PCB world in the next chapter (through holes go through layers!), and it means you can make your circuits on the top and the bottom and they will be separate. This in effect means you have a two-layer circuit board, which is great for flexibility, but something to be aware of because you could inadvertently connect the wrong thing, or not make a connection you thought you had. Also, a connection that passes through the hole, such as the pin on a device, definitely will connect the top and bottom layer since the solder will flow into the space and make the connection. This means you can connect to the top and bottom of a device going through the holes on the board.

This concept of layers is something that we will cover in much more depth in the next chapter, but for now, the most important thing to understand is that when connections between parts must cross, they need to be on a separate layer. You have two to work with and so you can

379

probably make some pretty complex circuits, but you will eventually hit a roadblock where two is just not enough layers. It is at that point that you will need to get into multi-layer boards. Again, we will talk about that in more depth later, and the examples for the lab are steered clear of anything that would need more than two layers. If your prototype is complex, however, this might lead to you needing to break out sections of the overall device onto separate protoboards and is just something to be aware of as you start translating your wiring diagrams into the 3D space of the circuit board.

So, with the protoboard, because the pads are all independent and not connected internally, how do you make this a completed circuit board? Well, the generally accepted, if somewhat "ugly," way to do it is just by making the traces, or connections, with wires, little cut-offs from resistors, very small gauge wire (like speaker wire), or any other relatively small metallic connector like on a breadboard. You may be tempted (as I was!) to try and make them with solder at first, but they will be VERY difficult to get right, and more likely you melt down the protoboard in the process (see Figure 11-13 for an example). It looks ugly with lots of wires looping everywhere, but the power flows and that's what counts. Figure 11-12 shows a completed circuit with the soldered connections. It's ugly but the circuit works, and it is much more robust than the one on the breadboard.

Figure 11-12. *Completed (if ugly) circuit. The back-side solder connections on the left and front-side connections on the right*

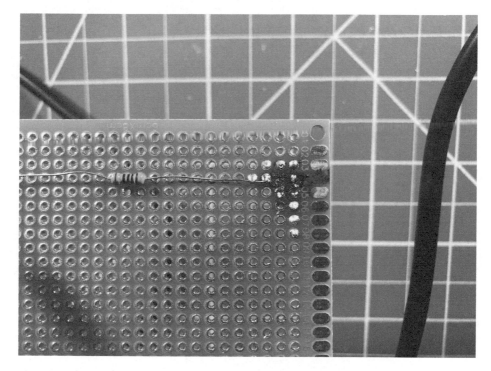

Figure 11-13. *Melted out perfboard from solder trace attempt*

I am going to give you a walkthrough of soldering up your first circuit, using a simple LED and battery pack just like we did in the first build lab. Now though, you do not need to worry about moving it around and having an LED disconnect or pulling out the wires. As much as it may not seem like it at first, you can actually build some really complex circuits on a protoboard and create some really cool layouts. This interim step is really important for understanding things like routing and layers and can really help you determine how hard or simple your final PCB will be.

An important note on your protoboard to be aware of: those pins sticking through the board? They are conductive, as is (at least minimally) most surfaces you will set it down on. Use caution with your protoboard when you set it down, and for real safety, use standoffs as seen in Figure 11-14 to make sure that nothing touches something it should not!

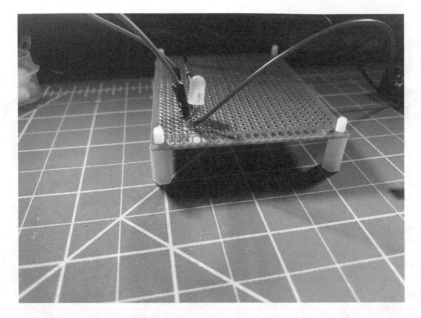

Figure 1-14. *Standoffs on protoboard*

So, as you can see from this, back to my original point about the circuit board you make from a protoboard vs. a PCB that is fully manufactured, there is no real way you are going to mass-produce this. Making all the traces out of solder is messy, and error prone, and frankly just a lot of work. That's what the PCB itself is for, and why I cover it in the next chapter. You will probably want to make one eventually, if for no other reason than you want more than one or two of the same devices. In the prototype phase though, the handmade circuit will provide you with a platform that is just permanent enough with the stability of solid connections to validate your idea.

Your First Circuit Board Lab

LET'S BUILD IT – HELLO WORLD – CIRCUIT BOARD EDITION!

We are going to revisit the basic LED circuit we built in the first section, and I will walk you through building out that most time-honored tradition of "Hello World" by lighting an LED on a semi-permanent protoboard circuit.

Figure 11-15. *The completed circuit with LED lit*

To make the circuit seen in Figure 11-15, you need the parts you can see in Figure 11-16:

- Protoboard (I used a big one, but any size is fine; there are not enough connections here to worry about pin counts or spacing.)

- 68ohm resistor minimum – I have used a 100ohm resistor here.

- LED (I used yellow because I hadn't yet in the book, but any color is fine)

- One MM wire (left out of the picture – remember this can be any connector; I have used the MM wire for convenience)

- 3V battery pack (two AA pack)

- Soldering kit

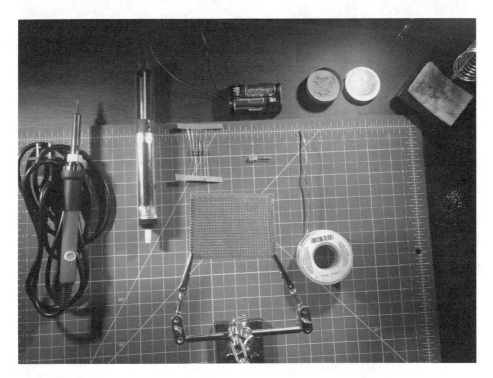

Figure 11-16. *Picture of basic circuit parts*

To assemble the hardware circuit, there are a couple of tips I want to give you. As a novice, the temptation is to try and "rig up" the whole circuit first and then solder it all at once. You CAN do this, BUT it often ends in frustration because gravity is annoying, and pins fall out of their hole and you end up faffing about to get everything in place. The less frustrating way is to solder the pieces on one at a time, get them attached to the board (a single pin will do this) and THEN worry about the connections. I have used this method (minus a couple of opportunities to do things at the same time) in this walkthrough. It is not the ONLY way, and maybe not even the BEST way, but it does avoid a lot of "dang it, where did that PIN go!?"

Right, so let's build this out!

1) Start by plugging in your iron and setting it to the recommended temp, and then while it heats up, putting your protoboard in your helping hands, if you have them – if not, you can set the board down after you put the pins through the holes, and gravity becomes an ally holding the board to the element. See Figure 11-17 for how this looks.

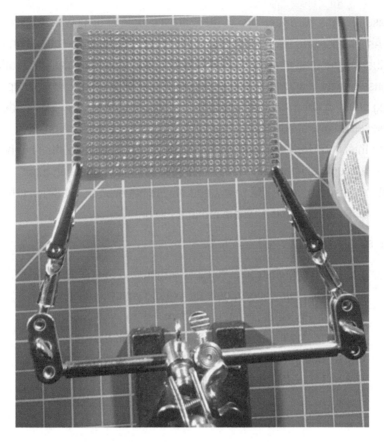

Figure 11-17. *Board in hands ready to go*

2)   We will start by putting the LED and resistor through the holes
      to position them for soldering (make sure to check the anode
      side of your LED – you can flip it around later, but it is more
      work with solder!). You can do them one at a time if you prefer,
      but because we can bend the pins to hold them, doing them
      both is a little timesaver. Figure 11-18 shows both elements in
      place through their respective holes – pins bent to hold them in
      place.

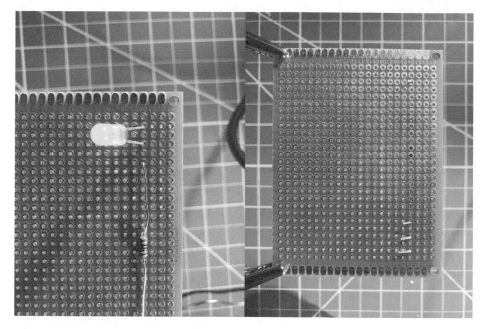

Figure 11-18. *The left is the "front" of the board, and the right shows the pins bent through the "back" to hold the elements for soldering*

3) Next we simply solder those four connections. Figure 11-19
    shows the finished product, and just remember that a little
    solder will make a nice connection. Putting on too much will
    make a blob on the other side of your board you have to clean
    up later.

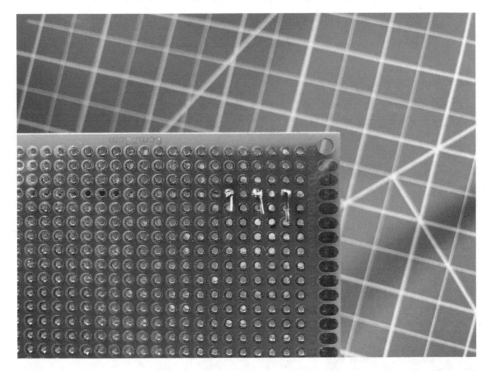

Figure 11-19. *pins folded down and soldered in place*

4)   Now that those connections are set, clean your iron and put it in
     the stand, and then put the wires from the battery box through
     their holes. I stripped off some extra on the wire to make this
     easier and would recommend for you to do the same. Tip: Wrap
     the wires around the pins for a better hold before you solder!
     Make sure the black wire is on the resistor end, and the red is
     on the LED end as in Figure 11-20.

Figure 11-20. *Leads from the battery case passing through the
breadboard*

5)   As before, you will solder the wire into its respective hole, and
     then put a bit of solder on the wire and pin from the LED and
     resistor. Figure 11-21 shows the soldered connection of the
     black wire in detail so you can see what the connections should
     look like in place.

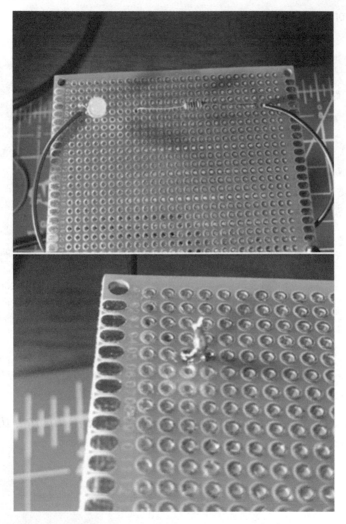

Figure 11-21. *The top shows the "front view" and the bottom is the
detail of the completed black wire to resistor connection*

6) Clean and park your iron in the stand, and you only have one last connection! Take the MM wire, which will form the last connection between the resistor and LED, and put the pins through holes next to the respective pins you want to connect, as in Figure 11-22. Tip: Bend the pins from the LED and resistor to be close to the MM wire pins, for easier connecting.

Figure 11-22. *Front view of MM wire in place*

7) As before, solder the pins to their hole first, and then make a solder connection between the resistor and one pin, and LED and the other respectively. You can see the finished (if slightly ugly) connections in Figures 11-23 and 11-24.

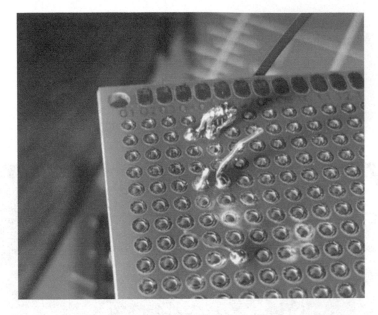

Figure 11-23. MM wire pin soldered to board near LED pin

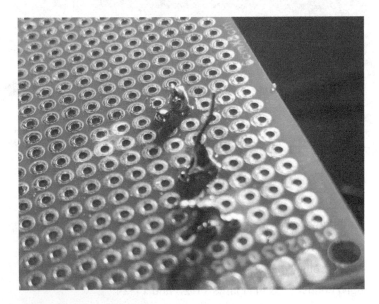

Figure 11-24. Both MM pins through and soldered to LED and resistor, respectively

8) One last thing to do, but first park your iron back in its stand, and unplug it for safety!! If you have some standoffs, you should put one in each of the four corner holes. While this is not explicitly required, and the voltages so low that you are unlikely to damage anything, it is safer for your circuit. If you have a metal workbench, you for sure need this! You can see what this looks like in Figure 11-25. It just holds the connections above the "ground" so that they don't touch and potentially short out.

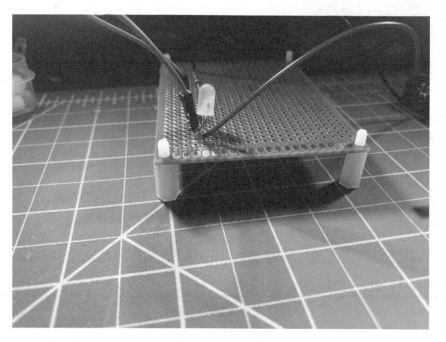

Figure 11-25. Standoffs in place to support the protoboard

Last step is to put the batteries in the box, and the LED should come on like in Figure 11-26. Congratulations, you have made your first "permanent" circuit. You can pick it up, move it, turn it over, and aside from dropping or throwing it, you should have nice solid connections that will stay put.

Figure 11-26. HELLO WORLD!

Note   If your LED did not light, there are three likely culprits:

1. Did you connect the battery pack wires the right way? If not, you can heat the solder and pull them off and change them around.

2. Pull the LED off and spin it around by heating the solder and pulling the LED out of the holes one at a time, back and forth to work it out.

3. Check that your solder connections are sound and not shorted.

Where to Next?

Well, this was a tough one for me too as I worked on the book and thought through your path as a learner. We started with the basics, some history, and then the electronics and components that make circuits work. We went on to the software side and worked through some of the parts of the smart system and highlighted some easy ways to get you started on the path to building with prototypes. Now we've come here to the point where you have a semi-permanent prototype that you can repeat a few times, validate your idea, and maybe move on. The moving on part is the question, and I leave it to you as the reader to decide what makes sense.

Maybe you want to stay at this point a while and start building and practicing and finding other resources to grow your general skills? Not a bad idea, and certainly there is no reason you have to go further than this to just build some things for your own use or friends, or indeed even small-scale commercial applications. However, the last chapter will walk through the last step in the maker's journey and take you down the road of the PCB. This topic is worthy of entire books on its own, but like the rest of this book I have kept it direct and approachable for you to get started and then grow beyond what I've given you here. The PCB is the final step in this journey, because once you have the PCB printed and done, it is fixed that way forever. Permanence and its unexpected consequences can often trip you up, and so having an idea of what to expect, how to handle it, and what a good PCB design looks like is important.

My recommendation, if I may, is to read it and then maybe put it on the shelf and get more builds going, experiment, and most of all learn more! Then when you are ready, the words will still be here, and you can come back and get going on to the world of PCBs and all that it can entail! Be warned though, PCBs can be addictive and designing them is a fun and interesting puzzle every time. That's before we even get into hyper custom boards, blinky lights, and the world of badge life.

CHAPTER 12

Your First Good PCB

Figure 12-1 shows one of my favorite PCB designs that I am fortunate to have (the one shaped like a skull). I did not make this design, but it is such a powerful example of the platform being designed for the purpose that I could not resist including it. Next to it is a circuit board that I designed myself, which as you can see is much simpler and more geometric, but it also illustrates the idea that the form fits the function. I am very proud of my design as well, and it served the thing I wanted it to do very well. My point in showing these two examples is to call out the difference between them which beyond their outward appearance, is nothing. Yes of course they clearly differ in size, shape, intended purpose, and so on, but in reality, they are the same: a collection of connection points for attaching the various components, traces to connect them together, and a solid and most importantly PERMANENT platform that means they can move around. In fact, the wiring diagram for a full PCB and for the previous circuit board and even the prototype on a breadboard is 100% the same. The difference is that this one can move without falling apart, and you can make hundreds or even thousands exactly the same.

© Christopher Harrold 2020
C. Harrold, *Practical Smart Device Design and Construction*,
https://doi.org/10.1007/978-1-4842-5614-5_12

Figure 12-1. Top Image: The front of my Garden Monitor PCB on the left and the Flying Badgers DC26 Badge on the right. In the bottom image is the back of each

When Bits of Resistor Just Aren't Good Enough

In the last chapter, I said that you could stop at the circuit board phase and not progress, and that is absolutely a true statement. In fact, both of these could have been made that way, but when you think about the skull shaped PCB, which is actually a fully working (when assembled) quadcopter, there is no way that would work with solder and bits alone. Just the weight would be a nightmare, never mind the need to have it be perfectly balanced! (In fact, when I finally get around to assembling mine, I will be VERY diligent about the soldiering for weight and balance reasons.) This is a prime example of where a PCB isn't just a nice to have, but a requirement for functionality. My board also would not have really worked as a solder-trace board because it was going to be subjected to heat and cold and had to be in a pretty tight box and I wanted it to be more rigid than a solder-trace board would be.

In the end, the PCB is about two basic things: consistency and rigidity. The printed circuit boards in Figure 12-1 will be the same no matter how many copies get made, because they are built using a long-established manufacturing process that lays down the pattern the same way over and over. This ensures that no matter how many you pump out of the process, they are all the same which, in the case of something like the two boards pictured, is REALLY important. That's because, as you can see, there are open spots on the boards for devices and components. Imagine trying to add in those things if the board was not the same down to the 100ths of a mm, you can't, and you'll see a couple of my board fails later that illustrate this.

The second bit, rigidity, is equally important because, again, imagine if the quadcopter wasn't a nice, rigid platform. Not going to fly very well with a lot of flex and movement, and the connections would be prone to detaching. Less than ideal for an object with high torques that is in flight, and probably results in putting our collective eyes out. Rigidity is important as well for the ability to mount the board into enclosures, such as what I wanted to do with my board. It was designed to fit into the enclosure with very little tolerance, and to be permanently mounted there. Something with too much flex could sag or bend in the enclosure and cause shorts or disconnections. Now that's not to say that PCBs are completely immune to the elements, in fact I had to straighten the skull PCB because it was in my hot metal mailbox on the hottest day of the summer. It had noticeably sagged and warped in the heat, and before it cooled off all the way I was able to manipulate it back to straight. This isn't a common thing of course, but something to know that even though they are permanent, they aren't indestructible!

On Closer Inspection

Let me take you on a guided tour of a PCB and show you the key features and components that make them up. Figure 12-2 shows a simple diagram of a two-layer PCB and the basic parts that make up those layers.

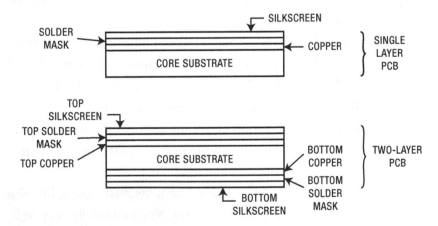

Figure 12-2. PCB cut-away view

What each layer does:

- Solder Mask Layer(s) – This is essentially a protective coating that keeps the heat of the solder from melting the substrate below and provides a measure of protection to the copper trace layer.

- Copper layer(o)   This is the actual copper that makes the "traces" or wires embedded into the board. When the board is printed, the copper is only applied to the board where you want it to form the connections you need, similar to a silk-screening process.

- Substrate layer(s) – In a two-layer board there is only one layer of substrate, and it is what gives the board its rigidity and form. To make a three- or even four-layer board, you simply add additional substrate and copper layers.

- Silkscreen layer – This is where your labels, cool pictures, inside jokes, and other decoration go. You can literally silkscreen just about anything onto a PCB in a two-color format (the board is one color and the screen is another, usually white although more and more multi-color screening options have popped up from providers).

The layers themselves are incredibly thin, but you don't need much to make the connections unless you are dealing with incredibly large loads. In that case you would expand the width of the connection by using wider copper traces within the connection layer (something you will see later in this chapter). There are two other key parts of the PCB that you will use and are important to understand, and those are the pads and through-holes. Pads are the copper on the top and bottom of the board that are exposed with no solder masking. That's because they are meant to have solder on them to connect the component that belongs on the pad or in that hole. You can have surface mount pads, which, exactly like they sound, are just exposed metal plates on the surface of the PCB and allow you to solder in surface mount components or external connections like wires. These are very useful for providing lighter and smaller components (surface mount components tend to be smaller than through hole in most cases) and also for providing possible expansion options for the future.

Through holes are just like they sound, holes drilled through the PCB. They pass through all layers of the PCB and are meant for standard through hole components, like the ones on your breadboard prototypes. The pad that is around the hole provides extra connectivity to the joint by ensuring that the solder touches enough copper and the component to make a good connection. There is no right or wrong to the components you use (through hole or surface mount), rather they are determined by lots of factors like form factors, weight, size, layout of the board itself, and so on. You will often find a mix of components on a single board due to what makes sense for the board itself, and various design constraints. One other type of through hole is the one with no copper pad. This is generally meant for things like mounting screws or standoffs to pass through the board and secure it to another surface (like an enclosure). There are several sizes for mounting screws, and you can simply use the correct size of hole on your PCB design, but connective through holes are all generally of a standard size. Figure 12-3 shows the various types of PCB connection options (pads and through holes).

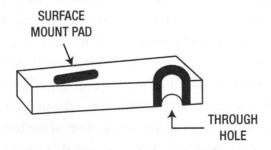

Figure 12-3. *Pad and through hole close-ups*

So now that you know the parts, how do you actually design one of these yourself? There are three steps to designing a good PCB, and you will have to go through all three to get the result you want:

1) You should draw out your circuit diagram and make sure you know all your connections and what goes to what, and what the different components on the board are going to be. You do not need to do this in a design tool, although it can be helpful. I generally work through my prototype on a breadboard, and then on a piece of regular sketch paper draw out the diagram. This step is worth doing because it can also help you identify errors in advance, something that when you move to PCBs can create a major headache!

2) You need to use a tool to actually draw the design and layout of the PCB itself. Thankfully there are some really easy to use and simple tools available for free to do this, and we will look at an example in this chapter. There are MANY tools that can perform this function, so it would be too much to put them all in a single chapter, but there are a couple that stand out for their simplicity and approachability for someone just getting started.

3) Lastly of course, you need to actually get the boards made. This last bit used to be difficult and expensive, and even today there are many hobbyists who make their own PCBs using chemical etching in their kitchens, but now there are several places you can design, validate, and order your boards all in one place, for relatively little money. This can also include full sourcing and assembly of the parts of the board, which means less soldering for you!

Taking this step by step, the first step takes us back to our regular wiring diagrams we talked about way back in the beginning chapters. This process is fundamental to making in all its forms and smart devices are no exception. Good wiring diagrams will help you identify the way things connect up and how the paths between connections will work. They will also help you start identifying where your layers need to be, because just like with your solder boards from the last chapter, the lines can cross on the drawing, but not in real life! You will need to understand the number of "crossovers" as that will help you in determining how many layers there need to be in your PCB. In reality, PCBs can be many layers thick, although the goal of generally accepted "good" design is to use the lowest number. This keeps the board thinner, uses less materials in the manufacturing process, and ultimately keeps the cost down for you.

The second step is really about deciding the physical size, shape, and orientation of the components and then drawing in the connections between them. I am not going to go deeply into the various design tools, as there are many other better resources for that online, and with the ease and simplicity of upgrading cloud-based software, the chance that my guidance is out of date too quickly is very high. I will talk through the basics though, and some tips for using them so that you can design with confidence. Laying out the components and the traces is really just a jigsaw puzzle of parts, and the orientations are all relative so there is generally no right or wrong way for them to fit. This freedom makes the layout part both interesting and challenging because you can find yourself in a spot where parts don't fit like you wanted and you have to reorient. Thankfully this is all virtual still, so you can simply delete and redraw lines until it all fits like you wanted.

The last step is pretty much just a couple of button clicks and a payment method with modern PCB manufacturing partners. The hard work done, you can sit back and wait for your board(s) to arrive and then get to soldering on components and testing and then using your PCB for many years to come. I have generally designed my PCBs using EasyEDA, and then just passed the order through to JLC which is their manufacturing partner. They have always been timely, the boards are good quality, and a 5 pack of a reasonably sized board (a few inches per side) generally run well south of $100 (even south of $50 for smaller and less complex designs). Another option is to use something like EasyEDA to do the design and layout and then export the files to give to any manufacturer. The standard output from the design tool that manufacturers expect is called a Gerber file (this is just a file type, like a word doc, but for PCB layouts) and you can upload that to any number of manufacturing outfits and order your designs. PCBWay is another company that specializes in custom PCB work and has a number of options for prototypes and small batches. I know several makers who use them and have been happy with them as well. In the end, if you are getting the board you want, it really is just what you feel confident using, no right or wrong!

Your First Traces

Because I genuinely do not want you to spend money on a worthless PCB for a lab, I am instead going to show you some basics of using one of the most popular design tools, EasyEDA, so you can translate this into your design in the future. I have chosen to do this in EasyEDA for two reasons: it is free and I find it to be really approachable for people just starting with PCBs. There are many other great tools, but I find many of them have really steep learning curves because they offer some really advanced features, or they are full-blown design CAD programs that also do PCBs. EasyEDA isn't probably the BEST design tool in those terms, but it works, is simple, and lives up to the name on the tin. The real power in using a tool like EasyEDA is just allowing you to visualize the design and layout of the PCB as you draw so you can modify it before you get it printed. Much better to have to delete a few lines on the screen than have a PCB that isn't wired up correctly. Figure 12-4 shows a PCB designed in EasyEDA from my own collection.

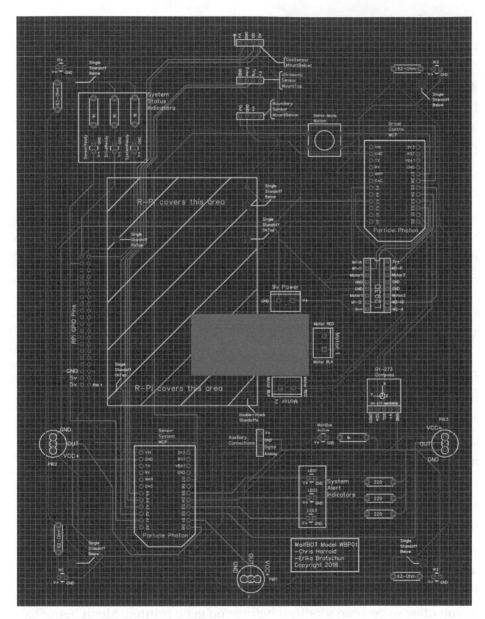

Figure 12-4. *Complex EasyEDA Design example*

For this simple walk through, I am just going to show you how to add traces, change the sizes, layers, and drop in a couple of components (an MCP3008 chip and an LED in this case). This will help you figure out the things that I kind of stumbled around with as I got started so that you can hopefully get to the design work without as much struggle! I am going to make the assumption that you signed up for your free account and ran through the basic tutorial to familiarize yourself with the interface. If you did not, you should, because the developers of the tool have obviously put a lot of work into usability and it is a nice simple walkthrough of the basics. For this little walkthrough, you can just create a default PCB layout of the default size. You can always modify the outline later for doing different shapes and indeed very complex designs. Once you have your basic board up you can start here to go through the steps.

Add a Component to Your Board

You are going to add a couple of components to your board, so you have something to connect! This is very easy to do, by following the steps here:

1) Right-click anywhere in the designer screen, and select "Place Component..." as in Figure 12-5.

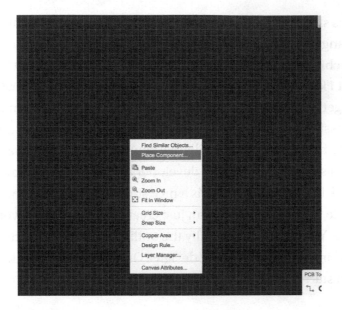

Figure 12-5. *Place component prompt*

2)   In the search field, type in "MCP3008" and click
     Search as you see in Figure 12-6.

Figure 12-6. *Search field for MCP3008*

3)   From the list, you can select the default MCP3008
     library for a through hole MCP3008. THIS IS AN
     IMPORTANT PART. I goofed this up a few times in
     my first designs and did not pay close attention and

chose the wrong one originally which will result in
your board not being right. The parts that have the
long lines going away from them are surface mount.
Make sure you choose one with holes as you can see
in Figure 12-7.

Figure 12-7.   *Through hole MCP3008 stencil*

4) Click "Place" and the search will close and you will
    be dragging the part with your mouse now. Put it
    somewhere inside the board outline by clicking on
    it, and then hit "Escape" on your keyboard to get rid
    of the part. Figure 12-8 shows the part on the layout.

Figure 12-8. *Placing the MCP3008*

5)   Repeat Steps 1 and 2 and change the search term
     to "LED" – again ensure you choose a through hole
     mount style as in Figure 12-9 (for this exercise the
     type really doesn't matter, but do note there are a
     LOT of types of LED, so make sure you choose the
     one that matches your design and component when
     you do this for a real project!).

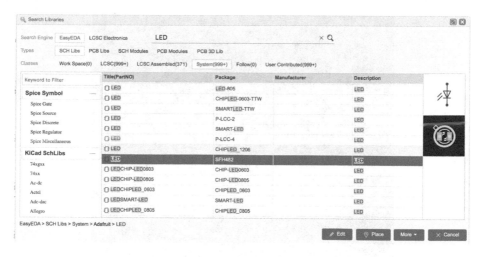

Figure 12-9. *Choose an LED*

6) You can see in the images I chose one with a nice
    silkscreen as part of it – I like having the extra visuals
    to go with my designs – simply click "Place" and
    then click on the canvas to drop one in as before.
    Figure 12-10 shows the LED and MCP3008 placed
    on the board.

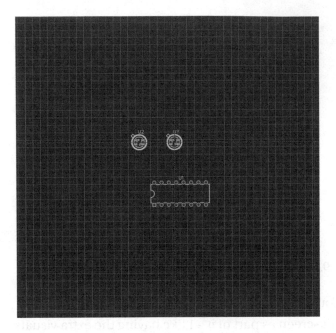

Figure 12-10. Components placed on the board

Now clearly these two components don't have much to do with one
another – you wouldn't generally connect an LED to an MCP3008 since
that's not what the chip is for, but these two components have the important
thing we need – connection points – and show you what to expect from
the search functionality and how to place components. One other thing to
note is that EasyEDA has a HUGE library of user contributed parts. I have
found a great many of needed components (MCUs in particular) in the user
contribution section. You can change the library EasyEDA uses by clicking
on the "User Contributed" link in the search box, just below the search field.
There are usually lots of them, and often they have nicer silkscreen visuals
than the built-in ones, but that's a personal preference thing.

Now that you have some components, you need to connect them
together so that the electricity will flow! We need to add some traces, and
we need them to be on the correct layer. As a general rule, I try (repeat,
TRY) to make my board designs with a power, ground, and "signal" layer.

This means that I can route power and ground out of the way of signal. If my board is very simple then maybe I only really need one layer, but generally you will find you probably need two at minimum. In EasyEDA the layer tool is super easy to use and understand.

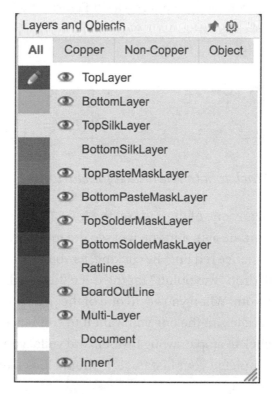

Figure 12-11. EasyEDA Layer tool

When you hover over the layer toolbox it will pop out to show you all the layers you have. You can rename them, hide them, and most importantly, select the layer you are "drawing" on. This will affect the tool and determine what it is you are actually drawing, silk screen, or traces or even the edge of the board itself. By default, the top layer is selected (noted by the little Pencil tip in the box), so I will have you draw your first trace there.

Add Your First Traces

1) From the PCB Tools toolbox click the "Track" icon (upper most left icon) – this is the "line" tool and will draw your copper traces – as in Figure 12-12.

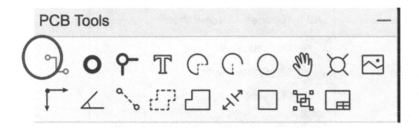

Figure 12-12. *Track tool (circle added for clarity)*

2) Click on any one of the pads on the MCP3008 on your board design, and you will see the tool starts drawing a nice red line. By clicking, as you move you will drop "waypoints" for the trace that it will extend from. When you get to one of the pads on the LED, click on the one you want it to connect to. Right-click to stop drawing further, and voila, you have completed your first trace. It should look like Figure 12-13.

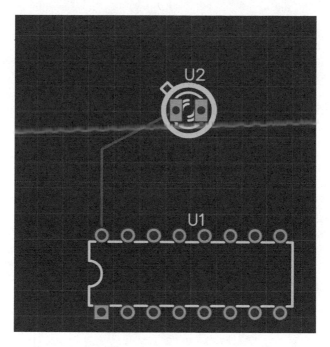

Figure 12-13. *Your first trace*

3) Now click on the "Bottom Layer" in the layer toolbox
    as in Figure 12-14.

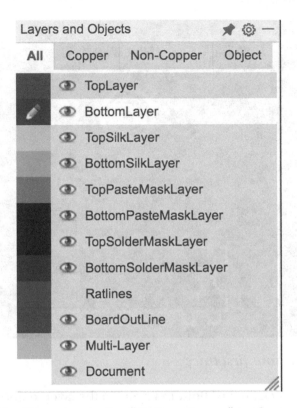

Figure 12-14. *Changing to the "Bottom Layer" in the toolbox*

4) Repeat the steps to draw a second line from the LED
    to another pad on the MCP3008 – this could be your
    "ground" trace from the LED to the ground out on
    the chip – you will notice it draws in a blue color to
    indicate it is on a different level as in Figure 12-15.

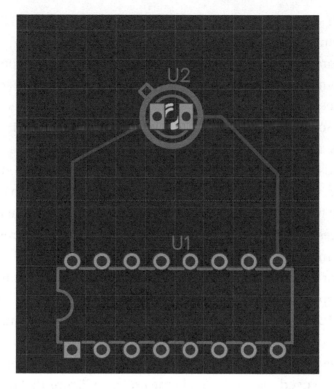

Figure 12-15. *Your Bottom Layer trace*

You will see that the tool tries to build relatively squared off lines with 45-degree angles to maintain a more consistent line layout. This will let you add more lines in parallel as you add more connections. Something to note about those connections is that they can be really close together – the tolerance is very tight, which allows you to add connections in close proximity. Something else to note about your traces, as I mentioned earlier, they can be made larger (thicker if you will) to handle larger current loads. This could be especially important in your ground plane, for example, where you may have a lot of devices dumping into a shared ground and want to ensure good conduction or heat management. Smaller copper traces may not allow as much current through (higher resistance) and so you may want to increase their size to ensure you have lower resistance of the path itself. This is very easy to do, by clicking on a trace, and in the upper right corner of the Properties box is a "Width" option. See Figure 12-16. The default size is 0.254 mm which is fairly small but enough for the small currents in question for LEDs and smaller MCUs. As discussed earlier, you can put in pretty much ANY size here that you need. For example, I used a size of 1 mm in the image in Figure 12-17.

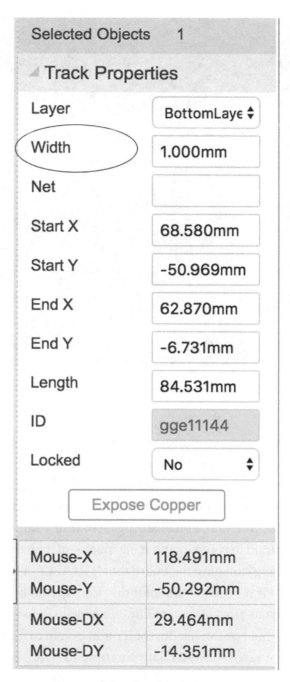

Figure 12-16. *Width option*

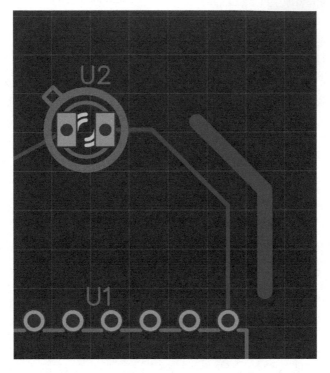

Figure 12-17. *1 mm Trace next to the one you drew earlier for comparison*

As almost trivially simple as it seems, that's pretty much it for the design phase. Drop in your components and arrange them on the board, connect the points that need connecting, and repeat! The challenges all come in the form of routing your connections, so they do not cross one another, making it all fit into the size you want, and ensuring all of your components fit on the board. Don't be afraid to zoom in and really pack stuff together, but a word of caution. Soldering stuff onto the board that is REALLY tight is also REALLY difficult because it is hard to get the soldering iron tip into tight spots. Where possible I try to make sure I leave a millimeter or so in between components at a minimum so that I can sneak the solder and iron in to make the connection. Figure 12-18 shows a relatively complex board I designed for a robotics platform, and you can see all the various component spots.

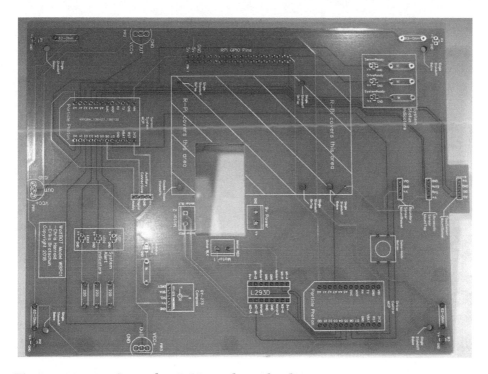

Figure 12-18. *Complex PCB with multiple components*

A Note on PCB Fails

You will make a PCB mistake, and it is OK. Even some of the truly gifted makers such as the ones I show in the later gallery have posted about mistakes, or errors in layouts. Manufacturing errors as well can impact your design, and you may find that things just do not work the way you laid them out. Sometimes you can recover from it with additional parts and bypasses. The board I showed from the robotics platform has an error that meant the power rail to all the outside sensors is the wrong voltage. Didn't catch it in design phase and had to correct it with some "after-market" add-ons as you can see in Figure 12-19 of the finished product. It works, but it is obviously significantly less elegant than I intended (the extra solderable circuit board in the middle there with the random resistor hanging off it? That should not be there...).

Figure 12-19. *"Fixed" robotics platform*

My point in illustrating this is, aside from letting you know you are not alone, is to let you know that many errors like this can be fixed. Traces can be shorted out with a drill and a little care and patience, meaning that connection is now broken, and can be rerouted with some clever use of wire and solder. Components can be removed from a board and replaced if need be (heat them up and pull them off and replace with the right thing). You can even get really creative and leave "open" pins for later add-ons or changes as I did. Ultimately you may come across something that you've done in error that you just cannot fix. If that is the case, you simply have some nice coasters and conversation pieces as I do in Figure 12-20, and you redesign and re-order. It can cost some extra money and time, but there is always this last option to get what you needed. By the way, the reason these are bad is I used the wrong stencil in EasyEDA for the MCU – when I got them, the one I was using didn't fit in the holes. It was crushing to say the least, but we learn from mistakes!

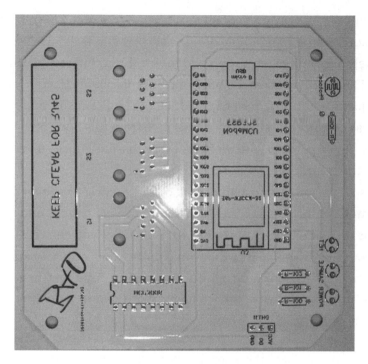

Figure 12-20. *"Bad" PCBs for my garden project, aka "coasters"*

Getting Fancy

In the end, once you have some mastery of PCB design down, the allure of building out amazing new designs and increasingly complex devices becomes a siren song that is irresistible. Before I end this book, I wanted to take you down one more road that I am sure many will find fascinating. Smart devices are meant to enrich and improve our lives, and surely even the basic projects we have built can be applied in a variety of simple ways to do so, but what about building devices for the sake of building them? What happens when tech and art cross paths? I find that the most illustrative answer to that takes the form of the parallel and overlapping disciplines of the Badgelife community and the maker community. I have

423

been privileged to meet and converse with many in both communities and see some of their incredible designs and creations. I have also spent a moderately silly sum of money on badges for things I haven't even gone to (like the Defcon26 badge at the beginning of this chapter). I did it because they are just plain funny, or nerdy, or cool, or represent something to the maker that I support. My last bit of guidance from this book is to let your creativity have a place in your work and designs, and make sure you think about all the elements of the form, and not just the function!

And so, I decided to close this book with a small selection of things that this talented community has created (that I have been lucky enough to get my hands on!), and that, with your newfound skills, you can create too. There is nothing in this gallery that you cannot build with the skills you have learned in this book, and a little imagination. That may be the most empowering thing about the smart device world; there is no limit to your creations and the power they have.

Figure 12-21. *"Bomberman" badge add-on by Twinkle Twinkie –*
note the surface mount LED components, and the use of the PCB itself
to provide diffusion for them. This is done by excluding the silkscreen
and mask layers from an area of the PCB

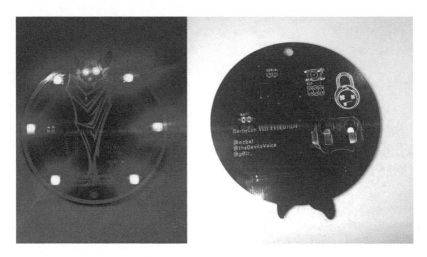

Figure 12-22. *The "Bat Badge" – a great example of a simple timer chip, LEDs, and a coin cell style battery to create some really nifty lighting effects. Badge design by The Devils Voice, MZ Bat, and P0lr*

Figure 12-23. *Another Twinkle Twinkie creation, the "Fat Pika" also uses surface mounts and PCB diffusion layers. This one does not have the components soldered in yet, so you can see the surface mount pads on the badge clearly*

Figure 12-24. *Last but not least, the "Chestoro" also by Twinkle Twinkie – another example of a great badge design using super-simple components (Timer chip, button, and LEDs)*

Index

A, B

AI-driven robotics, 141

Analog sensor, 148, 170–172

Analog to Digital
Converter (ADC), 149, 150

Arduino
board manager menu, 194
default sketch screen, 192
hardware/software, 191
install ESP32 board, 194, 195
libraries, 157, 158
machine setup, 191
NodeMCU, 190
preferences screen, 193

Arduino IDE
DHT11 library, 318
installation, 317
install button, 319
install support, 319
libraries, 317
pub-sub library, 320
Wi-Fi, 320

C

Capacitor
battery, 79
"downhill", 81

farads, 81
MOSFET motor controller
L298N, 84, 85
rate of discharge, 82
smoothing effect, 80

Capacitor test circuit, 129
assembling steps, 130
battery wires, 136
IC ravine, 131
LED, 134, 137
10,000 microfarad capacitor, 131
parts, 130
"–" rail, 133
resistor, 135
solar power, 129

cd smartdevicebook command, 211

cd temp command, 209

Circuit diagrams
adding resistor, 70
battery symbols, 69
close loop, 71
complex diagram, 68
LED, 71
symbols, 69

Circuits
basic circuit, 58
breadboard types, 63, 65
members, 58

© Christopher Harrold 2020
C. Harrold, *Practical Smart Device Design and Construction*,
https://doi.org/10.1007/978-1-4842-5614-5

Circuits (*cont.*)
   parallel circuit, 59, 61
   rules, 57
   series circuit, 59, 61
   series circuit broken, 62
   wire types, 66
Collector
   code, 313, 314
   DHT11, 293
   hardware circuit, 292
   LED, 294
   parts, 291, 311
   photoresistor, 293
   resistors, 295
Complex prototype, 360
Computer
   complex calculations, 4
   components, 5
   CPUs, 5
   EEPROM, 7
   magic device, 4
   MCUs, 6, 8, 9
   portable, 5
   RAM, 6
   ROM, 6, 7
   sensors/industrial control, 9–13
   usage of, 4
Connectors, 94
Consumer-grade sensors, 146

D

Dark themed dashboard, 352
Dashboard library, 328

Default dashboard, 349
delay() function, 201
Deploy button, 345
Deployment popup, 346
DHT11 wires
   MCU, 305
   pinout, 301
   power/ground, 303
Digital I/O, 169, 170
Digital sensor, 148
Digital systems, 141
Diode-based OR gate
   assembling steps, 122
   breadboard
      battery packs, 127
      button, 123, 124
      connecting rails, 126
      IC ravine, 125
      LED, 128
      resistor, 125
      wire connection, 124
   diagram, 121
   parts, 122
Diodes
   AN and OR gate, 89–91, 93
   definition, 85
   electronic components, 86
   forward voltage drop, 88
   LED, 87–89
   Schottky style, 87
   silicon-based PN diode, 86
DIY smart era
   hardware and software, 16
   MCU/Computer, 16

Minimum DIY lab (*see* Minimal lab)

Duplicate dashboard erratum, 348

E

Electrical Engineering (EE)
   analogy, 49
   circuit diagram (*see* Circuit diagrams)
   circuit (*see* Circuits)
   flow and resistance, 50
   forces, 49
   keys, 49
   Ohm's law, 50
   parameters, 52
   resistance
      components, 53
      electric flows, 53
      flow of, electricity, 57
      LED, 55
      Ω symbol, 53
      wiring diagram symbols, 54

Electrically Erasable Programmable ROM (EEPROM), 7

ESP32 analogue inputs, 315

ESP32 based build
   assembly
      GND pin, 267
      ground wire, 270
      LED, 272–277, 281
      MM wire, 269
      rail, 271

sensor on breadboard, 265, 266
sensor pegged high, 279
sensor signaling wire, GPIO 23, 277
VCC pin, 268
parts, 264
version, 263

F

Forward Voltage Drop, 88

G

General-purpose input/output (GPIO) pin, 77, 165
   callback, sensor pin, 261, 262
   conductive metal rod, 165
   MCU, 166
   power/ground pins, 166

git clone command, 211

GitHub repositories, 206

Good *vs.* bad solder joints, 368

Ground rails, 298

H

Hear sensor, 146

Home Network, 342
   configuration button, 342
   confirm settings, 344
   MQTT server IP, 343
   undeployed update, 345
   update button, 344

I

I2C bus
    ADC chip, 151
    functions, 152
    LCD displays, 152
    MCU circuit, 150
    multi-function sensors, 151
    single primary device, 151
Industrial Control, 9–13
Internet of Things (IoT)
    advantages, 38
    collecting data, 42
    connected world, 44
    future vision, 44
    hardware access, 43
    keys, 40
    output of, smart system, 40
    smart device, 39
    vector, 43

J, K

JSON file, 336
    configuration screen, 341
    import, 337, 338
    import flow, 339
    sensors, 340
    UI, 338

L

LED circuit
    front view, 390
    full view, 386

    HELLO WORLD!, 394
    lit, 383
    MM wire, 391
    parts, 384
    pin, 392
    soldering, 387
LED wires, 308, 309
Libraries
    Arduino IDE, 156
    code bits, 155
    Raspberry Pi, 156
    sensor, 155, 156
Light Emitting
        Diode (LED), 86, 87

M

Message count library, 333
Micro Controller Units (MCUs), 6
Minimal lab
    AA battery holders, 20
    breadboards, 20
    breadboard wires, 23
    DAOKI sound sensors, 30
    diode kit, 29
    Gikfun capacitive moisture
        sensor, 31
    home lab kit, 19
    LEDs, 21
    Light Dependent Resistors, 32
    MCU Kits, 18, 22
    10,000 Microfarad
        Capacitor, 24
    resistor kit, 21

Sensor Kits, 18

transistors, 28

voltage levels, 25

Wire kit, 26

wiring convenience, 27

software, 33, 34

mkdir temp command, 209

Moisture probe sensor, 311

MQTT Publishing
command, 316

N

Node MCU Circuit

Arduino IDE, 233–236

GPIO pin, connect, 231

ground pin, connect, 230

LED, 227

parts, 227, 229

power connector, 226

resistor connected, 232

NodeRED

canvas, 324

dashboard, 353

DHT11 temp, 354

File button, 335

flow, 322, 323

hamburger menu, 325

light sensor, 354

O

Ohm's law, 50, 51, 108

P, Q

Palette manager, 327

Parallel circuit, 103

assembling steps, 105

breadboard
resistor/LED, 105

second LED, 107

second resistor, 106

capacitor (*see* Capacitor test
circuit)

MCU pins, 108

Or gate (*see* Diode-based OR
gate)

parts, 104

transistor control (*see* Transistor
controlled circuit)

Photoresistor, 293, 295

Potentiometer, 170

Power rail, 299, 300

Printed circuit board (PCB)

badge designs, 426

Bat Badge, 425

BombermanBadge, 423, 424

bottom layer trace, 417, 419

component, to board, 407–410,
412, 413

consistency/rigidity, 399

copper layer, 401

designing, 403

diffusion layers, 425

EasyEDA, 404, 405

fixed robotics, 422, 423

Printed circuit board (PCB) (*cont.*)
    Flying Badgers DC26 Badge, 398
    multiple components, 421
    physical size, shape, and
        orientation, 404
    silkscreen layer, 401
    solder layer, 401
    substrate layer, 401
    track tool, 414, 415
    two-layer, 400
Programmable Logic Controller
    (PLC), 12
Protoboard, 361, 384
    PCB, 378
    side-by-side, 377
    simple circuit, 376
    standoffs, 381
Python code, blinking an LED,
    198–200
Python libraries, 158, 159

R

Random access memory (RAM), 6
Raspberry Pi, 204
    assembly, 242
        GND pin, 244
        GPIO header, 247
        indicator light, 247
        LED, 248, 250–260
        MF wire, 246
        power connected, 245
        sensor in place, 243
        sensor signal, 258

build, 241
circuit parts, 216–222
completed sound sensor, 240
confirm installation dialog, 186
DietPi, 180, 190
etcher selection screen, 182
first boot screen, 183
giclone, 211, 212
github repository, 210
GPIO pins, 223–225
install confirmation, 187
iso file, 182
LED, 215, 223, 239
LED and sensor pin, 281–283
loops, 237, 238
mkdir temp, 209
Node MCU, 214, 215
reboot confirmation, 189
reporting screen, 188
SD card, 181
software lists, 185
software selection screen, 184
SSH command, 222
wireless network credentials, 181
Raspberry Pi, installing Git CLI,
    207, 208
Read-only memory (ROM), 6, 7
Relative charge method, 75

S

Schottky style diode, 87
Secure Shell (SSH) command, 204
"See" sensors, 144, 145

Semi-permanent circuit board, 378

Sensors, 9–13

Series circuit, 97

    assembling steps, 99

    breadboard

        black wire connection, 100

        LED, 101

        red wire, 102

        resistor, 101

    parts, 99

Signal wire, 304

Silkscreen layer, 401

Smart device labs, 142, 149

    preprogrammed sensor/device, 161

    Putty connection wizard, 205

    Raspberry Pi, 204–206

    SSH command, 204

Smart software, 173

Smart system, 176, 178

    architecture diagram, 288

    Arduino-based devices, 178

    basic architecture, 178

    functionalities, 179, 180

    hardware, 289

    JSON objects, 286

    MCU, Raspberry Pi, 287, 288

    MCU options, 287

    MQTT server, 179

    NodeRED, 179

    parts, 285

    prototype, 179

    sensors, 290

Smart system architecture, 172

Smell/taste sensors, 146, 147

"Smoothing" effect, 80

Soil moisture sensor, 297

Solderable breadboard, 361

Soldering, 362

    bad connection, 369

    cleaning, 373

    components, 362, 364

    disposable components, 368

    kit parts, 364

    metal-on-metal connection, 366

    online resources, 365, 366

    oxidization, 370

    replacing, 374

    tip removed, 374

    tip tinning series, 371

Sound sensor reader, 202

SPI

    benefits, 153

    de facto standard, 152

    pin assignments, 154

    RFID reader, 155

    SD card, 154

Supervisory Control and Data Acquisition networks (SCADA), 12

System on a Chip (SOC)

    Arduino Nano, 163

    ESPxxx-based NodeMCU, 164

    Node32S, 163

    Raspberry Pi 3B, 163

    smart system, 165

    solar panel, 164

    types, 162

T, U

Tip tinning series, 371

Touch sensor
basic switch, 142
button, 143
measure conditions, 143
resistive screen technology, 143
vacuum's MCU, 143

Transistor
BJT (N-P-N or P-N-P)
advantages, 76
conventional flow, 75
GPIO pin, 77
PCB, 77
relative charge method, 75
software-controlled
devices, 76
uses, 74
FET
advantage, 77
gate layer, 79
MOSFET transistor, 78
starter kits, 79
MOSFET, 74
Transistor controlled circuit
activation, 120

assembling steps, 110
breadboard
battery pack, 119
button, 111
IC ravine, 114
10k resistor, 113
MM wire, 112
330 Ohm resistor, 116, 117
transistor, 115
diagram, 109
MCU, 109
parts, 110
Two-layer circuit board, 379

V

Validate Code button, 321
Visual Studio Code (VSCode), 175
Voltage divider
circuit, 296, 306, 307

W, X, Y, Z

Wi-Fi/MQTT settings, 315
Working code, blinking an LED,
196, 197

Printed in the United States
By Bookmasters